THE
PRIVACY
RIGHTS
HANDBOOK

THE
PRIVACY
RIGHTS
HANDBOOK

HOW TO TAKE CONTROL OF
YOUR PERSONAL INFORMATION

BETH GIVENS

and THE PRIVACY RIGHTS CLEARINGHOUSE
with Dale Fetherling

AVON BOOKS ▲ NEW YORK

PUBLISHER'S NOTE: This publication is designed to provide accurate and authoritative information in regard to the subject matter covered. It is sold with the understanding that the publisher is not engaged in rendering legal or other professional service. If legal advice or other expert assistance is required, the service of a competent professional person should be sought.

AVON BOOKS
A division of
The Hearst Corporation
1350 Avenue of the Americas
New York, New York 10019

Copyright © 1997 by University of San Diego
Interior design by Kellan Peck
Published by arrangement with University of San Diego
Visit our website at http://AvonBooks.com
ISBN: 0-380-78684-2

Library of Congress Cataloging in Publication Data:

The privacy rights handbook : how to take control of your personal information / Beth Givens and the Privacy Rights Clearinghouse, with Dale Fetherling.
    p.   cm.
Includes index.
    1. Privacy, Right of—United States—Popular works. I. Givens, Beth. II. Fetherling, Dale, 1941– . III. Privacy Rights Clearinghouse.
KF1262.Z9P72 1997   97-16596
342.73'0858—DC21   CIP

First Avon Books Trade Printing: September 1997

Contents

Part IV—Protecting Your Privacy on the Job

Part V—Guarding Your Personal Safety

Part VI—What More Can You Do Now?

Foreword

Anyone who lacks a sense of urgency about commercial and governmental invasions of the self—often called violations of our "right to privacy"—need only compare the twenty-year-old Privacy Protection Study Commission Report (mandated by Congress) to the new data in Beth Givens' alarming and prescriptive *The Privacy Rights Handbook*. Since the Privacy Act of 1974, intrusions on privacy have increased exponentially (consider genetic and medical data, for starters), yet the protections in law are no greater today than they were in the early 1970s. Zealous privacy intruders, driven by a frenzied race for profit and equipped with efficient advanced technologies, have overwhelmed our now quaint privacy protection laws. In their cumulative impact, these intrusions are enveloping Americans in what Aldous Huxley would recognize as a Brave New World.

The first hurdle in confronting the insidious spread of these processes is linguistic. The word "privacy" (and its companion phrase "the right to privacy") sounds like an indulgence. The expression "the right to be let alone" has a more serious ring to it, but even so evokes mainly an image of governmental harassment or offense. It was in this sense that the Bill of Rights was directed at protecting citizens from arbitrary government interference (no more King George III).

But modern global corporations now present a much greater threat to privacy than the British Empire ever presented to colonial Americans. Their influence is broad: on government itself, on our media, our universities, our children, on consumers and workers, on our health care system, and on science and technology. Intricate databases, assured of rapid expansion by ingenious technologies, are now proliferating. With few exceptions, neither the law, nor civic advocacy, nor the media have kept up with the changes. The computer and telecommunications revolution has created a personal data complex guided by the global business strategies of large corporations. In such a system, private citizens have little control over how their personal information is used.

Data on your private life can be used to sell, to intimidate, to retaliate, and to indoctrinate the young. And it can be gathered in ways of which you may be completely unaware. Interactive programs on the Internet feature cartoon heroes who "converse" with excited children, eliciting private information about their families that can be fed into a database. Car buyers complaining about "lemon" cars or improper repairs are told that if they persist, their credit rating can be damaged. Often, shoppers don't even have to be told directly. They know that complaining can put their names in a database that can be used against them. So they refrain from seeking justice.

Medical databases—potentially of great use in providing higher quality health care—can be a treasure trove of information for the health industry and associated business enterprises with mammoth mailing lists. Your health data are also of interest to employers, insurance companies, and government agencies. Out of control! The people are not organized, not equipped with the knowledge, tools, or skills to confront the invasions of the self they can see, let alone the far greater, more subterranean manipulation of (or negligence with) records, lists, and other kinds of surveillance. Talk about "invisible hands"!

Every day people are refused employment, denied insurance coverage, or rejected for promotion because of information about them stored in files or databases—information of which they are completely unaware. The efforts of all this have not been quantified, but they are pervasive. Think of how many more people decline to file complaints, speak out publicly, or even run for office for fear that someone will take revenge by divulging personal information about them or their family members.

Ironically, the very corporations that fight hard to invade your privacy fight even harder to maintain their own. They well understand that keeping the information they hold secret ("secrecy" is the institutional word for privacy) is essential to preserving their power, and they are willing to spend vast resources to protect the privileges that secrecy insures them. No matter that those privileges can involve polluting the environment, receiving corporate welfare, defrauding consumers and investors, of systematically invading the personal privacy of their employees and customers. By insisting on secrecy, they shield their crimes and misbehavior from law enforcement agencies and the public.

The struggle for corporate disclosure and open government is long-standing, and not without some victories: the U.S. Freedom of Information Acts of 1966 and 1974, the requirements of the Securities and Exchange Commission, and the acts of several safety regulatory agencies. But despite these victories, governmental and corporate secrecy continue to grow in scope and significance. As of this writing, corporate lobbyists are pushing one state after another to adopt their environmental audit privilege, which will keep internal audits of external pollution away from legal or media inquiries. Thus, with one hand, institutions undermine democracy by protecting their own privacy. With the other, they undermine individual privacy by claiming that databases of personal information constitute proprietary business information.

In the realm of privacy, the powerful contend daily with the powerless in order to seek maximum advantage. So it's vital to get *The Privacy Rights Handbook* to the millions of Americans still unaware of how these "invisible hands" manipulate their own lives on a daily basis. Beth Givens is one of the nation's leading students of privacy invasion. She has produced, under the auspices of the Privacy Rights Clearinghouse, many concise reports that show how to forestall or oppose these constant incursions into the realm of personal freedom. With this book, the knowledge and experience of Ms. Givens and her associates is available to you and your circle of privacy defenders.

As a consumer, taxpayer, and worker, you have tools at your disposal that you might not be aware of—tools that are vital if you are to preserve that legitimate autonomy of the citzen which is a precondition of a democratic society, one that balances properly the right to know and communicate with the right to privacy. *The Privacy Rights Handbook* will help you gain access to them. And what makes this book even more valuable is the opportunity it gives you, if you are so inclined, to go beyond your own personal concerns and, as a citizen advocate, advance the cause of individual privacy in American life.

—Ralph Nader
Washington, D.C.
May 1997

Preface

A unique experiment was launched a few years ago. The California Public Utilities Commission awarded a grant to the Center for Public Interest Law at the University of San Diego to establish a consumer-awareness program about privacy. The Privacy Rights Clearinghouse was the result.

A small team composed of law students, a project attorney and myself—a librarian with a second career as a telecommunications specialist—began researching the many facets of consumer privacy. We adopted as our working definition of privacy, *the right to determine when, how, and to what extent information about us is communicated to others,* penned 30 years ago by privacy scholar Alan Westin in the seminal work *Privacy and Freedom.*

We produced a half dozen publications, which we called "fact sheets," and readied them for the big day when the PRC's toll-free hotline was inaugurated in November 1992. While we thought we knew a thing or two about privacy, we weren't prepared for the flood of telephone calls that came into the hotline from all over the state. Our phones didn't stop ringing.

We have learned a lot from the people who called us to ask questions and to complain about intrusions into their privacy. And based on what we learned from callers and through further research, we went on to develop a series of 20 guides. These publications form the basis of this book.

Our philosophy has been to provide consumers with practical information on steps they can take *now* to exert control over the use of their personal information. We also wanted consumers to know about their rights as based in law, as well as the many gaps where there are no specific legal rights. Stories taken from the hotline logs have been used in this book to bring the facts to life, to show how ordinary people have seen their privacy abused.

The overriding theme is to take action. Remember the slogan from the '60s, "the personal is political"? We can apply this to privacy as well. If it's happening to you, it's probably happening to others, as the many anecdotes in the book suggest. And the only way we will stop this daily erosion of our privacy is to make our voices heard.

The main message of the Privacy Rights Clearinghouse, which you will see repeated in many forms in this book, is three-fold: be aware, be assertive, and be an advocate. This book will furnish you with strategies and resources to help protect your personal information and, if you choose, to become active in the cause of privacy.

A few words about how we've organized this book: each chapter is designed to stand on its own. That's so you can choose to use it as a reference tool to help you with a certain kind of privacy problem, rather than reading the book from front to back. Organizing it that way, though, means some points will be repeated in more than one chapter.

This book is the product of many hands. My sincere thanks go to the USD law students and staff members of the PRC who over the years researched the fact sheets and talked with, listened to, and learned from the thousands of callers who contacted the PRC: Brad Biddle, Charles Blevins, Valerie Breen, Lisa Briggs, Barry Fraser, Christine Harbs, Nieva Kelly, Judith Moore, Phil Peng, Kenneth Pomeroy, and Claudia Terrazas. And thanks to our tireless assistants who have mailed tens of thousands of PRC fact sheets to consumers: Andrea Brooks,

Bonnie Johnson, Barbie Miranda, Sarah St. Pierre, and Veronica Terrazas. Thanks also to Christina Maule for her research assistance, and Robert Ellis Smith for reviewing an early draft of the book. And, of course, my appreciation is deep for the many consumer advocates, government officials, and industry representatives who provided names, addresses, facts, and figures.

I also acknowledge those who have been instrumental in funding the PRC, in particular the Telecommunications Education Trust under the watchful eyes of California Public Utilities Commission Public Advisor Rob Feraru and TET Program Administrator Lynn Victor. Thanks also to the members of the PRC Advisory Committee.

A special word of appreciation to the many friends of the PRC at the University of San Diego. I am especially indebted to Robert Fellmeth and Julie D'Angelo Fellmeth of the Center for Public Interest Law for their guidance, support, and generosity. Thanks also to Michael Shames, director of the PRC's new parent organization, the Utility Consumers' Action Network.

And finally, my thanks and gratitude to writer and coauthor Dale Fetherling for taking our no-frills consumer education prose and shaping it into an entertaining yet informative book.

—Beth Givens, Project Director
Privacy Rights Clearinghouse

A Note on Using This Book

Many Internet Web site addresses are provided in this book. For example, here is ours: *http://www.privacyrights.org*. When a Web address falls at the end of a sentence, it is increasingly common to insert the words ''no period'' to remind the reader that the period is not a part of the address. However, because of the large number of Web addresses included in this book, we have chosen *not* to do that. Please note that although Web site addresses may contain periods, they never end with a period.

When a Web site address is continued on the next line of text, we have chosen to break the address at either a slash or a period rather than hyphenate it. Keep in mind that properly formatted Web site addresses do not contain spaces.

This book contains many organization names, addresses, phone numbers, and Web sites—information that is likely to change with time. So if you've ever been told not to write in books, forget that admonition, at least in this case. When you learn of new or changed information, write it in the margins. Alert us to such changes, too, by letter, fax, or e-mail. When we become aware of new information, we will post it on our Web site, so feel free to visit our site for updates.

Privacy Rights Clearinghouse
5384 Linda Vista Road, No. 306
San Diego, CA 92110
Fax: (619) 298-5681
Telephone: (619) 298-3396
E-mail: prc@privacyrights.org
Internet: http://www.privacyrights.org

Introduction

Who's Probing Your Private Life?

Each time you deposit or withdraw money at the ATM . . . visit the doctor . . . pay your mortgage . . . use a charge card . . . chat on the Internet . . . make a phone call . . . or do any of dozens of other routine tasks, you leave electronic "fingerprints." Nearly every quantifiable aspect of your life finds its way into a data bank somewhere. This staggering volume of information is sometimes scrutinized, other times ignored, and yet other times collected to be sold and perhaps resold again, all most likely without your knowledge.

This is not a conspiracy, but rather a product of our age. We are obsessive about numbers, insatiable about marketing, paranoid about crime, and endlessly seeking new conveniences, from cellular phones to interactive TVs. But each new electronic advance, whether for information, entertainment, or sales, can create yet more ways for business, government, or malicious individuals to collect our personal data. And once the much-vaunted Information Superhighway "is fully paved, everything you do will be recorded," as Georgetown University professor Mary Culnan has said in *The New York Times*.

In fact, almost 20 years ago, a federal privacy commission warned of an erosion of freedom caused by the merging of such record systems, "each of which alone may seem innocuous, even benevolent, and wholly justifiable."

And what has happened between *then* and *now*? In a word,

computers. We've entered the heralded Information Age, and as a result:

- Electronic record-keeping has exploded in volume.

- Computers are ubiquitous, operate at warp speed, and in many cases, are connected to millions of other computers all over the world.

- For the first time in history, almost every recipient of your data is a computer user, meaning he or she is also a potential publisher as well as a user or abuser of that information.

Each day people are silently victimized by those they never see. With as little as a Social Security number, it's possible to find out—and use—intimate details of almost anyone's life.
For example:

- Judith was electronically stalked for more than seven years. She changed her phone number 19 times, even moved repeatedly. But within 48 hours of each change, the stalker discovered her, apparently by accessing various computer systems, and made more than 1,000 threatening or obscene calls.

- After an auto dealership failed to shred old loan applications, an industrious "dumpster diver" got Fred's credit-card data and charged thousands of dollars worth of purchases.

- Laura, a physician in private practice, was puzzled about why she had trouble getting insurance for her office. Then she found out she'd been wrongly coded in a national medical records database as suffering from Alzheimer's disease and having had heart disease.

As those actual cases from the files of the Privacy Rights Clearinghouse illustrate, *1984* is for many Americans not an Orwellian nightmare but a shocking reality.

Even those of us who aren't being stalked or bilked or sty-
mied should be concerned. Unfortunately, the conveniences
we've come to enjoy—such as e-mail, wireless phones, and
banking by computer—can be used to sabotage us. Whether
intentionally or accidentally, legally and illegally, subtly and
blatantly, our privacy is threatened by the same innovations
we embrace.

Have nothing to hide? Perhaps so. But would you want a
prospective employer learning that you once took Prozac, or
that you are now on a fertility drug? Would you like your
insurer checking to see if you occasionally sky-dive on week-
ends? Would it be okay if your estranged spouse's divorce attorney knew instantly about that hot new stock you bought last
week? "Every sinner has a future and every saint a past" goes
an old saying. And, in truth, all of us can think of something
we would rather keep to ourselves.

Besides, on a broader civil-rights level, people in a democracy have a right to be aware if information is being collected
on them. Right now it *is*, and in many cases, no one is aware.

You may not realize, for example, that price scanners at su-
permarkets can link your name and address to your purchases,
yielding important facts for merchants . . . that contest entries
and product-warranty cards are often less about prizes and guarantees than about selling names and data to marketers . . . that
personal medical data from informal health screenings, such as
blood-pressure or cholesterol testings, may be passed along to
drug companies . . . that if you call an "800" or "900" line,
your phone number often is secretly recorded . . . and that
employers may legally retain and review your e-mail and voice-
mail messages even after you've deleted them from your office
computer or phone.

The point is, everybody from the local pizza parlor to multi-
national firms can easily and inexpensively capture, store, and
analyze information about you. And they *do*. Creating "data

warehouses'' is routine at most businesses and government agencies today.

RULES STACKED AGAINST YOU

Many Americans feel caught in the clash between two laudable national values: open access to information and the right to be left alone. In fact, 82% of respondents in a 1995 Louis Harris Poll expressed concern about threats to their personal privacy, and 80% said they believe consumers have lost control over how their personal information is used.

The rules are not stacked in your favor. Technology has far outpaced the law. There aren't nearly as many privacy-related statutes and regulations as you probably think, and even those are spotty in their protections. For example, the law grants your employer greater rights to infringe on your privacy than it gives to law-enforcement agencies.

Further, you may be surprised to find that the titles of the videos you rent are confidential—but your personal medical records may not be. Perhaps most chillingly, you also may be unaware of the degree to which personal data itself has become a commodity for sale on the open electronic market to anyone with a personal computer, and once created, such records rarely disappear.

In addition, you may not know that:

- It's possible to obtain not just credit reports but "investigative consumer credit reports," which can include hearsay information about character, lifestyle, and reputation as well as financial and work data.

- Though criminal-history information compiled by law enforcement is not public, increasing computerization allows some private firms to compile what amounts to a "rap sheet'' by piecing together bits and pieces from many different public files.

- Employers can choose not only to read what's on a worker's computer screen or in his or her files but may be able to monitor, for example, the number of keystrokes the worker makes per hour and the amount of idle keyboard time.

As online services become increasingly interconnected, affordable and fast, more and more personal information will be available. A *U.S. News & World Report* cover story put it this way:

> Your chances of finding work, getting a mortgage or qualifying for health insurance may be up for grabs, because almost anybody with a computer, modem and telephone can surf through cyberspace into the deepest recesses of your private life.
>
> A fairly accurate profile of your financial status, tastes and credit history can be gleaned from such disparate things as your ZIP code, Social Security number and records of credit-card usage.

ORIGINS OF PRIVACY

Many of us claim a ''right'' of privacy and take it for granted that there is such a thing. But, in truth, the word ''privacy'' does not appear in the Bill of Rights or, in fact, anywhere in the Constitution.

Instead, it springs from a visionary article published in 1890 in the *Harvard Law Review* entitled ''The Right to Privacy.'' Samuel D. Warren and Louis Brandeis, who was later to become a U.S. Supreme Court justice, asserted that the Constitution, as well as common law, implicitly protects our right to exclude unwanted people from our private lives. The pair also correctly prophesied that new technologies would threaten our control over private information about ourselves. *They had no idea!*

NEW TECHNOLOGIES

Surveillance and deception are becoming civilian art forms. In some cities, police cameras snap our license plates as we run red lights. Video cameras record us just walking around in stores. Employers can choose to observe what we do, say, and write—without ever telling anyone. Information brokers sell our unlisted numbers, our home addresses, and our preferences in what we eat, read, watch, and like to play.

Through mail-order catalogues and "spy" stores, you can purchase FM telephone kits that broadcast both sides of any nearby telephone conversations over FM radio . . . "stethoscopes" that allow you to listen to conversations through a wall . . . "voice changers" that allow a male caller to sound like a woman, or vice versa . . . "computer interceptors" that take advantage of Van Eck radiation to tune into other people's computer screens . . . laser-guided microphones that can pick up a conversation just by "listening" to vibrations created by voices on a window glass.

A few years ago, perhaps only law enforcement and a few semi-shady private investigators had reason to inquire surreptitiously into the lives of others. But now the kinds of lookers and the kinds of things they're looking for have grown.

In Southern California, it has become chic in some upscale neighborhoods to order computer searches of current or prospective residents. Gossip in one neighborhood, for example, had it that a resident was a mobster because he never worked but had a Mercedes in front of his big house. However, a private detective, after accessing bank records as well as the man's trash, learned the well-heeled neighbor got his cash from a trust fund, not from drugs or prostitution.

Obviously, the computer is at the core of many privacy threats. This same device that allows us to quickly search encyclopedias, keep track of our finances, entertain ourselves with electronic games, and chat with like-minded strangers continents apart also puts a galaxy of information at the fingertips of those who would pry. Now, not only can business, government, credit agencies, insurers, gangsters, and our enemies collect personal information about us without our consent, they can do so cheaper and faster than ever before.

Unlike the human memory, the computer has an infinite capacity to record characters and numbers. It's a whiz at finding patterns in raw data, making cross-referencing easy. Also unlike the human brain, it never forgives or forgets; it retains every awful detail of every painful divorce proceeding, property dispute, or other personal hassle. And finally, while your own memory is not transferable to others, the contents of a computer's memory can be mailed to others on disks, transmitted over phones, or printed out and passed around. Any sort of information, in any quantity, can be flashed from city to city, from nation to nation, without you or I knowing about it.

CORPORATE INFORMATION VENDORS

Orwell's vision of Big Brother was wrong in that it foresaw only Big Government burrowing into our lives. Increasingly, the threat is coming from the private side. "Big Brother has simply contracted out to corporate America," one congressman said as he introduced legislation aimed at helping consumers control their own personal information.

It used to be that people desiring privacy could, in large measure, get it by, say, unlisting their phone number and renting a post office box. Of course, it was still possible to track them down by following a difficult paper trail. Now information vendors—or you, if you buy the information vendors' service—can follow the same trail simply by pressing a few computer keys.

Corporate information vendors are compiling sophisticated, highly personal profiles listing your hobbies, court cases, buying habits, financial information, health data, computer usage, you name it. Dozens of these vendors are releasing these details about us without any restriction and, generally, without our knowledge.

A few years ago, for example, the magazine *MacWorld* experimented with trying to find information about 18 well-known individuals from the world of entertainment, business, politics, and sports, including football player Joe Montana, moviemaker George Lucas, Bank of America CEO Richard Rosenberg, and U.S. Attorney General Janet Reno.

The magazine used only legal methods involving online sources. Spending an average of $112 per subject, it was able to compile electronic dossiers that, for most of the subjects, included:

Biographies

Home address

Home phone

Social Security number (SSN)

Birth date

Tax liens/court filings

Driving record and vehicles owned

Commercial loans/debts

Real estate owned

Voter registration

The magazine's reporters made no tedious trips to distant courthouses and spent no time thumbing through dusty files. Instead, they just sat at a computer for slightly more than an hour for each subject.

As online services become increasingly interconnected and private information services proliferate, such searches will only become easier and cheaper. One writer called the surge in the sale of personal data "the electronic equivalent of the gold rush—few legal restrictions apply, and there's lots of money to be made if you own the mine."

One of the big "mine" owners is government. Increasingly, public agencies—especially cash-strapped local governments—are selling your information for commercial reuse. As a result, anyone with a computer and a willingness to spend a few bucks an hour can now search any of hundreds of databases for your personal information.

In Oregon, a Portland man recently paid the state $222 for the entire database of the state's department of motor vehicles. Then he put it on the Internet so that anyone could instantly look up a vehicle owner's name, address, birth date, driver's license, and title information. Data on any individual driver had always been available there to anyone who visited the Oregon DMV and paid $4. But putting the same information on the Internet raised a furor. People complained that their car could be seen, say, parked at a sporting event, thus tipping off burglars to an unguarded home.

Thus, ease of access becomes part of the problem, even with public records. It's one thing for, say, your divorce record—with its heated allegations and itemization of assets—to be on file at the courthouse. It's something else to have that same data available for individuals to pick through at their leisure while at their PC. But that's the direction in which we're heading.

THE WAGES OF PARANOIA

In short, technology has answered our call and is turning up in every facet of our lives. And such technology may yet be in its infancy. Where will this data collection eventually lead?

Will a life insurance company buy a database listing someone as a fan of Ben & Jerry's New York Super Fudge Crunch ice cream and then use that information to charge that person a higher premium? (That's not as far fetched as it sounds. The Selective Service once monitored the customer birthday lists of another ice-cream chain for young men who had turned 18 without informing their draft boards!) Will companies routinely monitor employees with locational badges that track their every movement, from the amount of time spent chatting with a fellow worker to the minutes spent in the restroom? Will Internet providers and Web-page operators trace every single click of your mouse in order to construct a detailed profile of you and your habits?

Others quite easily could have a sunrise-to-sunset trail of information about your whereabouts, what you're doing, what you're experiencing, with whom you're communicating. No public policy has developed yet to prevent that kind of scenario. And there's very little standing in its way except a more enlightened citizenry.

It pays to be a little paranoid, people sometimes say. That's true. But it costs something, too.

It'll cost you in a lot of little ways if you summon the courage to follow many of the suggestions in this book. In the short run, at least, it would be easier for you if you furnish your SSN when asked, don't gripe when your unlisted phone is called by telemarketers, fail to object when your county puts all its court and property records online, don't make a stink when bills are proposed to give police broad new surveillance powers, and keep your mouth shut when merchants want more information than you're comfortable giving before they'll cash your check.

It would be easier to be a sheep and go along. But, as this book makes clear, there's a price to be paid for that, too.

RELIEF IS POSSIBLE

All is not doom and gloom, though. In the chapters that follow, you'll learn ways to hone your sensitivity to potential privacy incursions. You'll learn steps to take to keep those incursions to a minimum. And, finally, you'll learn how to become an advocate and practitioner of privacy in the workplace, the marketplace, and in the policy arena.

While privacy intrusion is a rising tide, it can be stemmed. There's a need for changes in government and corporate practices. Before those changes will occur, individuals will need to fight back and seek to protect themselves. And you *can* do so. You can learn to be alert and be assertive about your privacy and that of others.

Slowly, people are waking up to this fact. For example, that same 1995 Louis Harris Poll showed that 59% of respondents—compared to 42% five years earlier—said they have refused to give information to a business because they thought it "was not really needed or was too personal."

Similarly, the three people mentioned earlier all sought and attained at least some measure of relief:

• Judith learned that her relentless stalker was a computer professional who felt romantically threatened. Judith and her husband obtained a restraining order against the woman and took her to court. The Privacy Rights Clearinghouse encouraged Judith to go public with her story so other stalking victims could benefit.

• Fred didn't have to pay for the purchases made by someone else with his discarded credit-card information. But he did face the prospect of a bad credit rating. So the Clearinghouse gave him information he needed to correct and monitor his credit report.

- Laura, the doctor denied office insurance because of erroneous health records, eventually got a policy, though at a higher premium. The Clearinghouse showed her how to check national health records so she isn't again falsely labeled. It also put her in touch with the media, which alerted other consumers.

As Marc Rotenberg, director of the Electronic Privacy Information Center, has said, George Orwell should be read "as a warning, but not a prediction. Today, we face a choice between technologies of surveillance of the type that Orwell correctly warned us and technologies of privacy that may allow us to keep our identity to ourselves in a very high-tech world."

Knowing how to walk that line is what the following chapters are about.

PART I

DEALING WITH INVASIVE COMMERCE

1

How to Turn Off the Junk-Mail Juggernaut

You say a small dog could be crushed if it were unlucky enough to be standing beneath your mail slot at the time of the daily deluge?

Like most of us, you are probably awash in catalogues, sale notices, pizza-parlor flyers, prize offers, car-wash coupons, postcards with pictures of missing children, investment solicitations, and political come-ons addressed either to you personally or to the ever-popular "Resident" or "Occupant." And you wonder *how do these people find me and what can do I about it?*

If you've asked yourself such a question, you're not alone. And you're not without recourse. There are ways to reduce, if not eliminate, a junk-mail Niagara, and this chapter will suggest an action plan.

And, be sure about this: If you find junk mail upsetting, you *do* need a plan. Because unless steps are taken, undesired—and sometimes highly undesirable—material will continue to flood in. In fact, as we'll see, it's likely to increase.

This chapter will spell out the 10 most common sources of names for junk-mail lists and how to deal with each of them. Since what's junk to some may be jewels to others, you'll also learn how to effectively pick and choose amid the commercial

15

avalanche. And at the end of the chapter, there will be a list of *Privacy Pointers* you can use to lessen your vulnerability.

FOUR TREES PER PERSON

Although your mother may have told you that a person's mail is private, in this day of computerized mailing lists, your name and address certainly are not. The direct-mail business has exploded. Sixty-five billion pieces of unasked-for mail reach American homes and offices each year. (The mailman bringeth, and the trashman taketh away—44% of junk mail is never opened.)

Junk mail averages about 30 pounds a year for every American. Or, to put it another way, estimates are that somewhere between one-half and four trees per person per year goes into making this tide of printed waste.

What's more, you can now get electronic junk mail. Millions of advertisements can be sent over the Internet at the push of a button. As with more traditional junk mail, e-mail advertisers can target specific audiences. But unlike regular, or snail, mail, you, in effect, may have to pay for reading unwanted advertisements if your online service charges by the hour or minute.

Technology makes it possible for companies to choose among more than 20,000 mailing lists. For just pennies per name, firms can precisely target recipients with mass mailings, either paper or electronic. As more and more addresses become computerized, this will become even easier to do.

What's worse, even though you can toss the printed material and delete the e-mail, *the computerized list that spawned them is practically immortal.* Once your name is on a mailing list, it can be "sold" over and over, until it's almost impossible to trace to the original business. (Actually, in direct-marketing parlance, lists are not sold but "rented." List purchasers sign a contract forbidding them from reusing the names. But if the consumer responds to the offer, then the mailer can keep that name for its own list—and perhaps even rent it to someone else. The going price for list rental is $50 to $150 per thousand, or five to fifteen cents per name.)

So even if you decide to stop giving out private information, even if you choose to wage war on those now annoying you, you'll probably still continue to receive *some* junk mail because of the ripple effect from the original list. In addition, some junk-mailers are just stubborn.

For example:

- Kevin, 37, has been receiving at least two mail solicitations a week from a medical plan for the elderly. Although he has repeatedly asked to be removed from these lists, the mailings continue.

- Since 1992, Evelyn has written over 2,000 letters to get her name off mailing lists. According to a log she has kept of her correspondence, the worst offender is the Republican National Committee, which, at last count, had not honored her 18 requests to be taken off its mailing lists.

WHERE DO THE NAMES COME FROM?

What's the source of all these names? Well, usually, it's *you*. You volunteer your name and address when, for example, you order from a catalogue, make a donation, subscribe to a magazine, enter a sweepstakes, join an organization, buy a car, or fill out a product-registration card. In each instance, your name is likely entered into a computer database that then takes on a life of its own.

Sandra, for example, paid $4,000 to join a dating service, but only after being assured that all the data she'd given them about her likes and dislikes would be kept in strictest confidence. Soon, though, she started receiving solicitations from other dating services. When she complained to the original dating service, she was told an ex-employee had obtained the mailing list and sold it.

Remember, too, that your name, address, and phone number are usually printed on your checks, giving that data to anybody you deal with. Such information can easily find its way onto a database for sending you that merchant's advertisements and coupons—and may be sold to direct-mail companies which, in turn, sell it to many more marketers.

Similarly, a lifestyle change can trigger junk mail. Get married, sell your house, change your address, or have a baby, and—*presto!*—another name is added to public records which then finds its way onto a mailing list, thanks to nearly 1,000 brokers and compilers of such lists.

While you may be the unwitting source of most of this traffic, remember you're also the one person who, if possessed of resolve and persistence, can do something about it.

GUARDING YOUR ADDRESS

Every time you fill out a form—whether it's to buy something, or enter a contest, or change your status (like getting a divorce or registering to vote)—you increase your chances of being added to one or more mailing lists.

Direct mail is a very lucrative industry, employing more than twenty million people and generating more than $600 billion in sales in 1996. Having your name on these lists is, naturally, good for the direct-mail companies. Thus, they're often reluctant to delete it.

So how do you fight back? Unfortunately, there's not one central clearinghouse. Most of the 10 sources of names and addresses cited below involve several organizations which must be dealt with individually. So, a number of letters or phone calls—perhaps *repeated* letters and phone calls—may be involved.

Let's look at the most common sources of names and addresses for junk-mail purposes, followed by what you can do in each case to reduce or eliminate your exposure:

1. Mail order and magazines. If you're a customer of one mail-order company, you're probably going to get offers from others. The same sharing goes on among magazines—and between magazines and mail-order firms. So . . . subscribe to a cooking magazine, and you may find yourself receiving mail-order catalogues for kitchen supplies and gourmet foods.

What You Can Do: You can remove yourself from most *national* mailing lists by contacting:

> **Direct Marketing Association**
> Mail Preference Service
> Box 9008
> Farmingdale, NY 11735

DMA will put you into its computerized "purge" file which is sent to its estimated 3,600 subscribing organizations several times a year. It may take a few months, but you should see a reduction in catalogues, magazine offers, sweepstakes, and other national advertising mail.

But that won't solve all your junk-mail problems because compliance is voluntary, not all companies belong to DMA, and not all junk mail is national. So, if after a few months you're still getting mail from some companies, notify the customer-service department of those firms and request they neither contact you nor provide your name to other companies. Also, contact magazines to which you subscribe.

Better yet, be proactive. When you first subscribe to a magazine or order from a catalogue, tell them up front you're withholding further use of your name. Include a copy of a letter forbidding them from giving your personal information to any other firm or organization. Your letter might say something like this: "Please do not rent, sell, or trade my name, address and phone number to anyone else," followed by your signature.

2. Phone books. If you are listed in the white pages, your name, address and phone number are, for all practical purposes, public record. Mailing-list companies collect this information and sell it to catalogue companies and marketing firms.

In addition, the phone company and others compile "crisscross directories" (also known as reverse directories), which are organized by address and phone number rather than by name. If you're listed in the white pages, you're probably also in one or more of these "street-address directories." (Information in such directories also finds its way to the Internet people-finders, which will be discussed in Chapter 10, "Privacy in Cyberspace: How to Protect Your Personal Computer.")

What You Can Do: Consider having an unlisted number. At the very least, ask your local phone company to omit your address. Also request the phone company to remove your listing from its "street-address directory."

Further, you can call or write to the major directory companies and ask that your listing be removed:

- **Haines & Company, Inc.**
  Criss-Cross Directory
  Attn: Director of Data Processing
  8050 Freedom Ave., NW
  North Canton, OH 44720
  (800) 562-8262
  Send a letter requesting your name be removed. Haines only accepts such requests in writing.

- **R. L. Polk & Co.**
  Attn: List Suppression File
  26955 Northwestern Highway
  South Field, MI 48034
  (810) 728-7000

3. Credit-card companies. Many credit-card companies compile lists of cardholders for promotional materials based on purchasing patterns, then "rent" their mailing lists to other businesses.

What You Can Do: You can request that your credit-card company not distribute your name. Also, some states—California, for example—require all credit-card companies to provide notice to cardholders if they disclose personal information for marketing purposes. Cardholders may prevent the release of this information by filling out a preprinted form or calling a toll-free number.

4. Credit bureaus. Companies you deal with provide data to credit bureaus on how promptly you pay your bills. These credit bureaus don't disclose specific information, such as names of your creditors and the amounts due, for marketing purposes. But often they do compile lists based on consumer characteristics. An example might be: people with incomes over $40,000 who regularly use credit cards and pay their bills on time. If you fall into a category like that, you probably receive numerous "preapproved" credit-card offers in the mail.

What You Can Do: Call or write the three major credit bureaus and ask to be removed from the mailing lists they make available for credit pre-screening purposes.

- **Equifax Options**
  Equifax Marketing Decision Systems, Inc.
  P.O. Box 740123
  Atlanta, GA 30374
  (800) 556-4711

- **Experian (formerly TRW)**
  Target Marketing Services Division
  Attn: Consumer Opt Out
  P.O. Box 919
  Allen, TX 75013
  (800) 353-0809

- **Trans Union**
  Name Removal Option
  P.O. Box 97328
  Jackson, MS 39288–7328
  (800) 680-7293

Depending where you live, you may be able to cite legal grounds. For example, California, New Hampshire, and Massachusetts require credit-reporting firms to delete any consumer's name and address from mailing lists if the consumer so chooses. Recent amendments to the federal Fair Credit Reporting Act require that the credit bureaus extend these opt-out opportunities to all 50 states.

5. Public records. Some government agency makes note of virtually every major event in your life. Many of these files are open to the public, such as birth certificates, marriage licenses, and real-estate transfers. Searching these public records is how companies selling baby items, for example, know to mail advertisements to new parents just days after a birth. It's how home-improvement firms, seeing you just bought a house, decide you might be in the market for some remodeling. (See also Chapter 6, "From Cradle to Grave: Government Records and Your Privacy.")

What You Can Do: You usually can't have government records about you kept confidential. Therefore, contact companies individually when they put you on a mailing list compiled from public records. For example, if you buy a house and receive mortgage insurance solicitations you don't want, write to the companies and ask to be taken off their mailing lists.

6. Charities and nonprofits. If you've ever donated money, chances are you've received fund-raising solicitations from many related organizations. That's because charities and nonprofit groups often rent or exchange each other's lists. For example, renting out lists of donors is a method increasingly used by political candidates to retire debts or fatten campaign coffers.

What You Can Do: When you give to a charity or nonprofit group, enclose a note requesting that the organization not rent, sell, or exchange your name and address with anyone else. When you receive solicitations from nonprofits, it may take a bit of detective work to be deleted from "their" mailing lists. That's because many nonprofits obtain lists from other groups, and thus, they don't keep the lists themselves and can't delete your name. (This is true of most mail solicitations, whether a charity or not.)

So save the mailing label and the "reply device" from these mailings. They are likely to contain codes which indicate the list your name came from. Ask the organization that mailed you the solicitation for the name of the organization that originally rented the list. Then contact *that* organization and ask that your name not be rented, sold, or exchanged.

7. Registration cards. Be aware that warranty, or "product registration," cards have less to do with warranties than with mailing lists. These cards, which the companies offer under the guise of "helping us understand our customers' lifestyles," ask about your education, your family income, whether you own or rent, how many people are in your household, and your hobbies—none of which the company needs to guarantee its product.

In fact, such registration cards are generally not mailed to the company that manufactured the product. Instead, they likely go to a Denver post office box of the National Demographics and Lifestyles Co. This firm compiles buyer profiles and sells the information to other companies for marketing purposes.

What You Can Do: When you buy a product, don't fill out the product-registration card, or at least don't fill it out fully.

In most cases, your receipt ensures that you are covered by the warranty if the product is defective.

For some products you may want the company to have a record of your purchase in case of a safety recall. If you decide to send in the registration, include only minimal information—name, address, date of purchase and product serial number.

Also, write to National Demographics and Lifestyles and ask to be deleted from its mailing list:

> **National Demographics and Lifestyles Co.**
> List Order Department
> 1621 18th St., No. 300
> Denver, CO 80202
> (800) 525-3533

8. Sweepstakes and prizes. You need to know that when you register to win that trip to the Bahamas or the nifty new sportscar, you're also adding your name to mailing lists used by other promoters of contests and sweepstakes. These may be legitimate and, at worst, may just add to your junk mail. But this can be fertile ground for scams, too. A sure sign of a rip-off is a requirement that you pay a fee up front to get the prize or gift. Be skeptical.

Older people, especially, are often targeted for scams and gimmicks. For example, Ellen's 90-year-old mother, who lives alone, has spent hundreds of dollars on fraudulent contests. And Joan's elderly aunt receives 25 to 30 pieces of junk mail daily. Finding it difficult to resist these solicitations, she's squandered much of her savings.

What You Can Do: To reduce mailings by prize promoters, avoid participating in sweepstakes and contests unless you're given the opportunity to "opt out" of any mailing lists that are created. (Look for disclosure notices in the sweepstakes and contest literature.) Because the mailing lists used to contact you are likely to be rented, save the mailing labels and reply devices, as indicated above, in order to find out how to contact the companies which maintain the lists.

To have your name removed from the major nationwide sweepstakes mailers, contact the following companies:

- **Publishers Clearinghouse**
  101 Channel Drive
  Port Washington, NY 11050
  (800) 645-9242
  Does not rent its list

- **Reader's Digest**
  Attn: Sweepstakes
  Reader's Digest Rd.
  Pleasantville, NY 10570
  (800) 234-9000
  Does not rent its list

- **American Family Publishers**
  Box 62000
  Tampa, FL 33662
  (800) 237-2400
  Does rent its list

9. Price scanners. A relatively new way of compiling mailing lists and buyer profiles is through price scanners. Scanners help businesses keep track of inventory and speed up service at the checkout counter. But they can also be used to link your name to your purchases, especially if you are using the store's "buyers club" card. Stores generally offer product discounts as an incentive to use the card.

When this card is "swiped" through the card reader at the checkout stand, your name and address, stored in the card's magnetic strip, can be matched against a record of the scanned items. The store is able to use this information to mail coupons and other special offers to you. But it may also sell the information to product marketers. So, for example, if you buy one type of soda, you might receive coupons from a rival soft-drink company to induce you to switch brands.

What You Can Do: If you don't want information compiled about your personal buying habits through the use of price scanners, check the "opt-out" box on the application. If there is none, don't participate in the store's "buyers club."

You may also want to pay cash at businesses which use scanners because technology may allow the company to store your name and address if you pay by check or credit card.

10. Data compilers. A number of companies purchase and collect information from government records, telephone books, association-membership rosters and other sources. They compile mailing lists and sell them for marketing purposes.

What You Can Do: To be removed from the lists of the major companies that compile and rent mailing lists, call or write to these firms. (Note that these companies also subscribe to the DMA's Mail Preference Service.)

- **R. L. Polk & Co.**
  List Compilation
  26955 Northwestern Highway
  South Field, MI 48034
  (810) 728-7000

- **First Data Info-Source**
  Donnelley Marketing, Inc.
  Data Base Operations
  1235 "N" Ave.
  Nevada, IA 50201
  (888) 633-4402 or (515) 382-8321

- **Metromail Corp.**
  List Maintenance
  901 West Bond
  Lincoln, NE 68521
  (800) 426-8901

- **Database America**
  Compilation Department
  100 Paragon Dr.
  Montvale, NJ 07645
  (201) 476-2000 or (800) 223-7777

- **Experian (formerly TRW)**
  Target Marketing Services Division
  Attn: Consumer Opt Out
  P.O. Box 919
  Allen, TX 75013
  (800) 353-0809

- **Trans Union**
  Name Removal Option
  P.O. 97328
  Jackson, MS 39288-7328
  (800) 680-7293

A NEW PHENOMENON: JUNK E-MAIL

Electronic mail (e-mail) is now used by millions of people around the world. The most widely used application on the Internet, it's another of those classic technological advances, offering great convenience but at a cost to your privacy.

Increasingly, e-mail serves as a means of tying families, colleagues, and friends together, and, in some cases, better connecting citizens with their government. But it's also a way for marketers to flood cyberspace with come-ons that cost them next to nothing, but cost you time, aggravation, and, often, money.

Junk e-mailers get e-mail addresses from a variety of sources. For example, they may comb postings to Usenet newsgroups, CompuServe forums, America Online message boards, and the like. Or, they may buy the addresses from e-mail address compilers.

Already, one such firm, the Bigfoot Directory, claims to have developed a list of more than 11 million e-mail addresses world-wide and is expanding by as much as a million entries per month. Bigfoot provides users with e-mail addresses as well as phone numbers, fax numbers, previous e-mail addresses, and mailing addresses—which can be accessed in any of six lan-guages. (It's also creating a "privacy list" of computer users who don't want to receive unsolicited e-mail.)

The growing use of junk e-mail has drawn intense criticism from independent-minded e-mail users. For instance, when two Arizona attorneys advertised their legal services to almost 6,000 discussion-group users over the Internet, they soon received thousands of furious e-mail messages from all over the world denouncing the pair for invading their privacy. So one way to fight back is by using e-mail itself as an instrument of protest.

In addition, some argue that unsolicited e-mail falls under a federal law, the Telephone Consumer Protection Act, that pro-hibits companies from sending unsolicited advertisements by fax. The rationale for government regulation of junk faxes (though some still are sent) is that companies are effectively shifting the advertising costs to consumers who pay for the fax paper involved on the receiving end. Privacy advocates say such strictures should apply to e-mail as well, because recipients usu-ally are paying for online time in order to read the messages. This theory is as yet untested in court, as of the production date of this book.

As entrepreneurs race to peddle their wares via modem, this issue will become even more important. There are some fledg-ling, nongovernmental efforts being made to deal with the prob-lem. Some junk e-mailers let you reply with a "remove" option to get off their list. Also, filters are already common in some of the better e-mail programs that may permit users to automati-cally segregate such messages or send them directly to the trash.

(For example, America Online has optimized a junk mail filter for their users.) In addition, some private individuals and privacy organizations are battling junk e-mail.

Adding to the murkiness is the fact that the issues are so new that judicial and legislative signposts are few, leaving scholars and activists to debate the search for solutions. (See *Privacy Pointers* at the end of this chapter for some actions you might take. See also tips provided in Chapter 10, ''Privacy in Cyberspace: How to Protect Your Personal Computer.'')

●Commonly Asked Questions About Junk Mail●

Q: Can I stop just *some* of my junk mail?
A: Yes. Junk mail is only junk if you don't want to receive it.

You may want to be on some mailing lists. If so, *don't* contact the Direct Marketing Association's Mail Preference Service. Rather, notify individually the companies sending you junk mail. Further, make it a point to tell the companies you do business with to keep your name and address private. A growing number of firms that rent their mailing lists are including statements in their literature to let you know you have this option. When such statements are not provided, add your own handwritten ''opt-out'' box.

Q: What can I do about local flyers and advertising supplements that don't emanate from a mailing list but are sent to "Occupant" or "Resident"?
A: Again, you must contact the companies responsible for the distribution list.

If you don't want to receive these flyers, get in touch with the individual company that's responsible for delivering them. Here are the steps to take to reduce this form of junk mail:

1. Look for a postcard that may accompany the flyers. It will have your address printed on it. Some postcards contain pictures of missing children. If you cannot find a postcard, then look for a mailing label attached directly to the flyer.

In either case, you will see the name of the distribution company near your mailing address. Find the "bulk rate" postage mark above and to the right of your mailing address. You will see the name of the company that distributes the flyers next to this postage mark.

These are among the major "resident" mailers:

- **ADVO, Inc.**
  List Service Department
  239 West Service Rd.
  Hartford, CT 06120
  (860) 520-3357

- **Harte-Hanks (Pennysaver or Potpourri)**
  2830 Orbiter St.
  Brea, CA 92821
  (800) 422-4116

- **Val-Pak Coupons**
  Direct Marketing
  P.O. Box 13428
  St. Petersburg, FL 33733
  Send the mailing label to Val-Pak to request name suppression.

- **First Data Info-Source**
  Donnelley Marketing, Inc.
  Data Base Operations
  1235 "N" Ave.
  Nevada, IA 50201
  (888) 633-4402 or (515) 382-8321

- **Carol Wright/Cox Direct**
  P.O. Box 13428
  St. Petersburg, FL 33733
  To opt out, send your request in writing. Include your mailing label.

2. Contact the company in writing or by telephone and request that your address be taken off the distribution list. When making a written request, send a copy of your mailing label along with the letter.

3. It may take four to eight weeks before you notice you are no longer receiving the packets of advertising flyers. You may have to notify the distribution company more than once.

4. If the distribution company can't or won't remove your address from its mailing list, please contact the Privacy Rights Clearinghouse. We want to know which firms don't honor such requests.

5. Train your mail carrier. This is often a tough task because of personnel switches and the sheer volume of deliveries. But if you persist, you can persuade the carrier to exclude you from unaddressed junk mail. Besides, it's against the law to deliver unaddressed mail. If need be, call the supervisor at the local post office and explain that you are no longer on the distribution list for advertising flyers and that they should no longer be delivered to you. In time, the mail carrier will catch on.

Q: Can I just send back the junk mail to the sender?
A: In some cases.

Envelopes with "Address Correction Requested" or "Return Postage Guaranteed" can be returned *unopened* by writing "Refused—Return to Sender" on the envelope. The company will have to pay the return postage.

Some people try to use postage-paid business reply envelopes to more aggressively fight the junk-mail onslaught. They stuff the contents of the mailing back into the reply envelope, along with a note demanding that their name be removed from the mailing list, and send it all back for free. This may feel gratifying, but it's unlikely to have much effect. Those employees who open the business reply envelopes are looking only for completed orders. Requests for name deletions are likely to be tossed away.

A more fruitful tactic would be to save the mailing label and reply device and contact the organization or firm which sent you the mailing. Give them the code that's printed on the mailing label or reply device. Ask them where they obtained the list that contained your name. Then contact *that* organization and ask to be purged from its list.

Q: **What are my legal rights if I am placed on mailing lists against my direct wishes?**
A: **Unfortunately, there are few legal protections, if any.**

Although some people have sued to stop junk mail, they have largely been unsuccessful to date. For example, courts thus far have ruled against a Virginia man who sued *U.S. News & World Report* for selling his name to other magazines. He argued that a state law, which had been interpreted to apply to celebrities, also prohibits the sale of names and likenesses without consent, whether a person is famous or no.

On the other hand, a San Diegan took several local merchants to small-claims court for continuing to mail unwanted solicitations to him after he'd written a ''contract'' on the back of checks which stated, in effect, that by cashing the check, they were agreeing not to send him any junk mail. When they ignored the contract, he recovered damages in court.

Legal challenges such as these will continue to be brought against the sellers of mailing lists until the thorny issue of ''ownership'' of consumers' names and addresses is resolved.

Q: What should I do if I receive unsolicited mail that seems obscene or illegal?

A: Questions or complaints about mail fraud, theft, tampering, or obscene or pornographic mail should be directed to the Postal Inspector at your local Post Office.

The Postal Service has two forms you can use to enforce federal laws designed to stop the delivery of certain objectionable material. PS Form 2201 will add your name to a list of persons who do not want to receive such sexually explicit ads from any mailer. PS Form 2150 should be used to prohibit a specific mailer from sending such material to you.

Thirty days after your name has been added to the list, mailers are barred from sending you such material. A mailer who violates either prohibition may face legal action by the U.S. government. If the mailings continue, you'll need to note the date you received the material, sign it, and take the envelope and contents to the post office.

On the other hand, if the communication is received via computer, the issue is much murkier. The question of who, if anyone, can or should regulate the Internet is still being debated.

Q: Is there any way I can tell who has sold my name to which company?

A: Only by keeping track of whom you send your name to.

While it's sometimes obvious how certain companies got your name (you subscribe to an outdoors magazine, for example, and soon receive catalogues for fishing and hunting gear), it's not always that easy. One of the simplest ways to track who sold your name is to use a fake initial or nickname when giving your name.

If you then receive unsolicited mail with this "new" name, you know who sold their list. You can then contact the original company directly and ask that it not give out your name in the future. Unfortunately, many lists are sold over and over again.

So while the original manufacturer may delete your name, the second and third companies won't receive your request. Again, persistence is the key.

Still, the best way to head off this problem is to be proactive. At your very first dealing with this firm, nonprofit, or publication, make it very clear that you do not want your name and address to be used for other purposes.

Q: Is there a way to lodge a complaint with the mail-order industry?

A: Yes.

The industry has a consumer-action desk to handle problems. Send the name and address of the company in question, details of the problem you're having, and photocopies of any relevant documents to:

> **Mail Order Action Line**
> Direct Marketing Association
> 1111 19th St., NW, No. 1100
> Washington, D.C. 20036
> (202) 955-5030

●Privacy Pointers: What You Can Do Now●

1. Pay cash whenever possible.

Checks and credit cards leave tracks. A company doesn't need to know your name and address if you're paying by cash.

Some, though, may still ask for that information. In fact, a Philadelphian, John Featherman, was so irritated by a major electronic retailer's policy of asking for a customer's name, address, and phone number on even the smallest cash purchases that he founded *Privacy Newsletter* to show consumers how to get privacy and keep it.

(The monthly newsletter takes a "how to" approach, providing practical tips for consumers on how to get privacy and keep it and, in Featherman's words, offer "hope, encouragement, and inspiration to individuals who seek freedom from Big Brother." For information, contact the newsletter at Box 8206, Philadelphia, PA 19101; $99/yr U.S. or $149 abroad; (215) 533-7373.)

2. Think twice before giving out personal information.
If you choose to fill out forms, such as product-warranty cards, give out only the minimum information sought: address, date of purchase, and product serial and model number.

3. Contact the following groups for more information on how to stem the flow of junk mail:

- **Stop Junk Mail Association**
  3020 Bridgeway, No. 150
  Sausalito, CA 94965
  (800) 827-5549
  This group, for a fee, seeks to substantially reduce your junk-mail solicitations. It also advocates for postal reform.

- **Private Citizen, Inc.**
  Box 233
  Naperville, IL 60566
  (800) CUT-JUNK
  http://www.private-citizen.com
  This group, also for a fee, will contact the eight largest direct-mail firms and ask that you be taken off their mailing lists. It also lobbies Congress to crack down on junk mailers.

- **Zero Junk Mail**
  405 Allen Dr.
  Charlottesville, VA 22903
  (888) 970-JUNK
  http://www.zerojunkmail.com
  This is a fee-based service with online access. It offers reduction of unwanted snail mail and e-mail.

- **Junkbusters**
  http://www.junkbusters.com
  This Web site offers a number of free services to help you get rid of unwanted snail mail and e-mail.

4. Learn how the direct-mail industry works.

Get a free brochure on direct-marketing practices by contacting the Direct Marketing Assn., 1120 Avenue of the Americas, New York, NY 10036.

5. Order an informative 20-page booklet "Stop Junk Mail Forever."

Send $3 to:

- **Good Advice Press**
  Box 78
  Elizaville, NY 12523.
  (800) 255-0899

6. Avoid using the post office's change-of-address form.

The Postal Service makes its change-of-address file available to the major mailing-list companies through the National Change of Address (NCOA) system. To avoid having advertising mail follow you to your new home, don't fill out the change-of-address form. Rather, notify friends, family, and business contacts of your move, but let junk mailers try to find you on their own. They likely will, but you'll lose some along the way.

7. Always look for disclosure notices and opt-out opportunities.

More companies are finding that offering privacy safeguards is good business. Many mail-order firms, magazines, and credit-card companies now provide a box to check if you don't want your information sold to other companies. If you don't see an opt-out notice, add your own.

8. Avoid entering sweepstakes or other contests.

Often the primary reason a sweepstakes or contest is conducted is to generate mailing or telemarketing lists. Politely, these are called "opportunity seekers" lists. They're also known as "sucker lists." If you're serious about stopping unwanted mail, you'll stay away from these sweepstakes or contests.

9. Guard your e-mail address.

For starters, don't buy anything advertised by e-mail. It will just encourage the junk e-mailers, and you'll probably get added to more marketing lists.

If there's an "opt out" alternative, be sure to take advantage of it. For example, the Bigfoot Directory says it's constantly updating its list of online users who don't wish to receive unsolicited e-mail. You can contact Bigfoot on the World Wide Web at: http://www.bigfoot.com. Some other big e-mail directories are Switchboard (http://www.switchboard.com), Four11 (http://www.four11.com), Whowhere (http://www.whowhere.com), and Infospace (http://www.infospace.com).

Also, use a separate log-on identity for some e-mail functions. Most commercial online services, such as America Online and Prodigy, allow users to establish multiple log-on identities. If you subscribe to one of those services, you might wish to adopt a separate identity for posting to public newsgroups, message boards, and the like, thus keeping your "real" e-mail address more private.

For other ideas on ways to thwart unwanted e-mail, visit these Web sites: http://www.mcs.com/~jcr/junkemail.html and http://www.coyotecom/jac/stopjunk.html.

CREATE YOUR OWN PLAN

To effectively control what enters your mailbox, you must come up with a plan and stick to it. You won't see a decrease in junk mail overnight, but in time, you can restrict the deluge of unwanted mail to a mere trickle.

There are three keys to doing so: be aware, be assertive, and be an advocate. You'll see those tips repeated in this book about other privacy intrusions. In the case of junk mail:

Be aware of all the ways that you give your personal information to others. At the very instant that you disclose such information—whether ordering something over the phone, making a donation to a charity, or paying by check in a store—tell the recipient you don't want them selling, renting or exchanging that information with anybody else. Make this a habit!

Be assertive about your desire to stop unwanted mail. If an organization doesn't comply, tell them, preferably by writing to the top executive, that you're taking your business elsewhere. Report uncooperative businesses to their trade association or to the Better Business Bureau or Chamber of Commerce.

Be an advocate for more control over your personal information. The consumer privacy issue is heating up. Add your voice to the choir by letting your federal and state legislators know you want say over how your private data is used, by whom, and for what purpose.

2

Telemarketing: What Happened to a Quiet Evening at Home?

When Margaret Davis became pregnant, she ordered a catalogue of maternity products. Suddenly, it seemed as if the whole world knew she was going to have a baby. The Burbank, California, woman not only got baby-product samples and more maternity catalogues in the mail, she received phone calls from at least five baby photographers as well as other infant-related businesses.

Unfortunately, Mrs. Davis miscarried. But despite her best efforts, that message never reached the solicitors. Salespeople would call about the time of the baby's due date and say, "Congratulations, we hear you've had an addition to your family." The continued deluge of calls and mail about the baby was not only irritating, but emotionally wrenching.

It went on for years. "What drove me to take strong action was a birthday card from a children's magazine that said something like, 'Happy Birthday, 2-year-old!' "

Davis tried contacting the solicitors by phone, requesting her name be removed from their sales lists. But the volume of baby-related calls and mail seemed to increase until, finally, Davis had to ask her husband to open all mail and screen all calls.

Eventually, she wrote a general letter to all the marketers, stored it in her computer, and then would print out a copy and mail it each time she was contacted. It threatened legal action if the solicitations didn't stop immediately. "I had to do something," she said. "I couldn't stand it anymore, and most of them wouldn't listen to a polite request."

Davis' struggle, which lasted more than three years, showed her "how it's very easy to get on these lists and how hard it is to get off them. I'd have taken action much sooner if I'd known it would have gone on so long. It's kind of like I have this phantom child out there in the world of marketing."

To a much lesser degree, most of us have experienced such unwelcome intrusions. Perhaps the phone rings just as dinner goes on the table. But then we find it's not a friend or family member, or even the office calling. It's someone—maybe even a machine—calling with "a terrific opportunity."

HOW DID THEY GET YOUR NUMBER?

Although you may not have heard of them, phone solicitors, or telemarketers, know about you. In many cases, they not only know your name, phone number, and address, but also your income, age, marital status, level of education, and maybe even your preference for such things as soap and cereal. Like junk mailers, telemarketers get your telephone number and other data from various sources, including you.

Some of the major ways they gather data are:

1. Phone book. If you are listed in the white pages, they simply may have looked you up. Similarly, several companies are in the business of compiling national phone directories, available in CD-ROM and computer databases, that are gathered from local phone books all over the country.

2. Reverse directories. The phone company and other businesses publish directories which list people by street address or phone number rather than name. Telemarketers frequently use these "street-address directories" when, for example, they want to call specific neighborhoods. If you are listed in the phone book, you are almost certainly in street-address directories, also referred to as "criss-cross" or "reverse" directories.

3. You. You may inadvertently give your number to telemarketers when you sign up for a contest or a drawing and include, as requested, your phone number. In fact, such giveaway promotions may have less to do with gifts than they do with obtaining your number for sales pitches.

Similarly, if you have your phone number printed on your checks, your name, address, and phone number can easily be entered onto computerized mailing/phone lists.

4. Automatic dialing devices. These machines are able to determine all possible phone number combinations, even unlisted numbers, and dial them in sequence much more rapidly than any person can.

5. "800" and "900" numbers. When you call these numbers, your phone number may be captured by what's called an "Automatic Number Identification" (ANI) system. ANI's equipment automatically identifies and stores the number from which you are dialing. (Even if you have Number Blocking, which is discussed later in this chapter, you can't keep your number confidential if you call an "800" or "900" line.) Marketers can often match your captured phone number with other computerized lists and street-address directories, thus adding your name and address to their database. However, it's now illegal for a company which captures your number to sell it to other marketers without your consent.

OTHER CONCERNS

For companies, telemarketing is a logical, efficient way to do business in today's technologically advanced world. But for most of us, it's usually a nuisance, at best. In fact, junk mail and telemarketing rank among the top five complaints received each year on the Privacy Rights Clearinghouse's hotline.

In addition to the nuisance factor, there are other concerns. On a broader, civil-rights level, there's the basic privacy question. "Using one's name without compensation or consent raises substantial privacy concerns," says Robert Ellis Smith, editor of the *Privacy Journal.* "People should have the right to know when information is being collected, and to choose whether to make it available."

(Published since 1974, his monthly newsletter reports on legislation, legal trends, new technology, and public attitudes toward confidentiality and privacy. The cost is $118 a year. For further information, contact P.O. Box 28577, Providence, RI 02908; (401) 274-7861.)

Further, telemarketing can be a fertile field for scam artists. The elderly, especially, seem ripe for commercial exploitation. A Southern California woman, for example, discovered that her 83-year-old mother, living alone and crippled by arthritis, had been targeted by telemarketers. They sold her stationery, although she found it painful to write, and hawked overpriced health products of questionable benefit. They also put her name on dozens of other marketing lists. As a result, her phone rang almost constantly, and salespeople were able to prey on her loneliness.

POLITENESS NO PANACEA

When a telemarketer calls for the first time, most of us try to be polite. "I'm sorry, I'm just not interested," may soon lead to, "Could you please not call during dinner time?" and perhaps eventually to, "Take me off your calling list or I'll sue!"

Threats rarely affect the determined, well-trained telemarketer:

- Clare was inundated with callers who would hang up as soon as they heard her answering machine engage. After asking the phone company to put a trap on her line to capture the number of the caller, she learned that it was a telemarketing company. It was using an automated random-digit-dialing device that would hang up when it detected an answering machine.

- Manny has an unlisted phone number, but that didn't keep telemarketers from pestering him about playing the stock market. Salespeople would greet him by name and ask about his wife, also by name. "I'm thinking I must have talked to these people. How would they know this?" he said, but "after I got the third call, I realized I've never talked to them."

- Greta was harassed by a local newspaper asking her to subscribe. It continued to call even after being asked to put her on its "don't call" list. So she took the company to small-claims court and won a $525 judgment.

Politeness often fails to bring results, but, as Greta learned, sometimes the law can. That's because in telemarketing, unlike the junk-mail arena, the legislatures and courts have taken some steps to help the consumer.

WHAT ARE YOUR LEGAL RIGHTS?

Both the federal and state governments regulate telephone solicitations, but as we'll see, there are big loopholes.

Two major federal laws govern telemarketing:

▓ The Telephone Consumer Protection Act

This 1991 law, monitored by the Federal Communications Commission (FCC), focuses on the use of telephone lines and requires telemarketers to follow certain guidelines. For example, they can't call homes before eight A.M. or after nine P.M. without permission, and they must put you on their ''don't call'' list if you so request. If you do ask and they don't comply, the law allows you to sue in state court, file a complaint with the FCC, or urge the attorney general in your state to file a suit against the telemarketer.

The law also prohibits telemarketers from using a fax machine to send an unsolicited ad and forbids them from using a prerecorded message except for emergency purposes.

However—and this is a big ''however''—tax-exempt non-profit organizations, research surveys, and firms that are phoning businesses (not homes) are exempted. Such telemarketers aren't required to have a ''don't call'' list and aren't forbidden to use prerecorded messages. And they're not bound by this federal law if they've had a prior business relationship with you.

▓ The Telemarketing and Consumer Fraud Abuse Prevention Act

Signed into law in 1994, this law is largely aimed at scams. It's enforced by your state attorney general or the Federal Trade Commission. The law requires the telemarketer to make certain disclosures, such as the identity of the seller and the total cost of any goods being sold. Though it also requires telemarketers to keep ''don't call'' lists, you can only sue in federal court and must show damages greater than $50,000. Again, nonprofits are excluded.

Many nonprofit groups raise money over the telephone and spend the donations responsibly, but they are almost totally unregulated, and thus, abuses do occur.

Some are quite willing to traffic in your generosity, renting your name and thus profiting twice from your gift. While most people seem to know their names are somehow swapped among catalogue companies, some are surprised to learn that charities and political groups do the same. In fact, it's a burgeoning practice.

List companies now offer more than 600 political lists, for example, permitting purchasers to choose from among all manner of donor/voters: gays, Jews, religious conservatives, tax protesters, liberals, whatever. It's big business, with each list being rented out repeatedly.

CALLER ID AND NUMBER BLOCKING

One of the newer twists in phone privacy, or the lack of it, is Caller ID. It may increase freedom for some consumers, reduce it for others, and, in any event, will likely prove to be a boon to telemarketers.

All states now allow homes and companies to buy an inexpensive device that displays the number of the person calling. That's true even if the caller has an unlisted number. Across the country, some 6% to 12% of residences and a somewhat higher percentage of businesses have subscribed so far.

The Caller ID device also captures the number in its memory for display at a later time. So, even if there's no one there to pick up the phone, your number can be viewed later. Businesses, for example, can record your number for future solicitations, or reverse trace your name and address to place you on mailing lists.

There's no way to know if the number you're calling subscribes to Caller ID. Remember: Your number will be transmitted even if you don't have the Caller ID service yourself.

However, along with this new technology comes another option, "Number Blocking," which allows consumers to place either a permanent block on their phone number, or selectively block their number from being transmitted on certain calls. However, no matter what equipment you buy, you can't block your phone number if you call an "800" or "900" number. That's another trump card for the telemarketers, because it allows them to build a database of numbers, regardless of what action you take.

If you choose Per Line Blocking, your phone number will automatically be blocked every time you call (unless, of course, you're calling an "800" or "900" number.) If you call someone who subscribes to Caller ID, the display device next to his or her phone will flash "Private," "Anonymous," or some similar word instead of your phone number.

If you choose Per Call Blocking, your phone number will be sent to the parties you call unless you enter a code (*67) to block an individual call. (Again, "800" and "900" numbers are excepted.)

Some phone companies offer call-blocking for free, others may charge. In any event, it's up to you to control who gets your phone number. Remember: unless you choose Per Line Blocking, which is the strongest option for those concerned about privacy, you will automatically be given Per Call Blocking.

Per Line Blocking is not available in every state, and in some states it is available for special cases, such as shelters for victims of domestic violence. To find out which blocking options are available in your area, call your local phone company.

So, which blocking option is best for you? It depends on the risk you feel if your number is revealed to someone else. For example, you might want to choose Per Line Blocking if you:

- **Have an unlisted number.**

    In other words, you've already decided that telephone privacy is important enough that you'll pay a monthly fee to keep your number private.

- **Belong to a profession that requires privacy.**

    Examples could include law-enforcement officers, judges, entertainers, mental-health care providers, probation officers, and teachers when they call from home.

- **May wish to report crimes anonymously.**

- **Operate a domestic-violence shelter or a safe home.**

    You'd want to safeguard the location of residents.

- **Sometimes call a "help" hotline and want anonymity.**

    Such hotlines include suicide-prevention, AIDS-information, immigration-assistance, or mental-health help lines. (*Note*: Your number cannot be blocked to 911 or to an "800" or "900" number.)

However, if few of those risks pertain to you, Per Call Blocking may make more sense. For example, if you:

- **Call mostly friends and family.**

    They may subscribe to Caller ID and may not want to pick up the phone unless they see a recognizable phone number.

- **Aren't sure which option you want.**

    You can choose Per Call Blocking on a trial basis to see how it works for you. You can change to Per Line Blocking later if you wish.

- **Won't forget to enter the Per Call Blocking code when you need to shield your number.**

    If you live alone and have few visitors who are likely to use your phone, this would make sense—*if* you're careful.

Caller ID promises to make some people feel more secure . . . and others less so. For instance, Caller ID can be used by people receiving harassing phone calls to decide whether to answer. But, on the other hand, most harassers probably will block their phone numbers or call from pay phones.

One Texas murder already has been indirectly attributed to Caller ID. In that case, a San Antonio man called by a former girlfriend recognized the number disclosed by the Caller ID. Knowing the corresponding address, he then went there with a gun.

Caller ID is likely to bring some cultural change beyond telemarketing. Imagine, for example, an employee trying to call in sick when the boss can see that he's phoning from, say, Las Vegas. Nor will the old dodge "I'm working late at the office, dear" work so well if the spouse's phone reveals the number of a saloon or, say, a lover's apartment.

HOW CAN I STOP SALES CALLS?

With all the trafficking in lists, it's difficult to completely eliminate sales phone calls. However, you can dramatically decrease the number of calls you receive by taking the following steps:

1. Have your name removed from national lists.

Sign up for the Direct Marketing Association's (DMA) Telephone Preference Service (TPS) to have your phone number added to the DMA's "don't call" list. The major nationwide telemarketers participate in this service.

Send your name, address and phone numbers, including your area code, to:

Telephone Preference Service
Direct Marketing Association
Box 9014
Farmingdale, NY 11735

Contacting TPS will help reduce, but not eliminate, sales calls because participation by telemarketers is voluntary. Further, the TPS doesn't stop calls made by random dialing devices.

2. Ask marketers to put you on their "don't call" list.

Federal law requires firms to maintain and honor such lists. If you are called by them—but don't want to be—you can insist on being added to the "don't call" list.

Keep track of who you've made this request of. If you're called again, you can sue for $500 per call.

3. Screen your calls with an answering machine.

Most telemarketers hang up when they hear an answering machine.

4. Get an unlisted phone number.

There are advantages to being listed in the phone book. But if you're tired of being called by telemarketers, having an unlisted number can reduce the calls considerably. Phone companies charge a monthly fee for unlisted numbers. To request an unlisted number, call your phone company's business office.

You can also request that your listing be removed from the phone company's street-address directory. In addition, write or call the major companies that compile reverse directories and request that your listing be removed:

• **Haines & Company, Inc.**
  Criss-Cross Directory
  Attn: Director of Data Processing
  8050 Freedom Ave., NW
  North Canton, OH 44720
  (800) 562-8262
  Send a letter requesting your name be removed. Haines only accepts such requests in writing.

- **R. L. Polk & Co.**
  Attn: List Suppression File
  26955 Northwestern Highway
  South Field, MI 48034
  (810) 728-7000

5. Opt for "custom calling" services or devices.

Your phone company may offer services such as Caller ID and Number Blocking, which can be used to limit unsolicited calls. Other custom calling services that may prove useful are Call Screen (which allows you to block calls from up to 12 phone numbers) and Selective Call Acceptance (which permits you to program your phone to accept up to 12 phone numbers). You must pay a monthly fee to your local phone company for these services.

Numerous private companies also sell special equipment that blocks or screens unwanted calls. (See also Chapter 8, "How You Can Stop Harassing Phone Calls.")

6. Be careful about releasing your phone number.

Be wary of giving out your phone number when making purchases. Don't have the number printed on your checks. Don't put it on contest or sweepstakes-entry forms.

Be sure the requestor has a reasonable need to obtain your number. And if you *must* give it out, consider providing your work number instead.

7. Demand privacy from "800" or "900" numbers.

When calling an "800" or "900" number, tell the representative that you don't want your name, address, or phone number rented or sold to others. You may also want to request that they not call you in the future. It's the law.

Evan Hendricks, editor of the bimonthly *Privacy Times,* a Washington, D.C.-based newsletter, suggests using different phones—such as a pay phone—when calling "800" or "900" numbers, thus thwarting the marketers' ability to capture your number.

(*Privacy Times,* which costs $250 a year, reports on privacy policy, primarily at the federal level, with a special emphasis on court proceedings concerning the Privacy Act and the Freedom of Information Act. For more information, contact: P.O. Box 21501, Washington, D.C. 20009; (202) 829-3660.)

●Commonly Asked Questions About Telemarketing●

Q: If a company doesn't comply with my request to be put on its "don't call" list, how much can I sue for?
A: It depends on your perceived damages.

Under the Telephone Consumer Protection Act, you can sue a telemarketer in small claims court for your actual monetary loss, or up to $500—whichever is greater—for each call received after your request to be placed on their "don't call" list. If the court determines that the telemarketer knowingly broke the law, the penalty is up to three times the actual monetary loss, or up to $1,500, whichever is greater. Similar penalties apply if automatic dialing systems or prerecorded messages are used illegally. You can also sue if you ask a telemarketing firm for a copy of its written policy and it fails to send it.

As mentioned, the Telemarketing and Consumer Fraud Abuse Prevention Act allows you to sue only in federal court and only if you can show damages greater than $50,000. In either case, you may want to contact the attorney general's office in your state to make a formal complaint. The office can sue for you if several complaints have been filed against the same company.

To document your case against the telemarketing firm, send it a certified letter, return receipt requested, demanding to be placed on the "do not call" list. Keep a copy of the letter and the return receipt as proof. Also, be sure to keep a log of all calls where you've asked for a policy statement or asked to be placed on the ''do not call'' list.

Q: **What do I do if I suspect fraud?**
A: **Contact your state attorney general and/or the National Fraud Information Center (NFIC) at (800) 876-7060.**

NFIC's toll-free service provides information on how and where to report fraud, advice to consumers, and direct complaint referral to the Federal Trade Commission's National Telemarketing Fraud Database. A project of the National Consumers League, NFIC doesn't disclose to any nongovernment organization the identity of persons filing complaints or reporting incidents.

Q: **How can I ensure that donations I make to phone solicitors from nonprofit organizations will be used responsibly?**
A: **Experts say the first rule is to avoid responding to such solicitations. But if you want to contribute, here are some safeguards:**

- Only give to nonprofits whose track-record is well known to you. Never contribute money to a stranger over the phone.

- Ask for copies of the nonprofit's two most recent IRA Form 990 filings and its last two annual reports.

- Ask if the nonprofit's mailing list is owned by its fundraiser and who earns money from the rental of donors' names.

- Ask for a copy of the nonprofit's contract with its fundraiser.

- If the nonprofit refuses to provide you any of this information, give elsewhere.

Q: What can I do about long-distance telephone companies which themselves seem to be aggressive telemarketers?
A: If you get a call—and don't want to change carriers—just say "No!"—and watch what else you say.

Some long-distance telephone carriers aggressively market their services by phone, trying to get you to switch from your present provider. Clearly tell them ''No'' if you don't want to switch, but also be careful about providing any information that might authorize a change without your knowledge. For example, don't give out or confirm personal information, such as birthdate or Social Security number, either of which might be used later in an attempt to verify that you authorized new service.

There are rules against unauthorized switching of service, known in the trade as ''slamming.'' But it does happen, so you and your family need to be vigilant. If your service is switched without your okay, report it to your local telephone company, ask to be returned to your original long-distance carrier, and make sure you get any switching charge removed. There is a ''lock'' you can put on your account, so that it can't be slammed. You can ask for it through the local business office.

You also should report the long-distance company's actions to the Federal Communications Commission's Common Carrier Bureau. Its address is listed in *Privacy Pointers* No. 4.

Q: Is it legal to use prerecorded messages for sales?
A: No—but . . .

Under federal law, a telemarketer can't use a prerecorded message unless you consent, or unless the call is an emergency. So why do you still sometimes get those annoying recordings? Probably because the calls fall under technical exceptions. For example, the calls might be from nonprofit organizations, or from someone with whom you've previously dealt.

Another possibility is that the calls don't specifically include an unsolicited sales pitch but some other inducement, such as a survey, contest or sweepstakes. Instead of trying to sell you something on the phone, the caller (that is, the machine) may ask for your name, address, or other information. If you comply, the phone problem then becomes a mail problem.

Q: **What if I choose the Per Line Blocking option, but some people with Caller ID won't answer unless they can see my number?**
A: **There's a code (*82) you can enter to selectively *unblock* your number and allow it to be transmitted.**

Q: **If my home has more than one phone number, do I need to choose a blocking option for each one?**
A: **Yes.**

Q: **Can I block my phone number when I call from my cellular phone?**
A: **It depends.**

Many cellular companies lack the technical ability to provide Caller ID or the blocking options at this time. But some can and more will as the cellular industry becomes increasingly digital.

It's worth investigating. If telemarketers latch onto your cellular number, it could cost you because you also pay for calls that come to your cellular phone. So ask your cellular provider to find out whether blocking is possible.

●Privacy Pointers: What You Can Do Now●

1. If annoyed, get serious about saying "no" to telemarketers.
The next time you're irritated by a telemarketing call, tell the caller to place you on their "don't call" list. Companies are required by federal law to keep these lists.
In addition:

- Send a certified letter, return receipt requested, to make sure they have received your request.

- Keep a detailed log. If a telemarketer continues to solicit your business even after you have asked to be placed on their "don't call" list, record when and how many times they call. If you are forced to sue, you will need this information.

- Ask for a copy of their written policy for maintaining the "don't call" list. (If they fail to provide the policy, that's also a violation of federal law, and you can sue them.)

2. Be firm about *your* "policy."

We've found it to be effective to say, "I never buy anything over the phone. Please take me off your list." By emphasizing that, as a matter of principle, you *never* buy from a telemarketer, many will decide you're not worth further effort.

3. Demand to know what your information will be used for.

When offered "free" premiums, rebates, and other incentives in exchange for giving personal data, find out who will use the information and for what purpose. If you want to participate, ask if you can do so by giving just your name and address.

If you choose to participate in marketing or public opinion surveys, verify that your answers will be used only in the aggregate. Your answers should be stripped of all personal identifiers so no personal information can be traced back to you.

4. Be alert to Caller ID changes.

Caller ID service is sure to change in the future. For example, a display of the *name* of the caller is one option that's now being offered in some states and is sure to be available in others.

You'll need to decide whether such features will enhance or harm your privacy. Be sure to read the monthly telephone inserts which come with your phone bill and/or contact the state agency which regulates local phone companies in your area.

5. Contact the following groups for more information:

FEDERAL AGENCIES

Federal Communications Commission
Informal Complaints Branch
Common Carrier Bureau
2025 M St., NW, Room 6202
Washington, D.C. 20554
(202) 632-7553
Hotline: (888) CALL-FCC (A national toll-free number.)
http://www.fcc.gov
The FCC is charged with enforcing the Telephone Consumer Protection Act.

Federal Trade Commission
Correspondence Branch
6th and Pennsylvania Ave., NW
Washington, D.C. 20580
(202) 326-2222
http://www.ftc.gov
The FTC is charged with enforcing the Telemarketing and Consumer Fraud Abuse Prevention Act. You can also call your local FTC office.

PRIVATE GROUPS

Center for the Study of Commercialism
1875 Connecticut Ave., NW, No. 300
Washington, D.C., 20009
(202) 332-9110, ext. 382
For $3, this group will send you a kit containing information, tips, and forms to keep track of "don't call" requests. It also provides advice on taking your complaint to small-claims court.

Private Citizen, Inc.
Box 233
Naperville, IL 60566
(800) CUT-JUNK
http://www.private-citizen.com
For an annual fee, this group will list you in its "don't call" Private Citizen Directory, which is distributed to the large telemarketing organizations. It also sells the book So You Want to Sue a Telemarketer?, *which provides legal forms. ($5 for members; $10 for nonmembers.)*

Zero Junk Mail
405 Allen Dr.
Charlottesville, VA 22903
(888) 970-JUNK
http://www.zerojunkmail.com
This fee-based ($15 per year) service contacts telemarketers nationwide to place you on their "don't call" lists.

Junkbusters
http://www.junkbusters.com
This Web service offers assistance in reducing the number of telemarketing calls you receive.

3

Paying by Check or Credit Card: How Much Information Do Merchants Really Need?

Choosing your personal checks isn't the most momentous event in your life. But if you're like most of us, you spend at least a few moments pondering what style or design best expresses your essence.

But do you give as much thought to what information you have printed on those same checks? Do you think about the person or persons unknown to whom you're furnishing your name, address, phone, and maybe driver's license or Social Security number (SSN)?

You *should*. Because it's fairly easy for someone armed with any, or all, such information to delve into your bank and credit records, or maybe even get a start on assuming your identity. Unnecessary disclosure of the SSN—because it's unique and used for so many different things—can be especially harmful.

Kathy, for example, applied for a loan and was turned down because of supposedly bad credit. Upon checking with the credit bureau, she learned someone in a different state had fraudulently used her SSN to obtain credit cards, and then failed to pay off the accounts. The unpaid bills eventually sabotaged Kathy's credit.

CUSTOMERS HAVE RIGHTS, TOO

Paying by check or credit card is so much more convenient than carrying around wads of cash. But there's a downside. The more checks you write or purchases you charge—and the looser you are with your personal data—the more danger you invite.

Although cash is virtually untraceable, your check and credit card numbers can be tracked by any company you do business with. Every time you write a check preprinted with your name, address, and phone number, and sometimes even your driver's license number, you are giving businesses much more information than they need. By paying with a credit card, you're making significant amounts of personal information available to marketers who solicit goods and services based on a profile of your purchases.

Most of us sympathize with businesses, which must guard against bounced checks and stolen credit cards. But customers have rights, too, and many merchants ask for far too much too often. In fact, repeat-visit establishments—such as hotels—are known to keep permanent files of customers' credit card, driver's license, phone, and Social Security numbers. It's not hard to imagine abuse by an unscrupulous employee.

This chapter will explain what a merchant can—and can't—rightfully ask for. You'll also learn what legal remedies you can seek if merchants do break the law. And, as usual, we'll add some *Privacy Pointers* which may give you more ideas for ensuring your personal information doesn't fall into the wrong hands.

PAYING BY CHECK

Though we're often told—and there's some evidence—that the world is moving toward a "checkless" society, personal checks are still the undisputed instrument of choice. In fact, Americans write more than 100,000 checks *per minute* every day.

When you write a check, it's a convenience for you—and a risk for the merchant. But, still, accepting a check doesn't give the businessperson a license to collect—and maybe sell—all sorts of data about you.

Wittingly or not, merchants often violate customers' privacy, and in so doing, expose those consumers to potential fraud. It has become more and more difficult to make a purchase with a check unless you present a major credit card. In fact, many merchants ask for two forms of ID before they will accept a personal check. Often, they require a major credit card, not only for identification, but because they believe customers with credit cards are more financially responsible and, thus, less likely to bounce checks. (According to the Bankcard Holders of America, this is a misconception. Nearly 90% of all bounced checks result from mathematical errors when consumers balance their checkbooks!)

Some merchants want to write your credit card number on your check. However, this can expose you to fraud, because anyone with access to such checks then would have your name, address, telephone number, and credit card number. Making matters worse, a number of states also put the SSN on drivers' licenses. With the SSN, plus the information on the check, it would be easy for a thief to apply for credit in your name.

The law varies immensely. Twenty-one states, plus the District of Columbia, forbid a merchant from recording a credit card number on a check.

In addition, the big credit card companies themselves—Visa, MasterCard, and American Express—prohibit merchants from charging a customer's credit card account to cover a bounced check. That being the case, there's no reason for a merchant to record your credit card number on a check. The merchant can't really use it.

So, you're within your rights in refusing to let a merchant write your credit card number on the front or back of your personal check. But unless you live in one of the 21 states where that's illegal, the merchant can refuse to make the sale.

There's probably no harm in allowing the merchant to verify that you hold a major credit card or even write down what kind it is. For your own safety, however, you shouldn't allow him or her to record your credit card number when you're making a purchase by check.

If you do resist and the merchant, in turn, refuses to sell to you, what do you do? You can tell the businessperson that Visa, MasterCard, and American Express forbid merchants from charging a credit card to cover a bounced check. And you can point out that he/she already has your name, address, phone number, and driver's license number, which should be plenty to track you down should the check bounce.

Most of us shy away from making a disturbance at the cash register. But many merchants are unaware of the potential problems caused by writing additional personal information on personal checks. It's up to you to inform store management.

PAYING BY CREDIT CARD

Credit cards were designed, in part, so that purchases could be made quickly, without need for additional information. It's supposed to be easier than paying by check. The merchant, if he or she correctly processes the bankcard transaction (by obtaining an authorization number and making sure the signatures match), is guaranteed to receive payment.

So why is there sometimes a hassle? Some overly cautious merchants have gotten into the habit of requiring consumers to provide a phone number, home address, or other personal information on credit card sales slips. However, requiring it as a condition of sale is actually prohibited by American Express,

MasterCard, and Visa—and it's against the law in 11 states and the District of Columbia.

If a merchant wants your personal information on a credit card sales slip, and if you're not comfortable giving it, you can decline. According to the rules of the major credit card companies, the businessperson can't refuse to sell to you because of that. Similarly, if the merchant asks to see your driver's license before he or she will allow you to make a credit card purchase, you can refuse. Again, the merchant can't turn thumbs down on the transaction for that reason.

As the consumer group Bankcard Holders of America points out, there really aren't any circumstances under which a merchant is required to locate a cardholder. If there's a problem with a transaction—such as the customer exceeding his credit limit—the card-issuing bank absorbs the cost. The merchant gets paid anyway. Thus, there's no need for the businessperson to require your personal information.

If a clerk insists on writing your credit card number on your personal check, or is intent on putting your address and phone number, for example, on a credit card slip, what can you do?

1. Ask to speak to the manager or owner.

Many clerks are just ill-informed and are carrying out what they believe is store policy. If the manager or owner is also uninformed, explain your rights and his or her obligations.

2. Find out why the merchant thinks he needs this data.

Some merchants aren't aware that they're exposing their customers to fraud by requiring unnecessary information. Maybe they'll change their policy if you alert them to the issues.

3. Report them to the credit card companies, if need be.

A merchant should be reported if he or she insists on using credit cards as backups for bounced checks or refuses to sell to you because you won't allow your personal information to be recorded on the credit card slip. That's a violation of the business' agreement with the credit-card company.

To file such a report, include name and location of the merchant and a copy of the credit card slip. Send it to:

- **Visa U.S.A.**
  Consumer Relations
  P.O. Box 8999
  San Francisco, CA 94128
  (800) VISA911
  http://www.visa.com

- **MasterCard International**
  Customer Service
  P.O. Box 28468
  St. Louis, MO 63146
  (800) 307-7309
  http://www.mastercard.com

- **American Express**
  Call the "800" number listed on back of the Amex card or on the monthly statement.

(According to the Bankcard Holders of America, Discover, which is the fourth major credit card company, does not offer cardholders the protections mentioned above. But, of course, Discover cardholders are protected in those 11 states which have laws prohibiting merchants from recording personal information in connection with credit card transactions. Those states are California, Delaware, Georgia, Maryland, Massachusetts, Minnesota, Nevada, New Jersey, New York, Pennsylvania, Wisconsin, and the District of Columbia.)

SIGNATURE-CAPTURE DEVICES

One of the newest forms of credit card-related technology is an electronic pad located at the cash register. When you pay by credit card, you're asked to sign the pad. It electronically captures your signature and sends it along with information about your purchase.

According to merchants, these signature-capture devices streamline operations by saving time and reducing the paper glut. If there's a dispute over a purchase, it's easier to retrieve the electronic receipt than look for a paper copy. Signature-capture devices, proponents also say, are likely to reduce fraud, because there's less paper floating around with sensitive information on it. Finally, they add, the devices usually encourage sales clerks to compare more closely the signature on the electronic pad with that on the back of your card.

Some consumers, though, feel uncomfortable about using the devices because of the obvious privacy issues. Will their signature be stored electronically? If so, how hard would it be for someone to enter the store's computer system, obtain these digitized signatures, and then copy them for fraudulent purposes? The technology is still too new to answer the question of whether these devices reduce, or increase, the risk of fraud— or perhaps have no impact at all. However, this much is clear: *you are not legally required to sign the pad.*

Sales clerks may be trained to encourage you to sign it. But if you're troubled by that prospect, request to sign a paper copy and, if necessary, to talk with a manager about the problem.

WHAT HAPPENS TO CONSUMER DATA?

Merchants are increasingly taking advantage of the power of computers to gather information about their customers. A growing practice among retailers is database marketing.

Using information gleaned from customers, the merchant can link actual purchases with the customer's name. Many retailers enhance their customer lists with additional data purchased from data compilers. This might include estimated income, ages of family members, hobbies and interests, and whether the family owns its home or rents. Retailers use this data to learn more about the types of customers who shop in their stores. They also use it to mail them notices of sales and special offers. Retailers claim that database marketing helps them improve service and develop a base of loyal shoppers.

Many consumers are concerned about what then happens to such data. Is it sold to other companies to generate unwanted mail and phone solicitations? Is it possible that someday this data might be used for purposes unrelated to marketing, such as government surveillance, employment background checks, law enforcement investigations, or insurance company research? While this may sound farfetched, there are no laws which prohibit such uses.

Ask to see the privacy policy of any store which compiles data about your purchases and links them to your name. More merchants, especially the larger chains, are spelling out their data-gathering practices and making those policies available to their customers. If you're not satisfied with the merchant's privacy safeguards, refuse to divulge personal information to that business.

THE CASHLESS SOCIETY

Futurists, financial experts, and computer scientists tell us that cash—now used for 85% of our daily transactions—may be an endangered species. Greenbacks and coins, they say, will gradually disappear, to be replaced by electronic cash.

Already, you can see this happening as various kinds of memory cards become more common. Memory cards have the potential to replace cash, and in rudimentary form, with the magnetic stripe cards that are so common today, they already are used that way.

Thus, the transfer of information replaces the actual handing over of cash when the card is inserted into an ATM-style machine. Examples include prepaid telephone cards, transit tickets on the Bay Area's BART or Washington, D.C.'s Metro, and other cards, such as those accepted by copying machines at large libraries.

The next step in the evolution of the cashless society is the use of "smart" cards, which contain microchips and essentially function as a personal computer in a card. Not only will smart cards act as digital cash, they could have many other uses as well.

Imagine yourself on a typical Monday morning in, say, 2002. Before leaving for work, you insert your smart card into a slot in your computer and download "cash" from your bank account onto the card. At the subway station you insert the card into a newspaper vending machine and buy the *Daily Times.* You then slide the card through the electronic reader at the turnstile before boarding the train, and the fare is deducted from your bank account.

On your way from the subway station to the office, you buy your morning bagel and latte with the card. The smart card allows you access to your office building and then into your office itself. Perhaps later that day you visit the dentist. There, your card retrieves your dental records as well as insurance information, then transfers payment from your bank account to the dentist.

After work, you stop at the library and check out a mystery you've been wanting to read, using the smart card to process the transaction. Employing the card again, you board the subway and head home. There, you register for a class at the community college by sliding the card into the slot in the front of your computer and sending a few commands from your keyboard to the school. And before turning in for the night, you make an online visit to the campus bookstore to purchase the texts for the class, using the card to once again transfer money.

Oh, yes, you almost forgot. You also contact the pharmacy and use the card to order a dose of the painkillers the dentist has prescribed to get you through the few rough days ahead until he can perform the root canal that you need.

It's been a cashless day. In fact, it's been a walletless day. The smart card has functioned as an ATM card, a credit card, a subway token, a security pass, a medical records file, a library ID card, a student ID, an insurance card and even a PC spreadsheet (keeping track of your bank account balance along the way).

Sounds great! How convenient to carry a multipurpose card that also eliminates the need for cash. But what about this scenario should give us pause? With each use of that smart card, you've left behind an electronic trail. The card has recorded that it's you, Mary Doe, who entered the subway at the uptown station at 8:14 A.M. leaving from the downtown station 17 minutes later . . . that it's you who bought the *Daily Times* at the Fifth Street vending machine at 8:35 . . . that it's you who picked up the bagel and coffee at the deli and entered the building a few minutes after that. All your transactions, all your comings and goings, from work to dentist to home to the dealings with the community college and the pharmacy, they're all recorded and, in aggregate, provide a very complete picture of your life.

Privacy advocates are uneasy about such a trade-off. They question whether the ease and convenience of the all-purpose smart card warrants creating a system in which an "electronic dossier" could so easily be compiled about any individual.

What would a preferred scenario be? Already developed is a system of electronic payment that provides both anonymity and, when needed, authentication—in other words, proof that you are who say you are without having to reveal your identity.

It's particularly effective in making payments from personal computers, via e-mail or the Internet, to online merchants.

In the transactions in our scenario where the card functioned as cash, Mary Doe would have made the purchase without revealing her identity or whereabouts, just as if she had paid with cash from her wallet. Where anonymity would have been appropriate, as when she checked out the library book, she would have retained her privacy.

But the specter of anonymous transactions is troubling to some. Government officials fear a host of potential problems, ranging from difficulty in collecting taxes to fighting organized crime to maintaining control of the nation's money supply. Lack of a paper trail could, some contend, make it easier to evade tax authorities.

Is there a happy medium? Will smart card technology be allowed to develop so that a modicum of anonymity will be built in, much as cash functions today? Or will smart cards be instruments of control, leaving behind traces of our every transaction?

As Ann Cavoukian and Don Tapscott say in *Who Knows: Safeguarding Your Privacy in a Networked World*, "There is a choice to be made between technologies of surveillance and technologies of privacy. One promises to collect vast amounts of personal information and track your movements and activities. The other promises anonymity, security, and the protection of your privacy. Both will get the job done. Both can be implemented. Which would you prefer?"

●Commonly Asked Questions About Checks and Credit Cards●

Q: Should I be concerned about my privacy when a merchant uses an electronic system to determine if my check is good?

A: Probably not. But you should know how it works because there always is a chance for mistakes.

When you pay by check, merchants often use one of two systems—*check-verification* services and *check-guarantee* agencies—to learn about your check-writing habits. A retail clerk usually runs the check through an electronic reader and enters your checking account number or driver's license number into a terminal, or calls a specific telephone number. The check-guarantee or verification agency then approves or denies the check.

A *check-verification* company provides an electronic database of people who've written bad checks or have had their bank accounts closed as a result of bad checks. The *check-guarantee* agency takes this one step further. It guarantees the check by pledging to reimburse the retailer if the check bounces. Retailers and banks pay a higher fee for this check-guarantee service.

Q: Why might my check be rejected?
A: Your check may be declined for a variety of reasons:

- You might not meet the check-guarantee/verification agencies' criteria (such as not providing a driver's license number or a home phone number).

- The agency might not have a file on you, or they might have negative information.

- Some agencies will look at how many times the individual has bounced checks (once, say, versus a history of check bouncing); others might look at the check number (low numbers might be rejected because they suggest a new, untested account).

Here's the rub: The databases of check guarantee/verification services are not perfect. You might find that you are listed as a bad-check writer by mistake, even though you have a perfect record. An error in computer-data input may have occurred. Or someone may be using your driver's license number or checking account number to pass bad checks. If so, you have a right to have the error corrected.

Q: What can I do if my check is declined?
A: The retailer will tell you the name of the check-guarantee or verification service that rejected your check.

Many states require that check-guarantee agencies provide the same protection as is required from the credit bureaus, including the right to access your report and have errors corrected.

You may call or write them to find out what information about you they have in their files, and if necessary, correct erroneous information. Their policies vary and are outlined below.

The major check-guarantee and check-verification firms are:

- **Telecheck**
  Consumer Affairs
  P.O. Box 17450
  Denver, CO 80217
  (800) 927-0188
  Telecheck will state the reason for the denial by phone if you call within 30 days of the denial. If it's more than 30 days, the firm will mail you the information.

- **National Processing Co.**
  Consumer Assistance
  P.O. Box 379
  Riverdale, NJ 07457
  (800) 526-5380
  National Processing will send you a letter explaining the reason for the rejection within three to five working days of your call. They may also be able to help you over the phone.

- **Equifax Check Services**
  Consumer Affairs
  P.O. Box 30032
  Tampa, FL 33630-3032
  (800) 437-5120
  Equifax will provide you with a written explanation for the decline of your check.

- **CrossCheck Inc.**
  P.O. Box 6008
  Petaluma, CA 94955
  (707) 586-0551
  CrossCheck requires consumer inquiries in writing. It will respond within 48 hours.

The following companies provide check-verification services only:

- **CheckRite**
  7050 Union Park Center, No. 200
  Midville, UT 84047
  (800) 766-2748
  CheckRite, a verification and collection company, provides information by phone and in writing.

- **Chexsystems**
  Consumer Relations
  12005 Ford Road, No. 600
  Dallas, TX 75234
  (800) 428-9623
  Chexsystems, which provides an electronic listing of closed checking accounts, will not release the information over the telephone, but you can request to have it mailed to you.

- **Shared Check Authorization Network (SCAN)**
  Electronic Transaction Corp.
  19803 North Creek Pkwy.
  Bothell, WA 98011
  (800) 262-7771
  SCAN will let you know if your check has been declined, what negative information has been reported, and by whom. Also, if you pay the outstanding unpaid check, your name will be deleted from the database.

●Privacy Pointers: What You Can Do Now●

1. Give only the minimum data required.

Leave all Social Security, home phone, driver's license, and credit card numbers off checks whenever possible. And don't give out such numbers for credit card purchases, either.

2. Be assertive when asked for information you don't feel is necessary.

For example, ask:

- Why is this information needed and what will be done with it?

- What benefit will *you* receive for giving your personal information?

- Who has access to the information and how will it be protected from unauthorized access?

- When and how will the records be discarded once they're no longer needed?

- Does the company have a written privacy policy? If not, encourage management to develop one.

Don't provide nonessential information unless you're satisfied with the intended use. And if you're not satisfied, take your business elsewhere.

3. For now, be wary of putting credit-card numbers on the Internet unless the transmission is secure.

The two leading purveyors of plastic—Visa and MasterCard—have joined forces to come up with technical standards that will make credit card purchases over the Internet safe from cyberthieves. The process involves creating encryption codes— long strings of numbers that essentially hide sensitive data— that are difficult for crooks to decipher. Many online merchants are already offering consumers the ability to send their credit card number via encrypted transmissions. Look for on-screen graphic indicators such as a picture of a complete, unbroken key, to determine whether or not the transmission is secure.

4. Learn more about digital cash and secure transactions in cyberspace.

Visit the Electronic Frontier Foundation's online commerce archives: http://www.eff.org/pub/Privacy/Digital_money

5. Be especially protective of your Social Security number.

Only give it out when you know it's required (tax forms, employment records, and most banking, stock, and property transactions). There's no law that prevents businesses from requesting your SSN. But, unfortunately, many of your financial records are linked to your SSN. Thus, if it falls into the wrong hands, you could become a fraud victim.

So ask if you can use an alternate number. You may need to be assertive and persistent. Or, you may need to take your business elsewhere.

6. For more information about protecting your rights in transactions with merchants, contact Bankcard Holders of America.

Bankcard Holders of America
524 Branch Drive
Salem, VA 24153
(540) 389-5445
http://epn.com/bha
BHA, a nonprofit membership organization of bankcard and credit-card holders, seeks to promote credit awareness. Among other activities, it produces a series of inexpensive pamphlets, one of which is "Consumer Rights at the Cash Register." It also produces an accompanying "action card" for your wallet, which summarizes your rights in dealing with a merchant.

●

PART II

SAFEGUARDING YOUR PERSONAL RECORDS

4

How Private Is Your Credit Report?

A few years ago, a magazine writer used $50 and his home computer to call up Dan Quayle's credit report. The resulting article showed that the vice president once had run up a $4,000 debt at Sears (later greatly reduced). More important, it showed how easily anyone can access a stranger's credit files.

Credit bureaus maintain files with more information (sometimes, *much* more) than you think and give it to more people than you realize. This chapter will explain what's supposed to be in a credit report and who's supposed to see it. It will also show you how to find out what's in your credit report and who has inquired about it. You'll learn what to do if you discover negative information or errors in your report.

In addition, you'll also learn how information brokers, also known as resellers or information vendors, buy credit reports to resell and how these credit reports are used for marketing purposes (that's usually the source of those "preapproved" credit cards). You'll also see how an "investigative consumer report" can contain information about reputation, personal traits, and lifestyle gathered by interviewing neighbors, friends, or acquaintances.

WHAT'S A CREDIT BUREAU?

A credit bureau is a company that's in the business of gathering and selling credit information. It would be far too costly and time-consuming for each creditor to gather information on each potential borrower. So these banks, finance companies, auto dealers, and others come to rely on credit bureaus, or credit-reporting agencies, to tell them how you've handled your current and previous accounts.

In addition, some credit bureaus evaluate credit files and provide "rating" services predicting how well consumers are likely to manage their credit accounts. These ratings, called credit scores, are generally not available to consumers, but are sold to creditors.

Banks, insurers, finance companies, employers, and merchants subscribe to a credit bureau as a means of gaining access to its files. In return, they submit their own monthly customer credit account records to the credit bureau.

In many cases, creditors will report to more than one credit bureau. Thus, you may be on file with several bureaus. Because all creditors do not subscribe to all credit bureaus, the contents of your file probably differs somewhat from one credit report to another.

There are three major credit bureaus: Equifax, Experian (formerly TRW), and Trans Union. About 3,000 smaller credit bureaus obtain information from the "Big Three" and sell it to their customers. Some of these smaller bureaus specialize in serving certain businesses, such as mortgage lenders or landlords. (To check the credit bureaus in your area, look in the Yellow Pages under "Credit Reporting Agencies.")

WHAT'S IN YOUR CREDIT REPORT?

Your credit report is actually a credit history and profile compiled from many different sources. The original idea was to furnish the basic information needed by credit card companies, present and potential employers, and property owners to determine if you're a high risk.

The report contains your name and any name variations, your address, Social Security number (SSN), employment information, and past and present financial situation. Your legal record may also be included in your credit report, including liens, bankruptcies, and other matters of public record which have an impact on your financial status.

According to Bankcard Holders of America, the information reported most regularly to credit bureaus relates to bankcards (such as Visa and MasterCard), travel and entertainment cards (such as American Express and Diner's Club), large-and medium-sized department stores, and judgments or other legal actions. Most mortgages are reported if they are more than 90 days late, and delinquent child-support payments may also be reported.

Accounts reported less routinely—but still commonly—include some auto and personal bank loans, student loans paid to a bank, and some credit union loans. Those not reported (unless they are past due and become a serious problem) are gasoline cards, utility bills, medical bills, rent payments, lawyers' bills, and most student loans.

Traditionally, this consumer credit report was used to predict how quickly you'd pay your bills. So your promptness—or lack of it—in making such payments was the main point of the exercise.

But now the process has gone beyond that. The trend is toward expanding the use of credit reports and adding to the types of financial data they contain. For example, some automobile insurers now use credit reports to decide whom to insure and at what rate. Credit reports also are being reviewed to pass judgment on your fitness for a mortgage loan, your employability, even your character.

Your bank may also inform the credit bureaus if you overdraw your account. Even worse, negative information—including financial problems you had as long as 10 years ago—can remain to haunt you today.

You also should be aware that some companies known as information brokers, or resellers, obtain credit reports from the major bureaus, then resell them. These brokers are regulated by state and federal laws, which limit the sale of credit reports to those with a "legitimate business need." In some states, such as California, the reseller must tell the credit bureau who will ultimately receive the file. This is to ensure the report is used for permissible purposes.

Basically, any personal information can be included if it is to be used for credit, insurance, or employment purposes. However, certain information cannot be included on your credit report. For instance, it *can't* contain:

- Medical information, unless the consumer consents.

- Adverse information, including bankruptcy, that is more than ten years old.

- Debts that are more than seven years old.

- If the report has been requested by a prospective or current employer, information about age, marital status, or race cannot be included.

The information that is included can be harmful if used by someone who has no right to your file. Carlotta, for example, was engaged to be married. When visiting her in-laws-to-be, she was shocked to discover they knew a great deal about her finances. She ordered her credit report and found that they had made an inquiry through a local credit bureau. Her future in-laws were given a copy of her report even though it was a stretch to say they had a "legitimate business need." Carlotta called off the wedding.

In truth, as the reporter showed with Dan Quayle's credit report, it's not all that difficult for a person with a little know-how, a computer and a modem to gain access to your credit information.

HOW TO PROTECT YOURSELF

Both state and federal laws govern credit bureaus. In addition, the credit bureaus themselves have adopted voluntary guidelines to improve consumer service. But the business is so vast and access so widespread that it's difficult to keep track of all the uses made of credit reports, legitimate or otherwise.

While laws can't always protect you, they can help alert you to activity concerning your file. Federal law gives you the right to know who has inquired about your credit file or requested your report over the last six months (two years for employment purposes); inquirers' names are listed on your credit report. Also, recent amendments to the Fair Credit Reporting Act require that job applicants consent before their credit report can be obtained for employment purposes.

It's wise to check your credit report for errors annually. For one thing, it's good to know who's been asking about your credit. Second, mistakes do happen. The most serious cause of error is fraud. But sometimes you can be mistaken for another person with a similar name, and that other person's information ends up in your file. Sometimes, pure sloppiness is at fault. Third, it's especially important to check your reports because they're now used by more and more people, such as potential employers.

If you find an error, contact the credit bureau and ask it to investigate. Send a letter or use the credit bureau's reporting form. State the points in dispute and outline the evidence. Keep a copy. Under the Fair Credit Reporting Act (FCRA), which governs credit-reporting agencies, the bureau is required to get back to you within 30 days. If you disagree with the result of the bureau's investigation, you have the right to submit a 100-word dispute statement, which the bureau must include in your file. Amendments to the Fair Credit Reporting Act now require the bureaus to develop a joint-error reinvestigation system.

It's also important to check your credit card bills carefully for any inaccurate information which could result in a delinquency being reported to the credit bureau. If you disagree with any part of the bill, send the creditor a *written* notice about the problem. The creditor can't report the disputed item to the credit bureau until the issue is resolved.

YOUR CREDIT AS A MARKETING TOOL

Like many businesses, credit bureaus sell information from their files. This is the source of those offers of "preapproved" credit cards—and it's *very* big business! Preapproved offers account for more than half of all new credit card sign-ups.

Although personal credit information is supposed to be private, the Federal Trade Commission allows credit card issuers to obtain it through a totally legal route. The card companies tell a large credit-reporting bureau that they want to deal with a whole class of customers—say, people who have big home mortgages but who are always on time with the payment. The credit bureau sorts through its files and spits out the names and addresses of those who meet those criteria. Then the credit-card companies send these people a preapproved offer.

Credit information, of course, shows only how a person uses credit, not his or her net worth. But it gives important clues that a card-issuer can use to estimate salary and net worth, such as the size of a home mortgage or auto loan. Data available from other sources, such as real estate information, ZIP code, and census-tract figures, can also help determine one's income level. So while the card-issuers may not know you personally, they have a pretty good idea of how you handle credit and how you will perform if they can entice you to take their card.

A recent amendment to the federal credit-reporting law requires the credit bureaus to maintain toll-free phone numbers to allow consumers to "opt out" of preapproved credit offers. Later in this chapter, you'll learn how to contact them.

INVESTIGATIVE CONSUMER REPORTS

Some companies which operate credit bureaus and back-ground-checking services also conduct investigative consumer reports. These are much more detailed than credit reports. Many of the same people who request credit reports—most commonly, employers and insurers—may also request this report, which contains material on your character, reputation, and lifestyle.

Such information is gathered through personal interviews with neighbors, friends, associates, or acquaintances, as well as through a search of public documents such as property and court records. It can't be used to grant or withhold credit.

Investigative consumer reports are governed by federal and state law. You have the same right to correct and dispute incorrect or incomplete information in an investigative report as you have in a credit report.

Chapter 11 ("What's Your Future Boss Entitled to Know?") discusses employment background checks. It contains tips on steps you can take to avoid unpleasant surprises if you're the subject of a consumer investigative report.

FRAUD AND YOUR CREDIT

One Southern California woman had more than $20,000 worth of merchandise and cash advances charged to her—even though her credit cards never left her purse. She never got any unusual bills because the crook registered a change of address to a fictitious place with each of her credit card companies. Further, the thief was careful not to charge more than the $5,000 limit on any one card. The upshot of the month-long spree was that the innocent woman's excellent credit rating was destroyed because someone obtained her credit card and Social Security numbers.

So, remember, whatever *you* can do as an individual, someone else can do *as you*. It starts when the crook gets access to your information. Maybe your wallet is stolen. Maybe there's an unscrupulous employee where you shop or work. Maybe your preapproved credit offer is lifted from your mailbox or filched from your garbage can.

But beyond the monetary loss (which is borne largely by the credit card issuer) and the sense of feeling violated, you'll be in for plenty of stress and anxiety if this should happen to you. Your credit report will likely be left in ruins. You'll face months of work as you make dozens of calls and write affidavits to creditors explaining your situation and reestablishing your identification.

Unless you're most fortunate, this nightmare can shadow you for years. You can't expect much help from authorities, because law-enforcement generally treats more seriously robbers who use guns than robbers who operate electronically.

Chapter 13 ("How to Cope with 'Identity Theft' ") will discuss in more detail how this could happen and ways to prevent it. For now, understand that credit card fraud losses are enormous, between $1 billion and $3 billion yearly.

●Commonly Asked Questions About Credit●

Q: How can I find out what is on my credit report?
A: By contacting one of the big three credit bureaus and ordering a copy.

Under federal law, credit bureaus must provide you with "the nature and substance of all information in its files" if you so request. Even if you have not been denied credit, it's still a good idea to check your report every year.

Experian (formerly TRW), Equifax, and Trans Union charge $8 for residents of most states. But if you live in Georgia, Maryland, Massachusetts, or Vermont, it's free. Most important, if you have been denied credit because of information contained in your report, the credit bureau must provide you with a free copy upon request within 60 days after the denial. Others who may receive free credit reports are indigent consumers, victims of identity theft, and the unemployed.

Check to see if there are any errors and who else has asked for a copy. If you see any errors, contact the credit bureau immediately. Instructions for disputing information are included with the credit report.

You can order your credit report from:

- **Equifax**
  P.O. Box 740241
  Atlanta, GA 30374
  (800) 685-1111
  http://www.equifax.com

- **Experian (formerly TRW)**
  P.O. Box 2104
  Allen, TX 75013
  (800) 682-7654
  http://www.experian.com

- **Trans Union**
  P.O. Box 390
  Springfield, PA 19064
  (800) 888-4213
  http://www.tuc.com

Q: What do I look for when I receive my report?
A: Anything out of the ordinary.

Start by carefully reviewing the basics, such as your name and address, SSN, employer, and the creditors listed. Be especially alert for accounts you did not open, incorrect payment history, and repetitive information, such as reports from a collection agency as well as from the original creditor.

Problems often occur when there's a mixup of names, such as father (''Senior'') and son (''Junior''), or very common names. Errors also occur when someone is defrauding another by assuming his or her name.

Q: Can I have negative information deleted if the entry is not an error?

A: Usually only by maintaining a good credit record.

Negative information—such as nonpayment of bills, over-drawn accounts, and high credit card debts—can usually only be removed by keeping good credit over a number of years. Be wary of companies or individuals promising quick fixes to your credit troubles. They're often fraudulent. Be especially wary of companies that promise to clean your record for a fee, or which offer you a major credit card but fail to adequately inform you about the up-front application fee, the ongoing annual fee, the percentage rate, or the grace period. A recent amendment to the Fair Credit Reporting Act prohibits so-called credit repair clinics from collecting a fee before completing the promised service.

Bankruptcies are reported on credit reports for ten years, and tax liens remain on your record for seven years after they're paid. In some cases, credit bureaus will stop reporting unfavorable information after only two or three years.

If there were strong extenuating circumstances that led to the reporting of accurate, but negative, information on your credit report, you may want to ask the creditor to help you get it removed. If the creditor agrees and tells the credit bureau the information is no longer verifiable, it will be dropped.

Q: What's a credit score and how can I learn my score?

A: It's a prediction about your ability to pay on time—but it's off-limits to you.

Credit bureaus use sophisticated computer models to analyze your payment history, your credit limits, and other factors. They assign you a number which indicates the level of risk a credit issuer faces if it grants you credit. Generally, the higher the number, the better you look and the less risk there is to the credit issuer. (For example, one scoring model gives a range of scores from 300 to the low 900s, with low-risk borrowers generally being above 800.)

More than 20 companies have developed computer-profiling software to create these scores. Credit bureaus can choose which firm's modeling method to use, so a score you're assigned from one credit bureau may differ from another. Your score may vary from day to day, depending on the data in your credit history at that moment. Further, individual lenders decide for themselves which scores are acceptable for different types of loans or credit.

Although the score is sometimes the *only* piece of information a lender receives about a consumer, the consumer isn't allowed to see his or her score. The Federal Trade Commission at one point decided consumers *did* have the right to see their scores and began working on rules to implement that requirement. But, later, it reversed itself for complex reasons, including pressure from the credit-reporting industry. That was a major blow for consumers, because more and more important decisions are being made about you based on that score.

Q: Why do I receive so many preapproved credit card applications in the mail?

A: Because credit-reporting companies are in the business of selling information, and the credit card industry is so highly competitive.

Receiving a lot of preapproved offers with tantalizingly high credit limits is the price you pay for having a good income and a clean credit record. Credit-reporting firms release to card issuers the names and addresses of people with good credit profiles.

The card companies especially like consumers who may carry a high balance, thus entailing interest payments. Some less than scrupulous card issuers may target consumers with poor credit in order to entice them into seemingly lower interest rates, which later increase.

If you want to opt out of preapproved offers of credit, contact the following credit bureaus:

- **Equifax Options**
  Equifax Marketing Decision Systems, Inc.
  Box 740123
  Atlanta, GA 30374
  (800) 556-4711

- **Experian (formerly TRW)**
  Target Marketing Services Division
  Attn: Consumer Opt-Out
  P.O. Box 919
  Allen, TX 75013
  (800) 353-0809

- **Trans Union**
  Name Removal Option
  P.O. Box 7245
  Fullerton, CA 92637
  (800) 680-7293

●Privacy Pointers: What You Can Do Now●

1. Check your credit report at least once a year.

We said it before, but it bears repeating: Checking your credit report is of paramount importance. With the uses of the credit report being expanded, keeping an eye on it is your best protection. Such scrutiny is the only way to determine if there's negative information or errors in your report.

You should also check your credit report when you know it's going to be used to make important decisions about you, such as applying for an automobile or home loan, renting an apartment, or applying for a job. At these crucial times, you don't want to be surprised to find negative information—especially if it's inaccurate.

2. Periodically follow up on the correction of any errors in your credit report.

Some consumers who have had errors corrected find the incorrect information reappears later in their files. Therefore, it's wise to periodically check your credit report to make sure the errors do not reappear. Under the Fair Credit Reporting Act, deleted information cannot be reinserted unless the credit bureau notifies the consumer and certifies that the reinsertion is accurate.

3. Don't fill out a credit application without good reason.

Sometimes merchants will insist you fill out a credit application even if you're paying for a costly item by cash or cashier's check. "It's just routine," they say, or "for our records."

Don't do it unless you're actually applying for credit. It will be listed as an "inquiry" on your credit report, and such inquiries may have to be explained later when you do actually apply for credit with someone else.

Be assertive about this. If you're paying by cash or cashier's check, that should be good enough to satisfy anyone. If you're paying by personal check, the merchant can easily verify that the check is good, or at the worst, you can agree to delay taking possession of your purchase until the check has cleared.

4. Destroy "preapproved" credit card and loan applications you don't want.

Rip them up, shred them, or burn them—don't just toss them in the trash, where "Dumpster divers" can retrieve them and possibly put your private information to their use.

Make sure the companies you apply for credit with, such as auto dealers, do the same. Unshredded credit applications are a rich treasure for those intent on fraud.

5. Remember: guard your personal identification numbers!

Your SSN is the key to defrauding you. With as little as your name and SSN, an unscrupulous person can apply for credit with your name and their address, then avoid the bills.

You may dutifully guard your credit card number and checking accounts, but if you cheerfully disclose your SSN to almost anyone who asks—insurance policies, club memberships, cable company, and the like—you're leaving yourself open to the possibility that someone else can tap into your good credit.

Other precautions include:

• Tear up carbons from credit card charge slips and take them with you.

• Don't throw away voided checks or extra deposit slips— rip them in half and discard the pieces separately.

• Examine every item on your credit card statements and every call on your phone bill. Look for anything unusual.

6. Educate yourself about your credit rights and responsibilities.

If you're bedeviled by a negative, though accurate, credit report, it will take time to change that. Let the credit bureaus see that you are actively trying to improve your credit, and eventually your bad credit report will become outdated.

Contact the following organizations for brochures giving in-depth information on managing your finances:

• **Bankcard Holders of America**
524 Branch Drive
Salem, VA 24153
(540) 389-5445
http://www.epn.com/bha
This is a national nonprofit consumer-credit education group.

• **Consumer Action Credit and Finance Project**
116 New Montgomery St., No. 233
San Francisco, CA 94105
(415) 777-9635
http://www.consumer-action.org

*A nonprofit consumer advocacy and education organiza-
tion, it offers several brochures on banking and credit, including "Establishing Good Credit."*

- **Federal Reserve System**
Publications Services
Division of Support Services
Washington, D.C. 20551
(202) 452-3693
Order its free booklet "Consumer Handbook to Credit Pro-
tection Laws."

- **Federal Trade Commission**
Public Reference
Washington, D.C. 20580
(202) 326-2222
http://www.ftc.gov
*Order its list of free publications on credit and other con-
sumer topics.*

- **U.S. PIRG**
218 D St., SE
Washington, D.C. 20003
(202) 546-9707
http://www.pirg.org
*This nonprofit advocacy group conducts research and is-
sues reports on numerous consumer issues, including credit
reporting and the problem of identity theft. Several states
also have PIRGs (Public Interest Research Groups).*

- *Read* The Ultimate Credit Handbook *by Gerri Detweiler
(Penguin Books, 1997). This is a thorough guide on reducing debt, dealing with credit bureaus, and obtaining and
keeping good credit.*

5

Is Your Medical Information Really Confidential?

When Nydia Velázquez first ran for Congress, she had to explain more than where she stood on the issues. The New York City Democrat had to defend her mental stability.

Someone leaked her confidential hospital records to the press. Those files showed that the former college professor had once attempted suicide and had fought depression with alcohol and drugs. Velázquez won the 1992 race anyhow, but only after enduring a news conference where she said that trying to take her own life had been "a sad and painful experience for me, one that I thought was in the past."

Velázquez is a high-profile example of how your medical or emotional history can be revealed without your knowledge or consent. You don't have to be a politician or a celebrity to come face-to-face with the fact that your medical records are probably not as private as you think. Consider the examples of Martin, Barbara, Anna, Doug, and Theresa, any one of whom could easily have been diagnosed as having an acute sense of false security:

- When Martin took a physical exam as part of an application for more life insurance, he offhandedly remarked to the doctor that he'd smoked marijuana about 20 years earlier.

Apparently, the doctor noted that remark in Martin's medical record because he was unable to get his insurance increased due to that and other old, or incorrect, information.

- Barbara donated plasma at a private center and was assured that none of the information she provided would be released. But when she returned to donate again, she noticed her name posted on a bulletin board as a donor. No big deal? Perhaps, but it ran counter to what she'd been told. Further, had there been a problem—say, blood contamination—would everyone have known?

- Anna's landlord is a medical doctor, and she sometimes babysits for his children. But after she went to another physician for treatment of a chronic back problem, she was shocked to learn that her doctor shared information about her condition with her physician-landlord. Her confidentiality was breached, she concluded, because her landlord feared he might lose his babysitter.

- Doug saw the company doctor and requested an HIV test. Doug later learned that the doctor gave that information to the firm's human-resources department, and someone there told his supervisor.

- Theresa, an attorney, was refused disability insurance after an insurer saw a physician's notations on her medical records that her father—not she—had Huntington's disease, a serious neurological disorder. The notation, it turned out, was in error. Theresa eventually had to change employers to get insurance.

Because we revere the doctor-patient privilege, we think of medicine as one of the few truly confidential areas in our lives. As those examples show, mistakes happen, the laws contain exemptions, and you usually must waive your right to confidentiality in exchange for insurance coverage. Also, patients may get complacent about their medical records.

Perhaps most alarming is the increasingly electronic nature of medical record-keeping. Although doctors and hospitals are well intentioned, computer hackers, private detectives, political campaign operatives, and healthcare insiders may be less scrupulous.

A crazy quilt of state laws provides scant protection against abuses such as these:

- A Massachusetts child-rapist obtained a job at a hospital. With an improperly acquired password, he allegedly gained access to nearly a thousand patient records and then made repeated phone calls to young girls.

- In Maryland, 24 people were indicted for a scheme in which clerks were accused of selling information about individuals in the Medicaid database to four HMOs.

- A Colorado medical student reportedly sold private patient hospital records to malpractice attorneys.

- A banker, also in Maryland, was accused of cross-referencing a list of cancer patients against a list of outstanding loans at his bank—and then calling in the loans.

While these kinds of cases may be rare, the truth remains that too often such data is shared by a wide range of people both in and out of the healthcare community. In fact, one recent study of a large hospital estimated that each patient's record was seen by an average of almost 80 persons. That included only the people inside the hospital, not insurance companies and other external reviewers.

This chapter will explain what is contained in medical records, who has access to them, and how those files can be protected.

WHAT MEDICAL RECORDS REVEAL

It's ironic that your medical records—which contain perhaps the most sensitive information about you—are also among the most vulnerable to outside scrutiny. Every ailment or disability you complain of, every illness you're treated for, every test you're given, and every bit of counseling you receive is probably in those files.

Records of your visits to physicians, nurses, dentists, or mental-health professionals may include your medical history, details about your lifestyle (such as smoking, obesity, substance abuse, or involvement in high-risk sports), laboratory test results, the outcomes of operations and other medical procedures, and family medical background. Your records can also reveal a history of family relationships, sexual abuse, abortions, and genetic diseases.

Much of this information—how you responded, say, to treatment for the flu or what your podiatrist noted about your fallen arches—might not trouble you if it were released. And who would care to know anyway?

But what if, instead of the flu or your flat feet, the records we're talking about include references to bed-wetting, or an abortion, or a sexually transmitted disease, or chronic depression? You probably wouldn't want many people knowing about those. There are folks—such as prospective employers or unprincipled acquaintances—who might well be interested.

While you may think that law and ethics would combine to keep this information strictly confidential, the reality is different. In fact, strange as it seems, the law puts stricter limits on the release of the titles of books you check out of the library than it does on your medical records.

As discussed in the introduction, technology worsens a potentially bad situation. Unauthorized access to paper records has always been feasible, but the computer magnifies the problem enormously. In fact, medical ethicists say the trend toward computerized record-keeping has gone so far that it's naive to think that what you tell your doctor stops there.

Increasingly, too, genetic information is being kept on file. Gene research offers hope for curing or preventing a wide range of diseases. But that technology also has enormous potential for fueling discrimination. What if you were shown to have inherited genes linked to cancer, muscular dystrophy, psychiatric disorders, and other diseases?

Though you may never suffer from any of those, the fact that those predispositions are in your DNA might be a factor in denying you insurance or a job. So what's in your medical file and who sees it isn't just a privacy issue; it can be an economic issue, too.

WHO GIVES PERMISSION?

Not only your doctors and nurses, but insurance companies, government agencies, and even marketers may have access to these personal records. And, perhaps surprisingly, permission for the majority of these people to see your records was probably inadvertently given by *you*.

In fact, sometimes even what you specifically ask *not* be included in your medical records can find its way into your file . . . and from there onto other places. Ellen, for example, always made a point of keeping a certain piece of personal information confidential—that she once had a child whom she put up for adoption. On her medical questionnaires, she was always careful to note that she had two children. However, she verbally told the doctor about the earlier child, asking him not to put this in her record. In the course of dealing with the insurance company following an auto accident, it became clear that the insurer knew about this third child, because the doctor *had* made a note in her file. Though the existence of this other child wasn't relevant to her accident claim, it was relevant to her emotions—and, potentially, to the emotional well-being of her family.

THE PROBLEM WITH WAIVERS

Generally, access to your medical records is obtained when you sign "blanket waivers" or "general consent forms" when you get medical care. When you sign such a waiver, you allow the healthcare provider to release your medical information to whoever shows a compelling need for it.

The most obvious, and the most expected, use of your medical records is for insurance purposes and by government agencies. Insurance companies want to see your records before they will issue a policy. For most of us, this seems a reasonable use of our confidential records. Governmental agencies such as Medicare, Social Security Disability, and Workers Compensation also have a compelling reason to see your records, because they're deciding whether to pay you money based on age and health.

Medical information gathered by one insurance company or agency may be shared with others through the Massachusetts-based Medical Information Bureau (MIB), a central database of medical information on some 15 million North Americans. About 680 insurance firms in the United States and Canada—virtually every major firm issuing life, health, or disability policies—use the services of the MIB.

MIB was created more than 90 years ago to make it more difficult for insurance applicants to fraudulently omit or conceal significant information. It now collects coded data in more than 200 medical categories (such as weight, blood pressure, and EKG readings) that relate to life expectancy and five nonmedical categories that could impact longevity (such as an adverse driving record and participation in aviation or hazardous sports).

When you apply for life, health, or disability insurance as an individual, you receive a brief written notice about MIB and are asked to sign a release allowing your MIB file, if any, to be seen by the insurer. MIB says a decision on insurability and premiums can't be made based solely on the MIB report; further investigation and tests are required. MIB emphasizes that it seeks data only on insurance applicants with "a condition significant to health or longevity." Further, it releases such information only to member firms, not to nonmember insurers or to credit- or consumer-reporting agencies, and that, in any event, data more than seven years old is automatically deleted.

If you have always obtained life, health, and disability insurance through a group plan, you are unlikely to be in the MIB database.

WHY EMPLOYERS NEED YOUR RECORDS

Employers also have access to your medical information. They often ask workers to authorize disclosure of medical records for one of two reasons:

- When medical insurance is paid in whole or part by employers, they may require insurance companies to provide them with copies of employees' medical records so the firm can see what it's paying for.

- Self-insured businesses may establish a fund to cover the insurance claims for employees. Because no third party is involved, the medical records that would normally be inspected by an insurance company are open to the employer.

Tying health care to employment, as our system does, greatly increases the problem with confidentiality. Because most insurance is paid by the employer, those firms assert they have a right to your medical information. That can work against you in the workplace—even though it's legally not supposed to.

There are, however, restrictions that the federal Americans with Disabilities Act places on employers. Generally, those state:

- Employers may not ask job applicants about medical information or require a physical examination *prior* to offering a job.

- Once a job is offered, an employer can only ask for a medical examination if it's required of all employees holding similar jobs.

- If you are turned down for work based on the results of a medical examination, the employer must prove that it is physically impossible for you to do the work required.

Despite these privacy protections, certain illnesses and medical conditions—sometimes as seemingly minor as backaches or allergies—can cause you to lose your job, or not be hired in the first place. That's because healthcare problems are costly, and insurers and employers don't want to take on high-risk individuals who might need expensive care in the future.

OTHER DISCLOSURES

Other ways your medical record might be disclosed would be if it's subpoenaed for a court case, if it's part of a research study, or if your treatment figures in the evaluation of a medical institution—say, a hospital or individual physician. Such evaluations are required for most hospitals to receive their licenses. However, your identity is generally not disclosed when medical practices are evaluated.

Occasionally, your medical information is used for health research and is sometimes disclosed to public health agencies such as the federal Centers for Disease Control. Again, specific names are usually not included with the information.

Much more troubling is the use of your private records for direct marketing. When you participate in informal health screenings—such as tests for cholesterol or blood pressure often held at pharmacies, health fairs, or shopping malls—your name and address may end up in databanks of businesses selling related products. Some consumer surveys, such as the Carol Wright Personal Preference Product Survey and the Buyers' Choice Survey of America, ask you to divulge information about your health, which is then sold to marketers.

THE FUTURE OF MEDICAL RECORDS

There's much debate over the future of American health care and medical record-keeping. The old, paper-based system of recording medical data—inefficient, perhaps, but easier to keep private—will soon be a thing of the past.

Massive computerized systems are being rapidly developed. They ultimately will allow physicians, insurers, employers, and others with an interest in the cost of medical care to access patient information from remote locations throughout the country. For example, instead of each of your healthcare providers keeping their own records in house, there might be one merged file with your complete medical history stored in a regional or national database. With a few computer keystrokes, your heart specialist, for instance, could review the notes of your general practitioner, obtain lab and radiology results, or even send a prescription.

Such technology promises not only to make the doctor more efficient but perhaps also help you better keep track of your personal information and monitor your records for mistakes. In this manner, proponents say, medical costs would be cut and patient care improved.

However, privacy advocates worry that having a comprehensive, computerized repository of cradle-to-grave medical records would significantly increase the risk of improper use. Data that can be accessed through a computer opens up the possibilities of unauthorized people seeing such data . . . and probably with a lot less effort than would be required for them to see paper records. You may not know who's looking at your file because, the way the law reads today in many states, no one will be required to tell you.

Though the public is being assured that electronically stored medical information won't be used for marketing or other non-medical purposes, it's clear that, on a broader level, medical information is becoming a commodity. Unfortunately, the law, as it now stands, isn't much of a protection.

Americans are uneasy about this. Without question, computerized medical records potentially can improve medical treatment and cut costs. But, according to a 1995 Equifax-commissioned survey, 74% of Americans are either somewhat concerned or very concerned about the "negative effects" of computerizing patient records.

There's a general consensus among policymakers, consumer advocates, and industry representatives that the privacy and confidentiality of health records should be addressed as part of revamping the healthcare system. Congress has been grappling with this medical privacy issue for several years. It has looked at ways to limit access to and uses of medical files, and provide criminal and civil penalties for those who violate the regulations.

Under most of the proposals, patients would be given the right to review their files, much as they now can with their credit histories, and make corrections if they find errors. But, predictably, each piece of proposed legislation is attacked by those in the medical and insurance communities, who say it goes too far, as well as by patient advocates who claim it doesn't go far enough in protecting patient privacy.

●Commonly Asked Questions About Medical Records●

Q: Can I get access to my own medical records?
A: Laws in about 20 states give you the right to see your medical file. You can also get a copy of the file kept by the Medical Information Bureau.

Many states require healthcare providers—such as doctors' offices, hospitals, mental health facilities, and clinics—to allow a patient to get a copy of all of his or her medical records. Even in states without such laws, it is the general practice to allow access.

The best way to get access is by writing the medical records department of your healthcare provider and requesting a copy. In states with access laws, the providers are given a time limit of a few days or weeks in which to comply with a request. They also may ask for reimbursement of reasonable copying and or clerical costs.

If you received care in a federal medical facility, you have the right to obtain those records under the federal Privacy Act of 1974. (See Chapter 6, "From Cradle to Grave: Government Records and Your Privacy," as well as Appendix A, which has sample request letters.)

Another route is to contact the MIB, the company that keeps medical records on many—but, by no means, all—Americans. About 160,000 people annually ask for a copy of their information. To find out if you're in MIB's database, contact:

Medical Information Bureau
P.O. Box 105, Essex Station
Boston, MA 02112
(617) 426-3660

Canadians may do the same by contacting MIB at:

Medical Information Bureau
330 University Avenue
Toronto, Ontario
Canada M5G 1R7
(416) 597-0590

If you are in MIB's files (about 1 out of 10 people are), you can obtain a copy. The fee is $8, including corrections, if needed. In addition, you'll be told the name of any MIB member or company that received a copy of your report in the preceding six months. If you detect an error, you can request a correction, as explained below.

Q: How common are errors in MIB files?

A: Percentage-wise, not common. But given the huge numbers of files involved, that can translate to thousands of incorrect records.

MIB President Neil Day has said he's proud that his database's error rate is less than 4%. But with 2.5 million new reports received by MIB annually, that still suggests odds high enough that you ought to check your records every few years.

If you request correction of an error in your MIB file, you'll be sent a ''reinvestigation request'' and a description of the reinvestigation process, which requires the insurer to check again with the medical source who provided the original information. Most reinvestigations are completed within 30 days.

If the rechecking confirms the error, it's deleted or amended. If the study substantiates the original report, you'll be allowed to file a ''statement of dispute'' that'll be included in your MIB record.

Similarly, you can ask your local healthcare provider to check your MIB record and seek a correction or amendment, if needed.

Q: Are records of my prescription drugs kept confidential?

A: Probably not.

Although health plans typically are administered by insurance companies, self-insured employers, in order to keep a lid on costs, have access to some records detailing workers' healthcare problems. Prescription charges often are among these. There have been cases of employers finding out from these records that employees had serious, but previously unreported, conditions.

In fact, such easy access to prescription records led, in part, to 17 state attorneys general pressuring one of the largest managers of prescription benefits (Medco Containment Services, a division of Merck) to change its policies. Under the agreement, self-insured employers still can look at prescription records, but Merck will encourage them to notify workers that such data is not confidential.

Q: Who can I go to for help if I think my medical records are being improperly released?

A: You first should contact medical authorities, then, if necessary, privacy advocacy groups.

If you have a dispute with a healthcare provider over improper release of medical information, or are having trouble getting copies of your medical records, contact your local county medical society for assistance, or call the state medical board.

In addition, the U.S. Equal Employment Opportunity Commission (EEOC) handles complaints against employers who discriminate against employees because of medical conditions. Local EEOC offices are listed in the U.S. Government section in the white pages of the phone book, or you can contact:

> **U.S. Equal Opportunity Employment Commission**
> 1801 L St., NW
> Washington, D.C. 20507
> (202) 663-4900
> http://www.eeoc.gov

The Americans with Disabilities Act (ADA) has also created regional offices to deal with consumer questions about such discrimination. These offices provide technical assistance and materials related to the ADA, including issues of medical records, physical and psychological testing, and employment. ADA regulations can be enforced by private lawsuits or by individuals filing complaints with the U.S. Attorney General, who then may file lawsuits to stop discrimination and obtain monetary penalties.

You can find out more by contacting:

> **ADA Regional Disability and Business Technical Assistance Center**
> (800) 949-4232
> http://www.pacdbtac.org

Other sources of information or assistance include:

- **American Health Information Management Association**
  919 N. Michigan Ave., No. 1400
  Chicago, IL 60611
  (312) 787-2672
  http://www.ahima.org
  This is the national professional organization of specialists in health-information management.

- **U.S. Department of Health and Human Services**
  Privacy Advocate
  200 Independence Ave., SW
  Washington, D.C. 20201
  (202) 690-5896
  http://phs.os.dhhs.gov
  The office of the Privacy Advocate serves as a resource for privacy issues regarding personally identifiable information about individuals in programs and activities of the DHHS.

In addition, a number of other groups have worked to develop federal legislation to strengthen patients' privacy rights in computerized medical records systems. They include:

- **American Health Information Management Association**
  1225 I St., NW, No. 500
  Washington, D.C. 20005
  (202) 218-3535

- **Center for Democracy and Technology**
  1634 I St., NW, No. 1100
  Washington, D.C. 20006
  (202) 637-9800
  http://www.cdt.org
  The nonprofit CDT has issued the report "Privacy and Health Information Systems: A Guide to Protecting Patient Confidentiality."

- **Consumer Project on Technology**
  Box 19367
  Washington, D.C. 20036
  (202) 387-8030
  http://www.cptech.org
  The CPT advocates for patient-centered federal legislation.

- **National Coalition for Patient Rights**
  405 Waltham, No. 218
  Lexington, MA 02173
  (617) 861-0635
  The Coalition is dedicated to restoring and preserving confidentiality and privacy in medical care.

●Privacy Pointers: What You Can Do Now●

1. Limit the amount of information you release to your healthcare provider.

When you're asked to sign a waiver for the release of your medical records, try to limit the information. Instead of signing the "blanket waiver," cross it out and write in more specific terms. For example, if the waiver asks for authorization for *all* information to be released by the physician, hospital, or other medical provider, specifically state where the records are to be released from, the dates you were treated, and the medical condition you were treated for.

> *Example of blanket waiver:* "I authorize any physician, hospital or other medical provider to release to [insurer] any information regarding my medical history, symptoms, treatment, exam results, or diagnosis."

> *Edited waiver:* "I authorize my records to be released from [hospital, clinic or doctor] for the [date of treatment] as relates to [the condition treated]."

Some insurance companies or businesses may not allow you to do this. If so, you'll then need to decide whether to go elsewhere and pay for treatment yourself, or let them have full access to your records.

2. If you want a specific condition to be held in confidence, bring a written request to your appointment with the health-care provider.

By bringing a written request specifically asking that a condition not be disclosed, you are withholding your permission for information from that visit to be passed on to the insurance company or your employer.

However, you will have to pay for the visit yourself if you don't want your insurer to know about your visit and/or subsequent treatment. To be doubly certain of confidentiality, you may wish to see a different physician altogether, as well as forfeiting reimbursement from the insurance company.

3. Question all questionnaires.

Find out if you must complete it, what its purpose is, and who will have access to the information. Also, before participating in informal health screenings and filling out consumer questionnaires, find out what uses will be made of the medical data collected.

4. Ask your healthcare provider to use caution when copying portions of your records for others.

Sometimes employees are careless and copy more of your medical record than is necessary. This can happen when, for example, they send it to an insurance company to settle a claim.

5. If your records are subpoenaed for a legal proceeding, try to limit what will become a permanent public record.

Ask the court to allow only a specific portion of your medical record to be seen, or that it not be open at all. The judge will decide what parts, if any, of your medical record should be considered private.

After the case is decided, you can also ask the judge to seal the court records containing your medical information.

6. Find out if your healthcare provider has a policy on the use of wireless phones or fax machines when discussing or transmitting medical information.

Cordless and cellular phones are not as private as standard "wired" telephones (see Chapter 7, "Cordless and Cellular Phones: Is Everybody Listening?"). Because wireless phones transmit by radio waves, phone conversations can be overheard by various electronic devices.

Fax machines offer far less privacy than the mail. Frequently, many people in an office have access to fax transmissions. Staff members at all levels of a healthcare organization should take precautions to preserve confidentiality when sending and receiving medical documents by fax machine. (See also Chapter 15, "Respecting Privacy by Being a Responsible Information Handler.")

7. Send for a copy of the brochure "Your Health Information Belongs to You" and "Is Your Health Information Confidential?"

They cost $1.55 each and are available from:

American Health Information Management Association
919 N. Michigan Ave., No. 1400
Chicago, IL 60611
(312) 787-2672 or (800) 335-5535.
AHIMA also publishes "In Confidence", a newsletter (bimonthly; $90/year to nonmembers) devoted to health-information confidentiality. For subscription information, call (800) 335-5535.

8. Seek a solid understanding with your doctor about what records are made available if you're injured or take ill while traveling.

Find out what his or her policy is about faxing records to out-of-town doctors or hospitals. Ask how rigorously your doctor seeks to establish the requestor's right to your file. Determine whether the entire record is sent, or just the portion relevant to your immediate problem.

There's a bit of a balancing act involved here. Obviously, if you're sick or hurt, you want the out-of-town doctor to have all the needed information, but establishing some ground rules with your own physician will help limit your exposure.

9. Remember whom your company doctor works for.

More employees are going to company doctors than ever before. Sometimes it's because they must have a preemployment physical or be examined for a worker's compensation claim. But many workers also are taking advantage of company "wellness programs" stressing preventive care. There's a lot to be said for that. These programs can save everyone money and time and, in many cases, provide excellent care.

But be aware that such programs may also maintain medical files on you. And be aware that there's a tangled web of legal and ethical issues that arise if, for instance, your tests disclose an illness that's expensive to cure. Lewis Maltby, director of the American Civil Liberties Union's workplace taskforce, says you could "lose your coverage or, even worse, your job" if management discovers a costly ailment.

Though it isn't supposed to happen, there have been cases, for example, where employees found out from a company doctor they were HIV positive and, as a result, suffered workplace discrimination. All employees should be aware of the economic relationship between the doctor and the company. "Anybody who uses a company physician in the assumption that person can be absolutely respectful of confidentiality as an outside person is foolish," Alan Westin, a respected authority on privacy and business, told the *New York Times*.

The moral: Think hard about when to take advantage of the affordable care that companies offer, and press your firm to clarify its policies and procedures.

10. Ask your doctors and your hospital about privacy safeguards.

Find out where and in what form your records are stored, and more importantly, who has access to them and under what conditions that access list will be expanded. Also ask about plans to computerize records and merge them with other systems.

6

From Cradle to Grave:
Government Records and Your Privacy

From your first breath to your last, the government keeps tabs on you. Somewhere, someplace, an agency has a file showing when and where you were born, went to school, got married or divorced, or served in the military. It knows what you paid for your house, what kind of car you drive and how safely you do so. It knows how much money you make and, in large measure, how you choose to spend it. It knows if your dog is licensed, what books you check out of the library, and whether you've had brushes with the law. *And a lot more.*

In truth, it has always known these things, but it has never been very good at retrieving these facts. Because each agency had its own dusty files of paper records, getting a nearly complete picture of anyone was next to impossible. In short, your privacy was largely protected by that old standby: bureaucratic inefficiency.

No more. Two trends are merging to make information about you both highly accessible and highly valuable.

First, these records are rapidly becoming digitized onto computers. Second, cash-strapped state and local governments are coming to see this data as a valuable commodity they can sell. As a result, many of these formerly disparate bits of information are now being compiled, either by the government or private information vendors.

It's the possibility of government and/or business pulling these bits and pieces of data together to build a kind of electronic dossier on each of us that causes the most concern. After all these years of our worrying about Big Brother, he could finally be quietly slipping in and taking a seat at the family table. The villain may turn out not to be Big Government as much as across-the-board data gathering and data merging by public and private entities. This trend, fueled by technology, is accelerating and may well be in full bloom by the year 2000.

This potential loss of privacy affects more than just those with skeletons in their closet. As we saw with credit reporting and other private records, errors happen, and it's often difficult, if not impossible, for the truth to catch up. Doubly ironic is the fact that sometimes it's more difficult for *you* to find out what's in your record than it is for *others*.

For instance, Dick, while divorcing his wife, was dating Helen. Helen's ex-husband looked up Dick's divorce file and contractor's license record, both public documents. Then he called Dick's estranged wife's attorney with allegations—untrue, it turned out—that Dick was hiding assets.

Deirdre, on the other hand, couldn't get information on the death of her son, whom the sheriff said committed suicide in jail. As she learned, government records can be withheld despite what seem to be compelling reasons for disclosure.

This chapter will show that there are few, if any, restrictions on the release of much of this information, especially at the local level. It's available to reporters, direct marketers, private detectives, law enforcement officers, or the guy down the street with a grudge. In fact, as more public records are computerized and go online, it'll become easier for anyone with a computer, a modem, and a little knowledge to compile detailed profiles on individuals.

This chapter will also explain what's confidential and what's not. You'll learn how to best protect your records, or in cases like Deirdre's, obtain records that are being withheld.

THE PERILS OF COMPUTERIZED DATA

In California, the Department of Information Technology is taking steps to create a single state database on individuals, replacing files now kept separately by as many as 123 agencies. As with so many of the potential intrusions into privacy, the motives aren't sinister. For example, the state has begun cross-checking state data against county data—something it couldn't do before relatively inexpensive, high-powered computers were available—and denying driver's licenses to those who fail to pay child support.

While most of us would applaud that goal, it doesn't take much imagination to see how government and computers could mix menacingly. Already, there are worrisome indicators around the country:

- In Illinois, a legislator proposed that the state furnish him and other elected officials its computerized master list of all operating businesses. That way, he said, he could use the roster for "official business," such as notifying firms of new laws or regulations. But much of the business community saw the request as an attempt to develop a campaign solicitation tool, an "incumbent-advantage kind of program," one businessman termed it.

- The IRS sometimes looks into lifestyles, using a variety of government and commercial databases to check standard of living against reported income. The agency as a whole doesn't have a policy on this, and the original, agency-wide proposal was met with cries of outrage from privacy advocates and civil libertarians. IRS officials explain that some regional offices do seek to measure group compliance by checking into aberrations. For example, if you're the owner of a certain kind of business, but your possessions or activities reflect a higher income than normally associated with that group of business owners, you may be investigated.

• As part of the outcry over illegal immigration, a national identity card is being suggested. The card, under some proposals, would need to be renewed annually and would include a digitized form of each citizen's vital statistics and be linked to federal computer databases. The question isn't, can it be done? The question is, would its use remain limited to catching illegal workers?

• The real-estate and publishing industries are giving us computer access to home-sale data, liens, mortgage-deed information, and other assessor's records. This could be a boon for the aware, self-reliant consumer or investor. But it also could be a leg up for the white-collar criminal who wants to take advantage of, say, rich widows or widowers. The scam artist could easily compile lists of recently divorced or widowed spouses, learn how much equity they have in their homes, then pick his targets.

Although much of this sort of information has been available for decades, it has been difficult to find and compile. It's legitimate to ask about the tradeoffs in privacy that easier access will bring.

Whether we're ready or not, governments are increasingly collating information—and in many cases, selling it. In part, that's because they face terrific pressure to cut waste and recoup costs. In addition, rising fraud and consumer demand for quick credit are spawning private firms whose business is finding answers locked away in government and financial records, such as: What do you owe? What liens are there against your business? Are you who you say you are?

Already, a dozen or more firms nationwide are putting government records online and then, of course, selling them. They buy public records—electronic and paper—from thousands of agencies and courthouses across the country and then feed the information into databases. As a result, some of them are able to conduct nationwide searches of court and other public records. Not only are banking, finance, and insurance companies interested in such information, so is law enforcement.

How much information will be given away or sold varies according to agency. As you go down the continuum from federal to state to local, information gets easier to obtain. Much of the real juicy stuff—property records, divorce files, court cases—is at the local level.

In some counties, for example, it's being proposed that entire court files—as opposed to just an index to those files—be sold to firms which will put them online. That may not seem like such a big deal until it includes your messy divorce, your battle for conservatorship for an Alzheimer's-stricken father, or your cousin who's being legally declared a sex offender.

True, those same records probably would be available now to someone interested enough to go to the courthouse and look through various paper files. It may be something else again to have those same records available to anyone with a personal computer. With just a few keystrokes, he or she can not only read your files but create copies and send them to anyone else with a computer.

HOW MUCH DOES THE GOVERNMENT KNOW?

Most Americans probably greatly underestimate the number of federal files they're in and how much information about them has been gathered and can be accessed in a matter of minutes. Obviously, if you pay taxes, the IRS has a file on you. If you were in the military, you're on file with the Veterans Administration. The State Department knows you if you've ever applied for a passport, and almost everyone is on file with the Social Security Administration. If you have or had a student loan, there's probably a file on you at the U.S. Department of Education. If you've ever contributed $100 or more to a political candidate or group, the Federal Elections Commission may have you on a list.

In all, estimates are that the largest federal agencies and departments maintain nearly 2,000 databanks. This is how our large, complex society keeps track of who receives farm subsidies or welfare benefits and who is eligible to vote in elections. It's what allows us to pay for goods and services with plastic cards rather than the more cumbersome cash, and to bank without going to the bank.

"No one is spying on us, exactly," writes privacy scholar David Lyon in *The Electronic Eye: The Rise of the Surveillance Society*, "although for many people that is what it feels like if and when they find out just how detailed a picture of us is available. 'They' know things about us, but we often don't know what they know, why they know, or with whom else they might share their knowledge."

It's the latter—"with whom else they might share their knowledge"—that most gets our attention. It's not just the concentration of and rapid access to government information that's ominous. It's that government increasingly is sharing it—often for a profit—with information vendors and private individuals, who are bound neither by federal privacy laws nor necessarily by even a sense of the common good.

This is a relatively new trend and, as mentioned before, not many have yet felt the sting of it. But they *will*. And, in fact, some already have. Kay, for example, was a salesperson required by the court to be electronically monitored as a result of a drug- and alcohol-related conviction. She was up front with her bosses about her brushes with the law, and they assured her she would not lose her job. In fact, she was considered to be a star employee, among the top ten in sales volume.

But an employee of the private company furnishing her electronic monitoring device gave further details of Kay's case to her employer, and she was terminated. Although the boss says the new information didn't affect his decision, Kay is sure the monitoring company's indiscretion cost her the job. Asked about why he divulged information about her, the monitoring firm employee said court cases are public records and, thus, he was under no legal or ethical constraints.

Kay's story underscores the debate between technology and privacy and the increasingly cozy relationship between government and private firms sharing the same information. Direct marketers, employers, private investigators, and reporters are increasingly going to be able to access your private information with the push of a button.

WHAT'S PUBLIC?

Public records are just that: *public*. Information from these records can be obtained by anyone from private citizens to the FBI. Let's take a brief look at the most common kind of public records:

▥Motor Vehicle Information

Some of the most easily accessible files in many states come from the department of motor vehicles. Those files contain names, addresses, birth dates, license numbers, physical descriptions, failures to pay traffic fines, and traffic convictions going back a certain number of years, depending on which state you live in.

DMV files also contain registration data, such as owner, license plate number, and previous owners' names. In addition, more than a dozen states display the driver's Social Security number on the license.

These DMV files are a special cause for concern, because in most states just about anyone has access to them. In fact, 33 states and the District of Columbia disclose such records without restrictions. Employers, insurance companies, attorneys, and private investigators can easily obtain DMV information, and such records are a gold mine for marketers. (However, a new federal law taking effect in 1997 permits drivers to "opt out" of having their identifying information sold to direct marketers by the state departments of motor vehicles.)

Big information companies love to get that kind of data, often reselling it for statistical purposes. If you wanted to open a foreign-auto repair shop, for instance, you might be willing to pay to know how many foreign cars are registered in your town and how old they are.

Similarly, people with less legitimate aims can get these records, too. Antiabortion protesters, for example, have obtained license plate numbers of doctors and women using abortion clinics and then harassed them at their homes. In Iowa, a ring of thieves took down license plate numbers off luxury cars at the long-term parking lot of an airport, retrieved home addresses from the department of motor vehicles, and then robbed the unoccupied homes.

▓Voting Records

Voting records are usually kept at the county clerk's or registrar of voters office. An index is available to the public that contains voters' names, addresses, and party affiliations. In many states, if a person believes that the release of voter registration data poses a danger to privacy, he or she can obtain a court order to seal the file, though a judge usually must be convinced that a life-threatening situation exists. People with sensitive positions in the criminal justice field and their families often seek to have their files kept confidential.

▓Birth, Death and Marriage Certificates

Birth certificates are on file in the county in which the birth occurred and/or at your state office of vital statistics. Birth records usually contain the name of the child, date and time of birth, the city and the hospital in which the child was born, the parents' names, the attending physician's name, and various signatures. Birth records can be ordered by anyone with sufficient identifying information.

Marriage certificates are usually filed in the county clerk's office where the marriage application was filed and/or in the state office of vital statistics. An index available to the public contains the bride and groom's names, the county where the application was filed, and the date of the marriage. Divorce records are considered part of court files and are available in the court clerk's office in the county where the divorce was granted and/or the state office of vital statistics.

Death certificates are kept on file in the county where the death occurred at the county clerk's office and/or the state office of vital statistics. The index of death certificates is available to the public and contains the name of the person who died, where the death occurred, the date, and the person's Social Security number.

▓Property Records

When you purchase a home or other real estate, a record of the transaction is made by the county assessor's office and the county recorder's office. The files maintained by the assessor, tax collector and/or recorder contain the location of the property, current owner's name and address, previous owners' names, dates of sale, description of the property, and its approximate value.

▓Court Records

A wide variety of court records are also open to the public, unless they involve a juvenile. Case files can be retrieved under the name of either the plaintiff or the defendant. A person involved in a lawsuit can ask the judge to have parts of a case file sealed. If the judge consents, that portion is no longer open to public viewing. In criminal cases, probation reports, medical information, and psychiatric information are removed from the file before it is made available to the public.

WHAT'S CONFIDENTIAL

While many government records are public, some are considered confidential. Generally, the confidential files involve:

▪ Social Welfare

These files, which include Medicare records and your Social Security earnings and benefits information, are usually off limits. However, social-service agencies must supply a list of benefit recipients and their Social Security numbers to tax authorities.

▪ Taxes

While you may have access to your Internal Revenue Service file, others usually do not. But again, there are exceptions. Your file can be disclosed if it's part of a court proceeding, if a government agency is trying to locate a parent who owes child-support payments, if you are applying for financial aid from the state, or if it's needed for statistical use.

▪ School Records

Schools keep track of a lot more than grades and discipline. Files on students may also describe emotional development, physical appearance, ethnic background, attitudes toward teachers and other students, psychological test scores, learning disabilities, or maybe even confidences shared with a counselor or school social worker.

Some of that data may be objective—such as test results and attendance records—while other information may consist of subjective impressions by teachers and administrators. Because most of us attend school for many years, and because our school records can affect such major events as college admissions and job prospects, the cumulative effect of these records can be tremendous.

The federal Family Educational Rights and Privacy Act (FERPA) governs schools which receive federal funds. Persons over the age of eighteen must authorize the release of their school records before they can be viewed by others, including parents. But if a student is under 18, such records can be released without consent to school officials, state or federal education authorities, state or federal financial aid programs, law enforcement officials for "child welfare" protection, or upon a judge's order.

Parents have the right to inspect all records a school has about their child if he or she is under 18, and to request that any errors be corrected. Schools must keep a log, open only to parents and school officials, which lists those who have received information from a student's record and how the information was used.

Parents or students over 18 can ask that incorrect or misleading information be changed. If the school refuses, it must notify the requester of a right to a hearing. (Parents or the students can't use FERPA, though, to challenge a teacher's judgment in deciding what grade was given for a course.)

The school may release directory information about students only after the parents (or the student, if over 18) have been notified as to the type of information to be released. "Directory information" includes the student's name, address, phone number, date and place of birth, major field of study, participation in school activities, weight and height (of sports team members), dates of attendance, degrees, awards, and similar facts.

Parents have the right to block the release of the directory information by notifying the school of their objection. Usually a notice dealing with this issue is sent home at the beginning of the school year.

▓Library Records

Forty-six states make public library records confidential. Such data may include information provided to receive a library card and a list of materials borrowed. Only Hawaii, Ohio, Kentucky, and Mississippi do not protect library records.

Also, privately funded libraries may not have the same privacy protections as those which receive public funds. You may want to request a copy of the facility's policies.

▓Criminal History

Records of arrests and prosecutions (called ''rap'' sheets) are considered confidential in many states and can only be accessed by the accused individual, law-enforcement agencies, attorneys working on a case involving the individual, probation or parole officers, a state agency that needs the information to license an individual, or under limited circumstances, employers, such as daycare providers.

Or, at least, that's the theory. In truth, with the increasing computerization of records, some private firms are able to compile their own ''rap sheets'' by searching those arrest records and court files which are public records. The information compiled by such firms is sometimes used by employers to run background checks on prospective employees.

HOW THE LAW CAN HELP YOU

There are two main federal privacy laws that, at first glance, would seem to contradict each other. The Privacy Act of 1974, enacted as part of the Watergate-era reforms, deals with keeping government records about individuals confidential, while the

Freedom of Information Act, first passed in 1966 and later amended, is used to open these very same records.

Both laws are important. Together, they balance the public's right to know what government's doing, on the one hand, with the right of citizens to keep their own lives private, on the other.

THE PRIVACY ACT

The Privacy Act requires federal agencies to collect only "necessary" information about individual citizens and gives them the right to see, copy, and correct those files. There's no response time mandated by the statute, but many agencies have instituted a ten-day deadline in which to reply to requests to see files.

The act attempts to ensure that people are not haunted by wrong or misleading agency records. However, intelligence and law-enforcement agencies can exclude entire systems of records, though some of these can be reached through the Freedom of Information Act.

On the positive side, the Privacy Act has forced most agencies to pay at least minimal attention to records management and observe basic protection for individual records. Thousands of people have gotten copies of their records and corrected inaccuracies.

On the other hand, critics say the act hasn't achieved its goals because it has been watered-down with exemptions, and there's no single overseer of compliance. Further, when the law has been litigated, the courts have often sided with the government.

THE FREEDOM OF INFORMATION ACT

While disclosing information can be a problem, so can withholding it. The Freedom of Information Act (FOIA) was de-

signed to improve citizen access to records of the executive
branch of the federal government. But as usual, there is a long
list of exceptions. Your request for information can be denied
if the records you seek fall within nine exempted categories.
These include information on litigation; internal agency memos;
trade secrets; law-enforcement activities; the CIA; classified
documents; personnel, medical, or other files which would invade someone's personal privacy; and confidential government
sources.

In addition, all 50 states have some type of open-records
legislation. Because of lack of manpower, and sometimes lack
of willingness, there may be long delays in getting documents
and, even then, significant portions may be blocked out. Despite
these exemptions and problems, though, these laws create a
strong right to see most government records.

The FOI Act, like the Privacy Act, sets up simple procedures
for obtaining access to documents. Many people seeking data
on themselves file joint FOIA and Privacy Act requests. (See
Privacy Pointers for more details on how to make requests, and
see Appendix A for sample request letters.)

●Commonly Asked Questions About Government Records●

Q: Why are government records mostly public?
A: It's the nature of our society.

The issue goes to the heart of our political system. The rationale is that public business—law-making, courts, public safety,
and the like—ought to be conducted in the open, not secretly.
Information should flow freely in a democratic society so citizens can keep an eye on what their government is doing. The
challenge to policymakers is to balance the public's right to
information with the individual's right to privacy.

The idea is that the average citizen will be better informed and can actively participate in the democracy. He or she will know how their tax money is being spent and reach an informed opinion about how government is performing. It's when the government acts secretly, when no one is watching, that abuses are most likely to occur.

Q: How do I get access to my own records?
A: It's up to you to identify which agency has the file you need, then request it.

There is no central index of government records about individuals. If you want to look at your records, you must first identify which agency has them. Then contact that agency directly in writing, using the Privacy Act or FOI Act, or their state equivalents, as the basis for asking to see your files. Most agencies are required by law to respond to your request within 10 working days.

As mentioned earlier, you may be denied access to your own records if what you want includes records pertaining to an ongoing investigation, the CIA, litigation, civil-service exams, or confidential government sources.

Q: How can I increase my chances of getting a quick, full response to my request for files?
A: Here are some tips from the Associated Press, which makes frequent use of the FOI Act for news-gathering:

- **Check first.**
  Call the public-information office of the agency you believe has the files and make sure you have the right agency and the right address. Ask if it will release what you're seeking without filing a request.

- **Be specific.**
  Give dates, titles, authors, addresses, and any other information you may have to help narrow the search. Also,

if you want field-office files checked as well as those at headquarters, mention that. Some agencies won't do that unless you ask.

- **Request a fee waiver.**
  Especially if you can rightfully claim that your use of the data will be in the public interest (say, in preparing an educational brochure or proposing legislation), you may be eligible for a waiver of search and copying fees. If such a waiver is denied, seek to set a limit on the amount you will agree to pay before further consent is required.

- **If in doubt, ask anyway.**
  If you want an item, ask. Let the government decide if it can or is willing to release it. Even exempted material can be released at the agency's discretion.

- **Seek to learn the reasons for any denial.**
  Request the agency cite specific exemptions for each item it denies you access to. That will help in your appeal, if any, and force the administrator to think through his or her rationale.

Q: What if I'm denied access to my records for what doesn't seem like a good reason?
A: Normally, there is an appeal process.

Usually, you can appeal administratively and, if that fails, through the courts. The denial letter will specify to whom the appeal must be sent.

Conversely, you may also sue a government agency if you believe it has improperly disclosed information about you, or if you want to block impending disclosures.

Q: Who can gain access to normally confidential files?
A: Mostly government and law enforcement agencies.

Supposedly confidential files can often be accessed by law-enforcement agencies and sometimes by other government officials (such as those with the CIA and IRS), attorneys working on cases, and even employers, under limited circumstances.

Q: Do the Privacy Act, the FOI Act, and their state counterparts cover local government?
A: Often, no.

In most states, city or county governments are free to make their own laws in many areas of privacy. As a result, that's frequently where abuses occur.

●Privacy Pointers: What You Can Do Now●

1. If you think a government file on you is incorrect, contact that agency immediately.

If you have reason to believe that an agency has inaccurate information about you, get in touch with it immediately. You have the legal right to have any mistake in a federal file about you corrected. (The *United States Government Manual*, available in most libraries, lists all federal agencies, describes their functions, and tells how to reach them.)

2. Contact the FBI to learn if it has compiled data about you.

Most Americans don't have an FBI file. But there are 9.6 million persons, living and dead, who do. Mostly, they are those who've been the subject of a criminal investigation, or who've been nominated for some position that requires a background check.

In either case, you can ask to review your files under the Freedom of Information and Privacy Acts, but don't expect a quick response. There are thousands of requests ahead of you and the FBI is notoriously careful about what it releases. As a result, you can expect to wait two years or more to get a peek at what's in your file, if you have one.

If you have a criminal history, ask for a copy of that record by writing to the Federal Bureau of Investigation. Include a letter stating why you are making the request, a set of finger-prints, and a check for $18. Mail it to:

FBI
Criminal Justice Information Services Division
935 Pennsylvania Ave., NW
Room 10104
Washington, D.C. 20535
(202) 324-5278
http://www.fbi.gov

If you don't have a criminal record, you can make a request under the Freedom of Information Act. That request also must be in writing and should include a complete name, address, date and place of birth and notarized signature. Send it to:

FBI
Freedom of Information Privacy Section
935 Pennsylvania Ave., NW
Washington, D.C. 20535
(202) 324-5520

3. Don't fill out the post office's change-of-address form.

Though the post office doesn't consider postal address infor-mation a matter of public record, data on its Change of Address form (USPS 3675) is available to many people. This can be an extremely important fact for anyone involved in a threatening or violent situation, such as a battered spouse who doesn't want to be located.

Prior to 1994, anyone could, for a small fee, get a copy of the change-of-address form you submitted. Because of concern about stalkers and harassers, the Postal Service changed its pol-icy so that ordinary citizens could no longer get that informa-tion. However, that data is still made readily available to mailing-list firms, direct mailers, and credit bureaus. The

Change of Address form carries a notice that the information you provide may be used by others. By filling out the form, the post office assumes you have read this warning and consent to the release of your information.

Obviously, you lack full protection. If you have any concerns, don't fill out USPS 3675, but notify your correspondents individually.

If you do file a change-of-address form and someone sending mail to your old address specifies "address correction requested," the Postal Service will release your new address to that sender for up to 18 months. A victim of a threatening or potentially violent situation can prevent the release of his or her new address by obtaining a temporary restraining order or court order and presenting it to the post office.

4. Read the fine print.

Under the Privacy Act, the federal government is required to list the principal purpose and any routine uses on all forms asking for personal information. If the form, or an accompanying tear-off sheet, doesn't list the purpose, ask to see the circular or regulation that the agency is required to publish. Sometimes these notices will indicate that some or all of the information requested is only "voluntary" and doesn't need to be given.

5. Write in limits.

Sometimes an agency will restrict further disclosure if you request it. As was suggested with medical-record waivers, you can write in what uses are acceptable to you. Your request may not always be honored, but it's worth a try.

6. When requesting records, ask for a list of all disclosures.

The agency is supposed to disclose the names and addresses of each agency or person to whom it has revealed your information, when, and the purpose.

7. Consult the following for more information about govern-ment records and their use:

- **Access Reports**
  1624 Dogwood Lane
  Lynchburg, VA 24503
  (804) 384-5334
  This is a newsletter covering open-government laws. Pub-lished twice a month, it costs $325 per year.

- **The Associated Press Stylebook and Libel Manual**
  (Associated Press, 1994).
  Pages 291–292 include a concise outline of FOI Act procedures.

- **A Citizen's Guide on Using the Freedom of Information Act and the Privacy Act of 1974** (Report No. 103–104, U.S. Government Printing Office, 1991).
  For a copy, write to:
  U.S. Government Printing Office
  Superintendent of Documents
  Washington, D.C. 20402
  (202) 512-1800
  http://www.access.gpo.gov/su_docs

- **The Reporter's Handbook: An Investigator's Guide to Documents and Techniques** by John Ullmann and Jan Colbert (St. Martin's, 1990).

●

PART III

THE PITFALLS
OF TELECOMMUNICATIONS

7

Cordless and Cellular Phones:
Is Everybody Listening?

Have you turned your home or car into a radio station?
Probably.

If you use a cordless phone, a cellular phone, a baby monitor, or a wireless intercom, you're sending your private conversations out over the airwaves where anyone with a decent radio scanner can listen.

The popularity of wireless communication is soaring. Tens of millions of Americans use these new phones and other devices, loving their convenience and believing they're as secure as traditional telephones.

But in truth:

- Others can easily listen to your conversations, accidentally or otherwise . . . and some pagers can be intercepted, too.

- It's almost impossible to know if your calls are being monitored.

- Some people make it a hobby to listen to such calls . . . and others may profit criminally.

In this chapter, we're going to look at this new generation of communication conveniences, their potential threat, the legalities, and the best ways to prevent calls from being over-heard.

CORDLESS VS. CELLULAR

Almost half of U.S. households own a cordless phone. Introduced in 1982, it's now the fastest-selling phone for home use. Of 1,000 households polled nationwide by the Electronic Industries Association, 40% said they owned at least one cordless phone and 9% had two or more.

In all, there are about 40 million cordless phones in the United States today. They work on standard telephone and electric lines, though you can carry around the handset—the part you speak into and listen from—for short distances.

Cellular phones, on the other hand, are not wired. So they're eminently portable so long as you're in an area where there's a cellular network of receivers and transmitters. Introduced commercially in the mid-1980s, they are a hot item, with perhaps 15% of homes having at least one. (Even a 22-year-old who was rousted by San Rafael, California, authorities for living in a tent under a freeway overpass had a cellular phone as well as a laptop computer.) By 1998, there are expected to be some 60 million cellphone users.

Both devices act like miniature radio stations. Basically, here's how they work:

> *Cordless phones* send signals from the base unit in your home to the detachable handset and back again. The transmissions can be overheard up to a quarter of a mile away, and sometimes as far as two miles. These signals can be picked up by a number of other devices, such as scanners, baby monitors, radios, and other cordless phones.
>
> Baby monitors, children's walkie-talkies and some

home intercom systems may be overheard in the same manner as cordless phones. If you are concerned about being overheard on one of these household devices, be sure to turn it off when it is not in use. You also might want to consider purchasing a "wired" unit instead.

Cellular phone signals travel to a low-power transmitter located within "cells" several miles away. If you're traveling as you talk, the transmitter you're using changes as you move. The effective eavesdropping radius is five to 10 miles.

Cellular calls, unlike those of cordless phones, usually are not picked up by unsophisticated electronic devices such as standard radios and baby monitors. But cellular signals may be received by radio scanners, or sometimes even by televisions.

One apartment-dwelling couple found out that the apartment manager and her son were using a scanner to listen in on many of their cordless calls, apparently just for amusement. The tenants hired an attorney to sue the manager for invasion of privacy.

In many instances, however, your cordless or cellular calls are probably overheard only briefly and accidentally. Some hobbyists think they're doing good deeds by monitoring calls and notifying authorities if they hear of a crime being planned.

But it's not hard to imagine more evil intent. For example, an eavesdropper might get your credit card information if you place a catalogue order over a cellular phone, or learn the dates of your vacation when you cancel your newspaper, or overhear you calling a cab to go to the airport, or arranging for something valuable to be delivered to your home.

ART AND CRIME

The ease of interception of cellular calls has spawned both art and crime. Robin Rimbaud, an English artist, musician, and publisher, has released three albums mixing music and pirated cellular telephone transmissions. Recording under the name of "Scanner," he melds his eclectic music with intercepted phone conversations ranging from amorous chitchat to drug transactions. His music has been described as an amalgam of "soothing ambient sounds and electronic caterwaul."

Of more serious concern, savvy criminals increasingly are turning to "cloned" phones—that is, cellular phones reprogrammed to use stolen numbers. One convicted cloner, for example, was caught with 22,000 stolen cellular numbers in his possession.

Such wholesale thievery means few are immune. In fact, a cellular number belonging to the Secret Service's Miami field office was cloned—and the Secret Service is the agency named by law to investigate cellular fraud! Executives of cellular phone companies and their families have been victimized, too.

Most victims don't even know their numbers have been stolen until the big bills start rolling in. Although the customer isn't usually liable for phone calls he or she didn't make, it's not always easy to spot the bogus calls. In any event, the cellular phone will need to be reprogrammed once it has been "cloned."

According to the Cellular Telecommunications Industry Association, the cellular industry loses almost $500 million a year—some estimates range to nearly $1 billion—to fraud, including "cloning." New York, California, and Florida are among the three biggest markets for cellular fraud. Florida is particularly susceptible because cell phones are very popular there, no mountains hamper transmissions, and the state's geographic narrowness means there's hardly an area beyond reach of a cellular site.

But it isn't just that calls from cloned phones are "free." It's that criminals—especially narcotics dealers and terrorists—use the anonymity of cloned numbers to hide from law enforcement. The scheme usually works like this: Cloners park near freeways or other high-traffic areas and use scanners to capture electronic serial numbers as drivers stream by. Phones don't have to be in use—just turned on—for a scanner to pick up the serial numbers. Then they can program those numbers into their own phones, thus billing their calls to you. One New York couple was arrested for amassing 80,000 cellular phone numbers by allegedly putting a scanner on the windowsill of their 16th-floor apartment to steal numbers from unsuspecting motorists driving past on a busy Brooklyn street.

Cloned phones are sold on the streets for a price cheap enough that they can be discarded before the first inflated bill reaches the victim.

Cordless phones that automatically switch between 10 or more channels are not as easily monitored as the older one- or two-channel models. Neither are the newest cordless phones which use the higher, 900-megahertz frequency and have as many as 30 to 100 channels. However, anyone with a good radio scanner can still eavesdrop on cordless phone calls even if you use a 10- or 100-channel model.

Digital cellular and *digital* cordless phones can give a high level of protection against eavesdropping. However, digital cellular is not yet available everywhere, and digital cordless phones are more expensive than analog models. When shopping for a cordless or cellular phone, insist that the manufacturer or salesperson provide you with clear explanations of any privacy protection claimed for their products.

Meanwhile, several manufacturers now report progress in making their cell phones clone-proof, and the cellular industry is making a strong effort to combat cloning through a high-tech monitoring system and by being quick to alert customers if an abrupt change in their calling patterns is noted.

THE LAW ON EAVESDROPPING

Federal law prohibits *intentional* eavesdropping on telephone conversations, including cellular and cordless ones. So if your neighbor, say, accidentally overhears your cordless or cellular conversation, that's not illegal. Even if someone is purposely listening, the difficult part, of course, is proving intent. (Penalties for intentional interception range from fines to imprisonment, depending on the circumstances.)

In addition, the Federal Communications Commission (FCC) ruled that as of April 1994, no scanners can be manufactured or imported that can tune into frequencies used by cellular phones, or can be readily altered to pick up those frequencies. However, scanners already manufactured and on the market or in use by then are unaffected.

A determined scanning enthusiast is not likely to be deterred. He or she can find help in electronics magazines or on the Internet for buying preban scanners or even modifying blocked ones.

THE DIGITAL WIRELESS FUTURE

Another type of wireless communication emerging today is the PCS, or Personal Communication Services. This is the generic name given to a family of digital wireless services that is already changing telecommunications through easy-to-use, lightweight, highly mobile devices. These small pocket-size phones, which cost less than existing cellular models, allow both voice and data transmission, and include Caller ID, short-messaging, paging, and other such services.

Unlike most cellular systems, PCS is based on digital technology, meaning it offers better voice quality and fewer dropped calls. Digitization also makes conversations more difficult to intercept and provides greater protection from fraud.

◉Commonly Asked Questions About Wireless Phones◉

Q: What is the best way to prevent my calls from being overheard?

A: Currently there is no inexpensive way to ensure privacy on either cordless or cellular phone calls.

If you are discussing a private matter, or you simply do not want others to listen to your call, it is best to switch to a standard "wired" telephone. Be sure both you and the person you are talking to are on standard phones.

These concerns will lessen as wireless communication gradually shifts from the present analog systems to digital.

Q: What does the law say about "cloning" of cellular phones?

A: It's a federal crime to use a "cloned" phone.

Penalties include up to 15 years of imprisonment and/or a fine of not less than $50,000 for knowingly and intentionally using a "cloned" cellular phone. The Secret Service is the agency principally responsible for investigating cellular phone fraud.

Up to this point, it has concentrated on apprehending manufacturers of the cloned phones, but, agents say, they've begun targeting users of the illegal phones in hopes they will lead them to the manufacturers.

Q: Is it illegal to intercept a pager message, too?

A: It depends.

The popularity of pagers has increased dramatically in recent years, with some 35 million Americans expected to use them by 1998. Though most pagers currently offer only one-way communication, they can receive signals over a larger geographic area and the cost can be significantly less than cellular or standard phone services. So if you worry about eavesdropping on your cellular phone, a pager might be worth considering.

Intercepting a signal from a tone-only pager, which sends out a beep to tell you there's a message, is not a violation of federal law. However, it is illegal to intercept messages from display pagers (which show the phone number of the person wanting to be reached), from voice pagers (which permit a spoken message), and from combined tone-voice pagers.

⬤Privacy Pointers: What You Can Do Now⬤

1. Most important: Watch what you say.

Never use a cordless or cellular phone to discuss financial matters, make a credit card purchase, or discuss sensitive personal information unless you're using a newer, digital system. Switch to a regular, ''wired'' phone if you must provide account numbers or expiration dates.

2. Always use the lock feature on your cellular phone when it's not in service.

Remember: Phones don't have to be in use for a scanner to pick up the serial number. Consider using a pager to receive messages and then turning on your phone only to return calls.

3. Be careful who has access to your cellular phone.

For example, don't leave it in your car if you're turning the car over to, say, a valet, a mechanic, or a car-washer. They might be able to get the electronic serial number and phone numbers.

In fact, never leave your cellular phone where someone might be able to get the electronic serial number off the battery, where it's sometimes printed. And don't ever give your cellular number to anyone who represents himself as a cellular technician ''testing'' the line. (There is no ''line.'')

4. Report frequently interrupted or dropped cellular calls.

Someone who has "cloned" your phone may be knocking you off the air.

5. Check your cellular bills carefully.

Do so even if they're not exceptionally high. That's because some "cloners" may be careful not to leave large charges or make international or other attention-getting calls.

6. Ask your cellular carrier what antifraud features it provides.

Many cellular phone firms are fighting back aggressively. Collectively, they've formed an industry-wide fraud task force, and they're working with the Secret Service to combat fraud.

In addition, some of the individual firms have installed software that detects unusual customer calling patterns. The software flags accounts that suddenly begin showing unusual calling patterns. Then the firm calls the customer to verify the calls. If the calls are found to be fraudulent, the company will change the number, or give the customer a specially programmed PIN (personal identification number) to lock out the counterfeiters.

Further, some cellular companies also are coming out with hard-to-clone identification numbers or other clone-resistant features.

7. Keep documents containing your phone's electronic serial number in a safe place.

8. Report a stolen cellular telephone immediately to your cellular carrier.

9. Contact the following for more information about:

CELLULAR REGULATIONS

Federal Communications Commission
Enforcement Division
2025 M Street, NW
Washington, D.C. 20054
(202) 418-0569
http://www.fcc.gov

PAGERS

Paging and Narrowband PCS Alliance
500 Montgomery St., No. 700
Alexandria, VA 22314
(703) 739-0300
PCS is by the Personal Communications Industry Association. See page 143 for more information.

CELLULAR INDUSTRY

- **Cellular Telecommunications Industry Association**
1250 Connecticut Avenue, NW, No. 200
Washington, D.C. 20036
(202) 785-0081
http://www.wow-com.com
CTIA's fax-on-demand service—INFOFAX, at (202) 736-3250—will provide you with a listing of the information the association provides. In addition, CTIA has a Fraud Task Force to deal with wireless fraud.

- **Electronic Industries Association**
2500 Wilson Blvd.
Arlington, VA 22201
(703) 907-7500
http://www.eia.org

This is the trade organization representing electronics manufacturers.

<u>PCS</u>

Personal Communications Industry Association
500 Montgomery St., No. 700
Alexandria, VA 22314
(703) 739-0300
http//www.pcia.com
PCIA is the trade association of the newest generation of wireless communications devices.

8

How You Can Stop Harassing Phone Calls

The phone rings, shattering your nerves as well as the silence. It might be that unknown caller again, speaking crude obscenities, or breathing heavily, or saying nothing. You're tied to that telephone, you need it. But it's become a weapon in someone else's hands.

Unfortunately, that's not an uncommon plight. Obscene or harassing phone calls are one of the most stressful invasions of privacy anyone can experience. They are also against the law.

So if the problem persists and you take appropriate steps to combat it, relief should be possible. This is one area of privacy where there are lots of remedies, which this chapter will detail. It will also tell you what makes a call harassing, what to do if it happens, and whom to contact.

Obscene and harassing calls are a serious problem. That sad fact is brought home almost weekly by news reports such as these:

- A San Francisco man was charged with making more than one hundred obscene phone calls to teenage girls. He called some of them as many as 15 times.

- The 13-year-old daughter of a Florida hospital clerk was

accused of rifling through computer records of former emergency-room patients and then calling them to say they'd tested positive for the AIDS virus. One recipient of the bogus news was so upset she tried to kill herself.

- A suburban Chicago woman called police after her tires were slashed by a man who'd been harassing her over the phone. In fact, the man even called while police were interviewing her.

- In Baltimore, a series of harassing calls to a Johns Hopkins University student ended when the harasser, a fellow student whose friendship had been rebuffed, shot to death a 19-year-old acquaintance.

When someone calls and uses obscene or threatening language, or even heavy breathing or silence to intimidate you, you are receiving a harassing call. It is against the law in most states to make obscene or threatening calls.

How many calls does it take? Just one unwelcome call can be harassing, but usually your local phone company or police will not take action unless the calls are frequent. However, if a call specifically threatens you or your family with bodily harm, a single call is generally enough to trigger immediate action.

FIRST-AID FOR HARASSMENT

Before you go to the phone company or to the police, there are steps you should take on your own.

First, simply hang up on the caller. Do not engage in conversation. If that does not work, record a message like this on your answering machine:

"I'm sorry I/we can't come to the phone right now but you must leave a message. I/we are receiv-

ing annoyance calls and the phone company has a trap on this line. If you do not leave a message I/we will assume that you are the annoyance caller and this call will be traced."

If you answer the phone and the harassing caller is on the line, you might say: *"Operator, this is the call."* Then hang up. Or say the word *"trap"* (which will be explained below) and give the time and the date, then hang up. Also, check the public service pages at the front of your phone book. Often they contain further suggestions for dealing with harassing calls.

Let's say you do those things and you're still receiving the harassing calls. Then it's time to contact authorities. Different phone companies have varying policies on whether to call the phone company or the police first. A wise first step is to find out your local phone company's policy by contacting its business office and asking for assistance. Some companies will first want to try to resolve the problem by using their "annoyance" specialists. Other phone companies may require you to file a formal complaint with local law enforcement before they will deal with the matter.

If your local phone company concurs that the calls are frequent and/or particularly threatening, it can set up a "trap" to determine the origin of harassing calls. For a trap to work, you must keep a log noting the time and date the harassing calls are received. Traps are free and are usually set up for no more than two weeks.

A phone company service called "Call Trace" may also be able to help track down harassing calls. If you receive a harassing call and have subscribed to Call Trace, you enter a code on your phone and the call is automatically traced. This is easier than using a trap because you don't have to keep a phone log and don't usually need prior police approval.

However, there are fees for Call Trace, and it's not yet available in all areas. In situations where the phone company would ordinarily use a trap, you might not be charged if the phone company suggests that Call Trace be used as an alternative.

The information collected from Call Trace or from a trap is turned over to law-enforcement personnel, *not* to the customer. Law-enforcement officers then try to stop the harassing calls by either warning or arresting the harasser. With both Call Trace and a trap, your phone conversations are neither listened to nor recorded by the phone company.

Even with the trap or new tracing technology, the harasser may prove elusive. For example, if the person making the calls uses a phone booth or multiple phone numbers, the phone company and law-enforcement officials may never get sufficient identification to take further action.

In cases such as these, changing your phone number might help. Also, you'll probably want to get an unlisted or unpublished number.

OTHER NEW METHODS

More Custom Calling options are constantly coming on line, offering further hope for the harassed. Fees are charged for these. But some of the new options you might want to ask your phone company about include:

• **Call Screen:** Your phone can be programmed to reject calls from selected numbers with a service known as Call Screen or, at some phone companies, Call Block. Instead of ringing on your line, these calls are routed to a recording which tells the caller you will not take the call.

With Call Screen or Call Block, you can also program your telephone to reject calls from the number of the last person who called. This allows you to block calls even if you do not know the phone number.

Call Block and Call Screen are not foolproof ways to stop

unwelcome calls, however. A determined caller can simply move to a different phone number to bypass the block. Also, this feature works only within your local service area and is not effective for long-distance calls. (Look in the front of your phone book for a map of your local service area.)

• **Special Call Acceptance:** This is the flip-side of Call Block, because it allows you to stop *all* numbers from ringing except those you specifically program your phone to accept. Up to twelve numbers can be chosen to ring through. All others are routed to a recorded message.

Not all phone companies offer this service, but if yours does, Special Call Acceptance can effectively stop unwanted or even harassing phone calls. Remember, it could also delay important or emergency calls, too. For example, a family member dialing from a pay phone would not reach you. An operator can override the service, but this would cause a delay in receiving the call. Like Call Screen, this feature works only in the local service area.

• **Call Return:** This service allows you to call back the number of the last person who called, even if you are unable to answer the phone. Some people suggest that Call Return can be used to stop harassing callers by allowing you to call the harasser back without knowing the phone number.

However, use caution with this method of discouraging harassing callers. It could actually aggravate the problem. For instance, if the harasser has Caller ID, he or she will know who's calling back.

Also note that Call Return only works in the local service area.

• **Priority Ringing, or VIP Ring:** With this option you program your phone to give two different rings. The special ring can be programmed either for calls you want to accept or for calls you do not want to answer.

There are ways callers can get around Priority Ringing when it is used as a screening device. For instance, if you program your phone for calls you wish to avoid, the person calling could switch phone lines and avoid the distinctive ring.

In the opposite case, if you program the calls you want to take, you run the risk of missing an important call dialed from a pay phone or another unknown number. This might happen, for example, if a relative or a friend were trying to reach you in an emergency.

As with the other Custom Calling features, Priority Ringing is now limited to your local service area. However, in time these features may be extended nationwide. Contact your phone company for details.

●Commonly Asked Questions About Harassing Calls●

Q: **What if I get calls that are annoying—such as telemarketers, frequent wrong numbers, or overly aggressive bill collectors—but are not personally threatening or criminal in nature?**

A: **There are steps you can take, short of calling the phone company or law-enforcement agencies.**

Only serious problems should be met with either a trap or Call Trace. But you can discourage unwanted calls by:

• **An answering machine.** This is one of the best ways to limit unwanted calls. It tapes messages when you're not available and can also be used to screen your calls. Similarly, you could hire a voice-mail service or an answering service to screen your calls.

• **"Inbound call blocker."** This is an attachment to the phone that allows only those callers who enter a special numeric code onto their touch-tone phone to ring through to your number. This device is highly effective in preventing unwanted calls. However, you must be certain to give the code to everyone you want to talk to. Even so, you could miss important calls from unexpected sources, such as emergency services.

See Chapter 2 ("Telemarketing: What Happened to a Quiet Evening at Home?") for other tips on dealing with telemarketers.

Q: Can I use Caller ID to stop unwanted calls?
A: Yes, but bear in mind, it's a two-edged sword.

Caller ID, which was discussed in Chapter 2, allows customers who pay a monthly fee and purchase a display device to see the number—and in some areas, the name—of the person calling before picking up the phone, even if the caller has an unlisted number.

Some people believe Caller ID helps reduce harassing or unwelcome calls, likening the service to a front-door peephole. Other consumers, however, raise strong privacy concerns and say Caller ID may exacerbate harassment because subscribers can capture others' phone numbers without their consent.

There's evidence on both sides. A Texas incident cited in Chapter 2 involved a violent ex-boyfriend with Caller ID. He recognized the number his former girlfriend was calling from, knew the address, and went there with a gun. On the other hand, in the Florida case mentioned earlier in this chapter, the young girl accused of making the bogus AIDS-notification calls was tracked down through numbers captured on a victim's Caller ID.

To answer privacy concerns, regulators in many states have required phone companies to offer number-blocking options (as detailed in Chapter 2). But blocking may not be a panacea. In New York recently, for example, a phone company admitted it accidentally failed to activate blocking for as many as 30,000 customers who had requested the protection.

Further, "counter-blocking" makes the situation more complicated. Some companies offer a service called "anonymous call rejection," which blocks any call which doesn't display the caller's phone number. Some phones also come with that capability. Callers who have blocked their number can't complete their call, and instead hear a message saying the recipient doesn't accept anonymous calls.

Q: Because harassers seem to lose interest when the thrill of the chase is gone, is there any way to fool them into thinking I've given up?

A: You could keep your same phone hooked up to an answering machine while switching to an unlisted number for yourself.

Though you end up paying for two phone lines and really only using one, this can act as a sort of a "safety valve," taking the pressure off you to deal with the harasser. He or she can talk to your machine while you use the other, unlisted phone for all other communication. Eventually, not getting a response, the harasser may give up.

◉Privacy Pointers: What You Can Do Now◉

1. Don't mention your phone number on your answering-machine tape.

By omitting your phone number from your answering machine's message, you prevent random dialers and people with Call Return from capturing this information.

2. For more information on Custom Calling options, talk to your local phone company.

If you're having a problem with unwelcome or harassing calls—or just want to take preventive measures—find out what Custom Calling options the phone company offers in your area.

Keep in mind, however, that these all cost money. Weigh your prospective monthly charges against the lower-cost solution that an answering machine alone might provide.

3. Be careful about giving out your phone number.

Sometimes we give out our personal information without much thought. It might be wise to wait a reasonable period of time before furnishing your number to new acquaintances. When you get a new, unlisted number to thwart a harasser, it would be wise to release it to only a few people at a time. That way, if you do start receiving harassing calls, determining the source might be easier.

9 |━━━━━━━━━━━━━━━━━━━━━━━━

Wiretapping and Eavesdropping: Should You Be Concerned?

Have a sensitive job? Involved in a controversial political or religious activity? Quarreling with a malicious relative or neighbor? Working on a high-stakes legal case?

Anyone in a position where others might benefit from listening to his or her conversations could be the target of wiretapping or electronic eavesdropping. Although relatively few wiretaps are legally authorized in the United States each year, improvements in technology have made it easier to *illicitly* wiretap, record, and eavesdrop on telephone conversations.

Unlike what's depicted in the movies, most wiretapping devices emit no audible sounds—so you're not likely to detect a tap yourself. In addition, false alarms are frequent. Many people think if they hear noises on the phone line—such as clicks, static, or voices—that the line is being tapped. That's usually a phone problem.

But if you do suspect such surveillance, this chapter will explain what to do and what the law has to say about legally monitoring phone conversations and recording calls.

LEGAL VS. ILLEGAL LISTENING

Americans have traditionally been zealous about their personal liberties and suspicious of authority, especially police. As a result, relatively few *legal* wiretaps are authorized, although the number is growing. In an average year, the courts allow about 1,000 phone taps by federal and state law-enforcement authorities after being told of evidence suggesting serious crimes are being committed.

Few citizens object seriously to those because, particularly as recent years have shown, there are some genuinely bad folks out there from whom we want protection. There really was an Oklahoma City federal-building bombing, a World Trade Center bombing, and terrorists who plotted to throw New York City into chaos by bombing strategic targets.

Of much more concern to us is that technology has made it easier to illegally wiretap, record, and eavesdrop on conversations of all sorts. People with sensitive jobs in business or government and those involved in fractious disputes—in or out of court—may have reason to be concerned about wiretapping and electronic eavesdropping.

Wiretapping is any interception of a telephone transmission by accessing the telephone signal itself. **Electronic eavesdropping** doesn't involve a phone line but rather the use of a transmitting or recording device to monitor conversations without the consent of the parties.

Eavesdropping or wiretapping can take many forms: industrial espionage, questionable police use, and monitoring in all kinds of personal disputes. (A particularly hot issue—eavesdropping by employers—is covered in Chapter 12, "Employee Monitoring: Is Your Boss Spying on You?")

Recent incidents reflect the range of possibilities:

- A Tennessee woman allowed her ex-husband to set up a computer system in her home so her ex and their son could exchange e-mail. But the father reportedly installed a duplex speaker phone system in the unit, and was able to access the computer remotely by modem and listen to what was going on in his ex-wife's home.

• A former executive of a tobacco company in Louisville was arrested for allegedly installing a sophisticated wiretapping device on his office phone. He'd supposedly bought the device for $5,500 in a spy shop in Manhattan.

• Investigators in Eugene, Oregon, listened to and taped an accused triple-murderer's confession to a Roman Catholic priest in the county jail. The act caused an ecclesiastical uproar because of the sacred nature of priest-penitent relationship, though Oregon law on the subject seems contradictory.

• A former University of Miami quarterback and his father may have secretly taped conversations with college recruiters, then sued when promises were not fulfilled.

• Two California men were arrested for allegedly manufacturing cellular-taping equipment so sophisticated that it could allow the user not only to listen to personal phone conversations but intercept others' pagers and faxes, and even call up victims' voice-mail messages.

WHAT IF YOUR PHONE IS TAPPED?

If you think your telephone is tapped, call your local phone company. Most phone companies will inspect your lines for wiretap devices at no charge. If a tap is found, the phone company will check to see if it's authorized and will alert you if the wiretap is illegal. It also will notify law enforcement and remove the device. In addition, you may want to consult an attorney; intentionally intercepting a private phone conversation can be the basis for legal action.

However, you will *not* be notified if the wiretap is legal—if it's made by law enforcement after being authorized by a court. Once a legal wiretap has been discontinued, the court must notify the tapped party that the wiretapping has taken place. Normally, this notice must occur within ninety days of the wiretap termination.

ARE YOU A VICTIM OF EAVESDROPPING?

As discussed in Chapter 7, the boom in wireless communications carries with it enormous implications for eavesdropping. Cordless and cellular phones transmit signals that are vulnerable to radio predators.

That threat hit the public eye in 1993 when British tabloids published the transcripts of a mobile conversation between Prince Charles and his then-married mistress, Camilla Parker Bowles. The conversations had been picked up on a scanner and recorded.

Sold at electronics stores for as little as $100, these scanners can home in on frequencies set aside for police, fire, and ambulance transmissions as well listen to private conversations on wireless phones. Some are as small as a walkie-talkie; other more powerful units come in desktop size. There are said to be 10 to 15 million scanner owners in the United States, and the devices have a pick-up radius varying from 100 feet to a few city blocks.

This is not all bad. Law-enforcement agencies were able to track down superhacker Kevin Mitnick in 1995 by monitoring cellular traffic. But there's enormous nefarious potential. Cloning cellular phones has become a vast, illicit operation, and if a criminal can pick up your cellular phone's ID number, he certainly can listen to your conversation, if he chooses to. For example, there have been reports of would-be investors monitoring cellular traffic to garner stock tips. There's even an audio underground where taped cellular calls are illegally copied and disseminated as entertainment.

You can minimize the threat of having your wireless phone conversations overheard by following the suggestions in Chapter 7 and the *Privacy Pointers* at the end of this chapter. Harder to overcome and potentially more distressing is the growth of sophisticated spying devices.

Not only may Big Brother be watching, but the boss, neighbor, spouse, family, colleagues, competitors, criminals, or the just plain nosy can now get into the surveillance game—and there is a raft of devices to allow them to do so. Among the devices available in the marketplace are radio transmitters disguised as pens, pocket calculators, phone jacks, and light sockets.

Vendors of surveillance and countersurveillance gizmos are burgeoning. There's even Surveillance Expo, an annual exhibition of high-tech equipment held each year in Washington, D.C., to display state-of-the-art snooping, spying, and eavesdropping equipment.

●Commonly Asked Questions About Wiretapping/Eavesdropping●

Q: If I suspect a wiretap, I go to the phone company. But what if I suspect electronic eavesdropping?
A: Consider an attorney and/or a private investigator.

You may want to consult an attorney and/or a private investigator who specializes in eavesdropping cases. Be sure to check for references and proper licenses. Get all fees and conditions in writing before acquiring the assistance of a legal or investigative service.

Q: Aren't there products I can buy to detect phone taps or eaves-dropping equipment?

A: Yes, but . . .

Devices can be purchased that supposedly detect wiretapping or electronic eavesdropping. You can find them at electronics shops and through catalogues and magazines that cater to private investigators and security services. Some of them are designed to sound alarms—or even vibrate noiselessly in your pocket or purse—when an eavesdropping "bug" is detected. One advertised device claims not only to detect wiretapping devices but then "jams them to oblivion."

But . . . let the buyer beware! Experts advise against relying on such devices that claim to detect wiretaps by noting when voltage drops occur on the line (a possible sign that someone is listening on the same line). Although these devices can detect amateur wiretaps, experts say, often the devices give false-positive readings caused by normal voltage flucuations. Further, they are ineffective in business environments with electronic phone systems and multiple lines.

Q: Who can legally monitor phone conversations?

A: Law-enforcement officials may tap telephone lines only after showing "probable cause" of unlawful activity and obtaining a court order.

The unlawful activity alleged must involve certain specified felony violations. The court order limits the surveillance to conversations related to the unlawful activity and to a specific period of time, usually 30 days.

Generally, federal law and federal crimes take precedence. For example, federal agents may go to federal court and obtain a warrant to place a wiretap, even though state officials may be barred by state law from obtaining a wiretap under similar circumstances.

Either federal or state law-enforcement officials may eavesdrop on and record conversations without a court order under the so-called "one-party consent provision." In other words, if state or federal authorities have the consent of one party to a conversation (such as a government informant), the conversation may be monitored. This provision applies only to eavesdropping by *law-enforcement* officials.

Telephone-company employees may listen to your conversations when it is necessary to provide you with service, to inspect the telephone system, to monitor the quality of telephone service or to protect against service theft or harassment. Also, employers may monitor and even record their employees' phone conversations with few restrictions as will be discussed in Chapter 12.

Q: Can digital telephone communications be monitored?
A: Yes.

In 1994 Congress passed the Communications Assistance for Law Enforcement Act, also known as the Digital Telephony Act. The law seeks to assure law-enforcement officials that they'll be able to "tap" any communications incorporating new digital technology. These transmissions include both voice communications transmitted in digital format as well as text and data sent via computer communications.

Traditionally, law-enforcement agents accessed phone conversations by tapping the line and simply listening in. However, with digital communications, a code is used that's impossible to "listen in" on. The Digital Telephony Act requires all phone companies to make digital communications available to law-enforcement officials in the same manner that traditional voice transmissions are currently accessible.

When first introduced in Congress, the Digital Telephony Act sparked controversy among civil libertarians because it sought to significantly broaden the wiretapping capability of authorities. In its final form, such new capabilities were restricted somewhat, but the law is still being contested as this book goes to press. Up-to-date information about the Digital Telephony Act can be found at http://www.eff.org and http://www.epic.org.

The law specifically states that it doesn't alter or expand the ability of investigators to wiretap. Instead, it allows them— in the event a legal tap has been approved—to access digital communications in the same way as voice communications. Furthermore, telephone companies aren't required to unscramble encrypted communications unless the phone company itself provides the encryption service. Finally, the federal government must reimburse the phone companies for many of the modifications necessary to comply with the law.

Q: Is it legal for individuals to tape-record telephone calls?
A: In most cases, no.

The Federal Communications Commission (FCC) and state regulatory bodies restrict tape-recording by non-law-enforcement personnel.

California, for example, doesn't allow tape recording of telephone calls unless *all parties* to the conversation consent or are notified of the recording by a distinct ''beep tone'' warning. However, in California, if an individual or members of one's family are threatened with kidnapping, extortion, bribery, or another felony involving violence, the person receiving the threats can make a tape recording without informing the other party.

In all, a dozen states require consent from both parties to record phone conversations (with an exception for law enforcement).

The FCC requires that notice of any recording of a telephone conversation be given to the other parties involved. This can be done by telling them at the beginning of the call, or using of a periodic beep tone. (These regulations don't apply to law-enforcement investigations, emergency situations, or patently unlawful conversations.)

However, the FCC acknowledges that these rules are hard to

enforce, and violations are virtually impossible to detect. So you shouldn't be lulled into a false sense of security that your call is private simply because there is no notice of recording.

Further, whether state or federal law applies depends on where the call originates, why the recording is being made, and who places the call. In short, to stay within the law, you'll probably want to avoid taping calls you make, unless you first consult a knowledgeable attorney, but be aware that others could be recording your conversations with them.

Q: Aren't there ways to record phone activity without actually listening in on conversations?
A: Yes.

Certain devices, when attached to a phone line, allow the phone numbers of incoming or outgoing calls to be recorded. A "pen register" device records numbers dialed out. A "trap and trace device" records the numbers from which incoming calls are dialed.

Employers often use pen registers as a means of managing the use of their own phone systems. In nonworkplace situations, before either of these devices can be attached to someone else's phone line, a court order must be obtained, according to federal law. An exception: telephone companies may use these devices without a court order to protect against theft or fraudulent use of the telephone service, or to protect customers from harassment.

These devices may only be used to obtain the *phone number* of the calling party, not to listen to the actual conversation or to pinpoint the location of the called or the calling party.

●Privacy Pointers: What You Can Do Now●

1. Use a prepaid phone card with an 800 number.
A telephone debit card can be purchased for cash at many locations. You scratch off the surface that covers the personal

identification number (PIN) on the back of the card, then place a call to an "800" number that's listed on the card and punch in the PIN. The call is made by the service instead of by your home or office phone.

The prepaid cards also offer more privacy than calling cards because you don't get a bill listing the numbers you called. However, privacy is not absolutely guaranteed. The FBI used records from prepaid phone-card calls to identify a suspect in the 1995 bombing of the Oklahoma City federal building.

2. Get an inexpensive voice mailbox.

One way to preserve the privacy of your own phone is to use a voice mailbox service and use that number on business cards, stationery, and checks. For as little as $10 a month, you can get one from a private voice-mail firm not connected with the phone company. You can find them under "Voice Mail" or "Answering Services" in the Yellow Pages.

3. Fax safely.

As mentioned in Chapter 5 ("Is Your Medical Information Really Confidential?"), faxes aren't very private. Your message can easily fall into the wrong hands, either as a result of dialing a wrong number or because the machines are usually in an open office where incoming faxes can be seen by coworkers or others.

If trade secrets are at issue, one answer could be to obtain a fax machine with security features, such as "keylock" or "confidential mailbox." The keylock prevents any information from being transmitted or received unless the machine is "unlocked" by an authorized person. The confidential mailbox feature stores the transmission within the memory of the fax machine until an authorized receiver enters a password.

While impractical for general office use, these safeguards do provide maximum security for confidential fax transmissions.

For more details on fax security, see Chapter 15 ("Respecting Others' Privacy: How to Handle Information Responsibly").

4. Remember: even if you play by the rules, others may not.
Cellular and cordless phone conversations are easily monitored. Also, long-distance calls which travel by microwave or satellite links are susceptible to monitoring. Those to whom you're talking on a wired phone may be ignorant, or contemptuous, of the complex web of regulations that generally require notification if your conversation is being recorded.

Privacy in Cyberspace: How to Protect Your Personal Computer

Personal computers give us a marvelous window to the world, causing cyberspace poets to wax rhapsodic about how we can gaze out upon a vast global village. In reality, though, the PC can also offer a window to others who want to look *in*. Cyberspace is a worldwide public place where strangers can meet—and as in the real world, some strangers may abuse the rights of others or even break the law.

Consider the woman who came to Intuit, producer of a popular personal-finance software program. She complained that her computer had locked her out for not knowing a password—yet she had never activated her PC's password feature. According to *Forbes* magazine, Intuit's engineers found that a burglar had broken into her machine, written a check to himself in the amount of her entire checking account, and then covered his tracks by inventing a password of his own. He was caught and convicted. But the story is chilling because it shows our vulnerability to clever computer thieves and vandals. There are threats from more "legitimate" trespassers, too.

This chapter will discuss not only technical intrusions but also social dangers—such as harassment or stalking—that can occur as millions correspond with others whose identities may not be what they appear. You'll learn how to become more vigilant by protecting your password, guarding your files, watching for suspicious activity on the screen, being more careful about what information you send out, and exploring encryption and other devices to heighten security. We will also give you ideas for keeping a closer eye on your kids' computer habits.

Computers, unlike leisure suits and hula hoops, are more than just a passing fancy. If you follow the trend of your fellow Earthlings, soon you will be putting your personal schedule, your correspondence, your private notes, your bank records, your brokerage dealings, your travel reservations, and maybe your company's trade secrets on your computer. Your computer may even be a notebook-sized one that you'll carry with you and leave in insecure places, such as hotel rooms and the backseat of your car.

Imagine the possibilities for convenience—*and* malice or mischief. Not only can your privacy be invaded, some "hackers" get a perverse joy out of committing electronic vandalism by making viruses disguised as legitimate computer programs available for downloading.

THE THREAT OF CONNECTEDNESS

More than one-third of the nation's households now have a PC, and according to a recent survey, nearly three-quarters of those computers are connected to a modem. On a typical day, the average e-mail user sends three messages and receives five. Yet most of us don't realize the threats inherent in that increasing connectedness.

If your computer is hooked up to a modem (a device that lets your machine "talk" to other such machines), then you have the capability to go online. That means you can, via your PC, send and receive material—text, pictures, even sound—from your computer over telephone or cable networks. You're potentially connected to anyone else in the world who has a computer and a modem.

There's a vast—and rapidly growing—array of entertainment, education, government information, and shopping available online. You can exchange messages, trade documents, and teach others and learn from them in ways not possible even a few years ago.

This is a tremendous capability. But, as we've seen throughout this book, great leaps forward in electronic technology often bring with them what are potentially at least a few steps backwards as far as privacy goes. This is no different.

The Internet is making a reality of one-stop information shopping, but because it's so vast and undisciplined, it raises some unique privacy concerns. From the comfort of home or office, the computer user can search for people from coast to coast. Data once considered private, or at least hard to get, now may be readily accessible.

A recent, alarming case highlighted the Net's potential impact on personal privacy. Yahoo!, a popular system for finding material on the Internet, and Database America, a New Jersey direct-mail marketing list wholesaler, began making available to computer users the names and home addresses of Americans with unlisted phones. Assembled from credit reports, product warranty cards, driver's license data, and magazine subscriptions, the list included some very private people, such as police, judges, crime victims, corporate executives, and a host of others who had taken steps to keep their home addresses to themselves.

After inquiries from the press, the unlisted home addresses disappeared from Yahoo!'s "People Search" service after just two weeks. However, the incident again clearly showed that while computers can bring people together, that proximity can be a mixed blessing.

THE MAJOR PLAYERS

Each computer—or network of computers—is capable of capturing and storing our online communications. These networks interact both with their users and with one another in various ways. For example, the mother of all computer networks is the Internet, which is not operated by anybody. It's the cyberspace equivalent of anarchy, and it's growing at a phenomenal rate. No one knows the total number of users, but 1996 estimates were that the Internet consisted of 60,000 networks worldwide, with more than 50 million users.

You can use various routes to access the Internet. You might communicate online by dialing into the Internet through a local or national Internet Service Provider (ISP), a commercial online service (such as America Online, CompuServe, Microsoft Network, or Prodigy), or a BBS. Increasingly, the differences between ISPs, the commercial services, and BBSs are blurring.

Each ISP, commercial service, and a BBS is managed by a different "sysop" (systems operator) or systems administrator, each of whom may have different attitudes toward online privacy. This makes it imperative that you research thoroughly any ISP, online service, or BBS you are considering joining.

WHO SEES WHAT?

Information sent over this huge network may pass through dozens of different computer systems on the way to its destination. Although it may not seem like it, you are being followed through cyberspace.

Each time you retrieve a file, look at an image, send e-mail or visit a Web site, a record is created somewhere on the Internet. These online activities can be monitored, either directly or indirectly, both by your own service provider and by the systems administrators of any sites on the Internet which you visit.

A growing number of Web sites ask you to register with them. In many cases, registering brings real benefits, such as discounts, access to special areas, and timely information.

Often, these sites are merely collecting names, addresses, phone numbers, and other information to create marketing lists. This direct approach also provides the site's operator with a detailed picture of how you use the site.

You also may reveal information indirectly, because most sites keep an electronic log of all visitors. They record which site you just viewed previously, what kind of software you are using to view their site, and other details.

To see this in action, check the Web site of the Center for Democracy and Technology (http://www.cdt.org). One of the things you can see is a display of some information it's gathered about you just as a result of your visit there. CDT's system is a rudimentary one. Provided that you log in from your own ISP and are using your primary e-mail account, a Web site operator with the right equipment and the desire to do so can easily obtain your e-mail address, the exact files you viewed, and other detailed information without your knowledge.

In addition, many kinds of Web-browsing software deposit on your hard drive information (called ''cookies'') about your visit to that site. When you return to that site, a ''cookies'' reader will scan your hard drive to find out if you've been there before.

Often, these browsers invisibly provide Web site operators with information about a user's service provider and with information about other Web sites the user has visited. Some Web browsers are programmed to transmit a user's e-mail address to each Web site visited. (For information about a ''cookies'' blocker and other types of online filters, visit http://www.pgp.com/products/PGPcookie-info.cgi and http://www.wizvax.net/kevinmca.) Both Microsoft Internet Explorer and Netscope Navigator now provide the option to block cookies.

Thus, systems administrators, if they choose to keep track, can tell whom you connect to online, what you look at there, and what you download. The practice of collecting these browsing patterns is increasing, and you should be aware that this could pose a significant threat to online privacy. It's a good idea to contact your service provider and ask whether the system captures this type of information.

Some online services will ask you to submit personal profiles when you join, although most services do not require these miniprofiles for membership. These bits of information, reflecting subscribers' interests, can potentially be used to create valuable mailing lists for advertisers and target marketers. Usually, the specific online bulletin boards and forums used by those subscribers are not revealed.

Further, the services may also offer subscribers the option of being excluded from all of these mailing lists they sell or rent. If you're at all concerned about your privacy, you should take them up on that offer.

WHAT HAPPENS TO YOUR INFORMATION?

Much of this material may never be used. The fact remains, you have too little control over what, if anything, is done with your personal information. Put in the hands, say, of a marketer with a powerful computer, this record of your online activity can be used to build a detailed profile of you.

Understand, virtually no online activity or service comes with an absolute guarantee of privacy. It's up to you to be vigilant. You can't count on the service provider, and as we'll soon see, you can't count on the law.

Regardless of a service's privacy policies and whether you complete a personal profile, you need to keep in mind that anything you put online is vulnerable. Even your supposedly "private" message typed live to the computer screen of another person in a so-called private "chat" room, for instance, can be easily captured by someone in the "room" and forwarded to multiple recipients. Don't send anything you wouldn't mind seeing widely disseminated.

In fact, many online activities are actually intended for multiple recipients. Online newsletters, for example, are usually sent to a mailing list of subscribers via e-mail. If you wish to privately reply to a message posted in an online newsletter, be sure you address it specifically to that person's address, not to the newsletter address. Otherwise, your message may be sent to everyone on the newsletter mailing list.

Even if an online service or BBS requires a password to participate, that doesn't mean your privacy is protected. Communications made in these forums may initially be read only by the members with access.

Again, there's nothing preventing another member from recording your communication and then transmitting it elsewhere. Additionally, much like e-mail, these activities can be legally monitored in some cases, as will soon be explained.

THE INSIDE STORY ON E-MAIL

Virtually all online services offer some sort of "private" activity which allows subscribers to send personal e-mail messages to others. The federal Electronic Communications Privacy Act (ECPA), passed in 1986, makes it unlawful for anyone other than the sender or recipient to read or disclose the contents of an electronic communication, such as e-mail messages.

However, there are three important exceptions:

- The service may legally view and disclose private e-mail if *either* the sender or the recipient consents. Many commercial services require a consent agreement from all new members when signing up for the service.

- Though random monitoring of e-mail is outlawed, an online service may view private e-mail if it suspects the sender is attempting to damage the system, harm another user, or engage in illegal activity.

- If the e-mail system is owned by an employer, the employer may inspect the contents of employee e-mail on the system. Therefore, any e-mail sent from a business location is probably not private. (See Chapter 12, ''Employee Monitoring: Is Your Boss Spying on You?'')

Law-enforcement officials may also access e-mail, but only after receiving a court-ordered search warrant.

Again, remember that your e-mail message typically travels through many computers to get where it's going. Thus, the people who run these computers (sysops, or systems administrators) may read, copy, or store your messages. When it arrives, your message can be copied and distributed widely by the recipient. It's wrong to assume your message is necessarily just a short, private exchange between two people.

Another false assumption about e-mail and other computer communications is that once you delete them, they're gone forever. Not so.

For example, a New Jersey man sued his wife for divorce after accusing her of having an affair online. Although his wife assumed her e-mail messages could not be recovered, her husband was able to retrieve them from the computer and store them on a disk. The dozens of e-mail messages were included in the court case.

You should also be aware that vast streams of e-mail can be scanned for key words. It's quite feasible to set up a computer to scan all messages passing through some chosen mail path, thus ''trolling'' for some interesting topic. This can be done fairly cheaply, so almost anyone with technical know-how can scan many separate mail streams.

The moral of the story is that for a variety of reasons, your private e-mail generally isn't private. Unless it's encrypted, which will be explained later in this chapter, your e-mail can be transmitted to others without your knowledge, monitored by person or persons unknown, and resurrected even after you believe you've deleted it. So, be discreet!

CRIMINAL ACTIVITY

As the technology grows, the capacity for crime grows, too. Whereas once computer hackers were considered largely a threat to businesses, now that individuals are relying more and more on computers for their financial dealings, the targets have broadened.

Security experts say that dialing software is one tool hackers use. It automatically and continuously dials up phone numbers, searching for the telltale tone of a modem. When they get that modem tone, initially, they don't know if it's an individual or a business, so they may go in and snoop around. Sometimes they'll take credit card numbers and use them, or perhaps post them on a bulletin board.

A motivated, knowledgeable computer user can potentially access your files, steal your Social Security number and credit card number (if stored in files on your hard drive), or even stalk you through your computer activity.

While you cannot fully protect yourself from these dangers, you can take these precautions:

- Never transmit your credit card number over the Internet or any other public e-mail system, unless it's encrypted.

- Don't post your Social Security number in any communication, either e-mail or otherwise.

- Be on the lookout for suspicious activity on your computer. Unfamiliar commands on your screen, the appearance of new files, or changes in your memory could mean an intruder has accessed your files.

- Never forget that one of the advantages of the Internet is anonymity and that not everyone is who he or she claims to be.

TWO KINDS OF STALKING

Computers raise the stakes for stalking. This will be discussed further in Chapter 14 ("Protecting Yourself from a Stalker"). For now, be aware that the computer makes this heinous activity easier and more invisible. It also makes it possible to stalk someone without ever coming near them.

A 1995 *Newsweek* poll showed that 80% of respondents were concerned about being harassed by "virtual stalking" through unwanted messages on the Internet. Similarly, 76% worried about harassment by real stalkers whom they first meet on the Internet.

A determined, skilled stalker can locate every word you type on, say, the Usenet—a global bulletin board made up of more than 15,000 separate discussion groups—and on other public online forums. A new, powerful generation of search programs (such as Deja News, Alta Vista, or HotBot) have been created to allow a systematic indexing of the contents of Usenet postings, making it possible to find just about anything you have ever communicated in these forums.

Where once it would have been almost impossible to read through the millions of messages posted daily to the various newsgroups to find one by a particular person, search services now can sift through that data in seconds and supply an "Author Profile" of any given person.

John Kaufman, a San Francisco writer, was stalked that way. An obsessive admirer tracked down almost everything he'd ever communicated on the Internet and, at one point, sent him a three-page letter that essentially was a pieced-together dossier of his entire life gleaned from postings he'd made. "When this thing flashed on the screen, my mouth dropped open," Kaufman told a reporter. "Here was a total stranger who knew my cat's name."

In other words, if you say something impolite on the Usenet about a political candidate, or make irreverent comments about, for example, General Motors or Vanna White—those words are not gone forever. They can be retrieved over a period of years and assembled under your name.

Worrisome? Maybe not now. But it could come as a shock if you later try to get a job with that politician, or have a beef with General Motors, or want to try a spin on "Wheel of Fortune," and find out someone has exhumed your words.

THE RIDDLE OF ENCRYPTION

The need for better computer security is obvious—and so, in large measure, is the solution: encryption. Encryption is the scrambling and then un-scrambling of the text so only the sender and intended recipient of a message can read it. It's the best tool for protecting computer privacy.

The technology already exists, as André Bacard makes clear in *The Computer Privacy Handbook*. In the near future, for example, "smart" disks with built-in encryption will be almost universally in use. Meanwhile, a continuing tug-of-war between the government and the software manufacturers and consumers has slowed down the spread of encryption systems.

The U.S. State Department, the National Security Agency, and the FBI oppose unchecked public use of encryption. They seek to minimize the chances that spies and criminals will have superior codes. At issue is how complex—and thus, effective— the encryption can be in software shipped overseas. Right now, the most effective systems are classified as "munitions" and barred from export. But, reflecting the global promise—and problems—of the Internet, there's still no clear ruling as to whether making software available on a global network is equivalent to exporting it.

Though there's dispute about what level of encryption should be allowed for export and how—if at all—government should be allowed a "backdoor" to unscramble encrypted messages, even domestically, few are saying encryption should be eliminated. Even if they were saying that, it probably wouldn't make any difference. Clearly, encryption is an idea whose time has come. In fact, millions already use it to some extent unawares. For example, it's now being woven into some software. And it's being routinely used on Web sites conducting online commerce where credit card numbers are transmitted.

ONLINE RISKS TO YOUTH?

Already some four million youths use the Internet, according to the publisher of the monthly *Digital Kids Report*, and that figure will soar as every state seeks to get more schoolchildren online. On one hand, that's reason for rejoicing. Clearly, computers and the Internet will become increasingly important not only for learning and careers but for everyday activities, such as banking and shopping. Children and teenagers are going to need to master the Internet because, in large measure, that's how the future will work.

On the other hand, kids are especially vulnerable to being taken advantage of in cyberspace. Some companies see young computer users as consumer trainees, and the past few years have seen a dramatic increase in the amount and detail of personal information collected from children. While many adults are aware of the ways in which this is collected (such as magazine subscriptions and surveys), children are not.

Although we teach our children not to talk to strangers, most kids don't consider a favorite toy or cartoon character a stranger. Thus, when they log onto a Web site featuring these characters, they probably won't hesitate to provide whatever personal information is requested. That data then may be used for marketing by the company that developed the Web site, or sold to other marketers.

"Never before has there been a medium with this kind of

power to invade the privacy of children and families,'' wrote the
Center for Media Education in a 1996 report. It says children as
young as four are being asked to provide detailed information
about themselves before they can enter a Web site where games
and entertainment await them. The companies, while conceding
that some sites ask children to provide information—such as
name, sex, age, e-mail address, favorite TV show, and musical
group—maintain that the identities of the children are protected
and their lists are not sold.

The dispute also enlarges the debate over regulating the Internet. Until now, that concern has centered mainly on fears
about criminal activity and pornography. Now the Center, along
with the Consumer Federation of America, the National Parent-
Teacher Association and other advocacy groups, have asked
the Federal Trade Commission to regulate electronic advertising
aimed at kids. The FTC polices false or deceptive advertising
claims—including appeals to children on television and in magazines—but as yet has no specific rules for Internet advertising.

But the threat is greater than just marketing overkill. For
example, a Los Angeles television reporter, Kyra Phillips, purchased for $277 a mailing list of 5,500 children living in nearby
Pasadena from Metromail, a Chicago mailing list company. She
gave the name of the buyer as Richard Allen Davis, an infamous
California child molester and child murderer. No one questioned
his right to have the list. Thus, physical molestation, or worse,
is a potential threat. In a few cases, pedophiles have used online
services and bulletin boards to gain a child's confidence, then
arrange a personal meeting.

Teenagers are particularly at risk because they frequently use
the computer unsupervised and are more likely to participate in
''adult'' exchanges online. However, children of any age could
be exposed to indecent or inappropriate material, such as that
containing sex or violence, or they may see e-mail or bulletin
board messages that are harassing, demeaning, or belligerent.

STEPS PARENTS CAN TAKE

There's no substitute for parental control. To tell children to stop going online isn't very practical.

Most online service providers allow parents to limit children's access to certain services, such as adult-oriented ''chat'' rooms. Check for this when you first subscribe. In addition, there are now software programs designed specifically to prevent children from accessing inappropriate materials on the Internet—for example, Cyber Patrol, Surfwatch, Net Nanny, and Cybersitter. Ask your computer retailer. Such tools aren't foolproof and aren't a substitute for parental involvement. Further, some such filters have been criticized for prohibiting access to sites that parents might consider worthwhile for their children.

By far the best way to assure that your children have positive online experiences is to spend time with them and have them show you their activities.

Further, you can establish family rules for online computer use. Among those suggested by the National Center for Missing & Exploited Children:

- Tell your children never to give out identifying information—such as home address, school name, or phone number—in a public message. They shouldn't even reveal such data in private e-mail unless they're sure whom they're dealing with.

- Never permit a child to arrange a face-to-face meeting with another computer user without your attending.

- Warn your children not to respond to messages or bulletin board items that are threatening, suggestive, demeaning, or otherwise make you or the child uncomfortable.

- Set reasonable rules, including time limits, for your child's use of the computer. Watch particularly for excessive use

of online services late at night. That could be a tip-off that
there's a problem.

• Try to make online use a family activity. Keeping the computer in a family room rather than the child's bedroom
  might be wise.

• Get to know your children's online ''friends'' much as you
  try to get to know their other friends.

PROTECTING YOUR FILES

Despite the dangers at home and at the office, there are ways
to protect your personal computer files. Data encryption, anonymous remailers, password generators, and firewalls, are among
the means available to ensure the maximum privacy possible.

Encryption

As discussed, this involves scrambling e-mail messages or
files, making them unreadable to anyone who intercepts them.
An encrypted e-mail message cannot be read by the online service sysop, or any third party who has obtained the message
legally or illegally.

Although its legal status, particularly as to export, is still
unsettled, there's no doubt that encryption for personal, domestic use is legal, available, and usually effective.

Anonymous remailers

These programs, in effect, ''launder'' your e-mail by strip-
ping off all identifying information, then forwarding the mail
to the appropriate address. Generally, this is a free service that
allows you, the sender, to remain unknown.

Why would you want to do that? Well, perhaps you're a
stalking victim seeking help from others who've experienced
similar harassment. Or maybe you're a whistleblower who

needs to retain anonymity while passing on information to authorities. Or you might want to place a controversial personal ad, share your strongly held beliefs on some incendiary topic, or simply post anonymously on Usenet.

In any of those cases, using an anonymous remailer might make a lot of sense. To learn more about anonymous remailers, visit André Bacard's Web site at http://www.well.com/user/abcard/remail.html. For a list of reliable remailers, visit http://www.cs.berkeley/~raph/remailer-list.html.

You should investigate any remailer before sending sensitive material. You'll want to know how they operate. Are they easy to use? Are messages forwarded in a timely manner? Find out if they keep logs of the messages or leave other tracks. Try to determine their stability, the length of time they have operated. Do they use cryptography if traffic to the site is monitored?

Proxies

When you're surfing the Web, you can create an anonymous identity by using the Anonymizer, created by Community ConneXion. Log on to this Web site (http://www.anonymizer.com) before visiting other sites. It shields your personal information from other Web sites that you visit, and you don't have to be concerned that your ''clickstream'' is being tracked along the way.

Password Generators

Passwords are a big source of security problems on any network. Because many people forget their passwords, computer companies often build weak password systems. Furthermore, to help those same absent-minded users, password-recovery software is effective and popular.

Of course, that's a two-edged sword. The same program that can help you retrieve your password can help snoopers unlock your files.

One way to guard privacy and get around the traditional password weakness is to use programs known as one-time password generators. These produce one-time-only passwords, making them invalid at the end of the user's session. The downside is that such a system adds complexity and cost.

▓Firewalls

This protection, more relevant to companies than to individual PCs, offers an even higher level of security by acting as a buffer between the Internet and all other computers within a system. It sets up only one point of entry by an unauthorized user. That one point then can be monitored and defended, and many firms place their firewall computers in a physically secure room.

However, firewalls work both ways, limiting access from the inside while blocking intruders from the outside.

●Commonly Asked Questions About Computer Privacy●

Q: How common is it to track and record a user's various on-line visitations?

A: Web site tracking services are increasingly being used by Web site owners and advertisers to monitor the browsing patterns of visitors.

It's possible to record many online activities, including which newsgroups or files a subscriber accesses and which ads are read. Records of these browsing patterns—also known as "transaction-generated information" or the "clickstream"—are a potentially valuable source of revenue for online services. Auditing services like WebTrak and DoubleClick record who reads specific ads, create demographic profiles of users, and report such data back to the advertisers and Web site owners.

This data is useful to direct marketers, who can develop highly targeted lists of online users with similar likes and be-haviors. It also creates the potential for junk e-mail. Additionally, this information might be embarrassing for users who have accessed sensitive or controversial materials online.

To address these concerns, the Electronic Frontier Foundation and a group of companies involved in electronic commerce have joined forces to develop a system of ratings that tell users what level of personal data is being collected when they visit Web sites. Called eTrust, the system enables vendors to communicate to customers what personal information is being collected and what is done with it. The rating system, which uses graphic symbols, is backed up by an auditing and certification process. To learn more, visit the eTrust Web site at http://www.etrust.org.

Another emerging privacy-enhancing tool being developed for online users is the Platform for Internet Content Selection (PICS), a project of the World Wide Web Consortium (W3C). This international industry group is developing common protocols for the evolution of the Web. PICS allows online users to control what is accessed on the Web by associating labels with Internet content. It was originally designed to help parents and teachers control what children access.

An extension of PICS, called the Platform for Privacy Preferences (P3), will enable online users to communicate their privacy preferences and Web sites to indicate their information practices on the Internet. Information about P3 can be found at http://www.cdt.org. Learn more about PICS at the W3C Web site, http://www.w3.org/pub/WWW/PICS.

Q: Can my online service or the Web sites that I visit access information stored in my computer without my knowledge?
A: Yes.

It is *technically* possible for online services and Web sites to access subscribers' computers. Many of the commercial online services automatically download graphics and program upgrades to the user's home computer. Web sites attach ''cookies'' and other ''applets'' such as Java and ActiveX programs to your hard drive. These programs gather details about your visit to

Web sites so that when you visit again, you do not have to reinput your name and profile.

Online services deny prying with malicious intent. But an applet in the wrong hands could be used to gain access to your hard drive and retrieve its contents.

Q: How can I make sure my password is secure?
A: The more complex and obscure your password is, the better.

There are several ways to make your password uniquely your own. First, don't choose ordinary words. Computer hackers can use automated programs that test every word in the dictionary at lightning speed. If possible, use at least eight characters; the longer the password, the harder it is to crack. Never use obvious, guessable passwords such as your name, birth date, license plate number, or nickname.

Second, combine letters (both upper and lower case) and numbers, and include special characters if possible. For example, the password O2*weFF& is much harder to detect than a simple word or alphanumeric combination.

Third, don't record your password where people can find it, including in your wallet or desk drawer. Don't lend your password to someone else or give it over the phone or in e-mail messages.

Fourth, change your password frequently. The ultimate protection would be to change it each time you log-on to your computer. Watch out for someone looking over your shoulder as you enter your password.

Fifth, report any unusual log-on usages immediately to your online provider.

And, finally, be aware that instances of "password fishing" have been reported. That's when a hacker, posing as an online-service employee, tricks you into revealing your password and other information. Six major online companies have begun an effort called "Project Open" to educate users how to keep themselves safe online. For more details, see:
http://www.isa.net/project-open.

Q: Why should I care if somebody accesses my old Internet messages?
A: Maybe you wouldn't care about many of them. But think about those you might.

Your public postings may be archived and saved for posterity. For example, it's possible to search and discover the postings an individual has made to Usenet newsgroups. These then can be used to create profiles of individuals for a variety of purposes, such as employment background checks and direct marketing. You might want to be careful about revealing acts (such as crimes or love affairs) or feelings (such as depression or suicidal thoughts) that could come back to haunt you.

Q: My e-mail inbox is cluttered with junk e-mail. What can I do?
A: Fortunately, the Web offers "spam"-fighters many tips to keep unwanted junk e-mail at bay.

We recommend that you visit the many Web sites dedicated to the eradication of junk e-mail. For starters, see John Rivard's "Stop Junk E-mail" page at http://www.mcs.net/~jcr/junkemail. html). Coyote Communications' site also offers useful strategies (http://www.coyotecom.com/jac/stopjunk.html), as does CNET's site (http://www.cnet.com/content/features/Howto/Spam) and Voters Telecommunications Watch (http://www.vtw.org/uce). These sites provide links to many other online resources. Junkbusters (http://www.junkbusters.com) provides a "Spamoff" service and suggests a legal strategy to pursue. And Bigfoot offers a list of abusive bulk e-mailers (http://www/bigfoot.com).

To summarize the tips offered by these sites:

• Don't buy anything advertised by junk e-mail. This only encourages the practice.

- If you're an AOL user, take advantage of its mail filtering services.

- Surf the Web anonymously by using the Anonymizer service (http://www.anonymizer.com). This prevents your e-mail address from being captured while you browse from site to site.

- Remove your e-mail address from the many "people-finder" tools on the Net. These include Four11, Whowhere, Switchboard, and Bigfoot; their Web addresses are listed at the end of this chapter.

- Learn to decode the mailer's "header" to determine the real identity of the junk e-mailer and to find out who owns the machine that sent the solicitations (a complex process described in John Rivard's site). When you have learned the host's identity, send a complaint to "postmaster@*host. domain*". You can also try "root@*host.domain*" or "abuse@ *host.domain*" (no quotation marks). Some online services and Internet providers have local e-mail addresses where you can report abusive "spam" mailers.

- If the solicitation contains a phone number, fax number, or "snailmail" address, register your complaint with the mailer by using one of those means.

And finally, complain loudly to policymakers. Let your state and federal legislators know that you want relief from this growing online nuisance. Several state legislatures have already introduced bills to curtail unwanted solicitations. Report illegal activities to the National Fraud Information Center (http:// www.fraud.org) and the Federal Trade Commission (http:// www.ftc.gov).

●Privacy Pointers: What You Can Do Now●

1. Research the privacy guidelines of your present or future online service.

Most online services now provide users with a statement of their privacy measures. Most services require new subscribers to allow e-mail to be monitored as part of the sign-up process.

Avoid services that do not have a well-defined policy. Make sure the policies are consistent and wide-ranging. If a service doesn't have a written policy, don't sign up.

Shop around. Investigate new online services before subscribing to them. One way to check them out is to post a question about a service in a dependable online forum or newsgroup. Another method is to visit the Web site of the Center for Democracy and Technology (http://www.cdt.org), where privacy policies of commercial providers are listed.

2. Invest in encryption or some other privacy-protection system.

Check with your computer retailer about the kinds of programs available. This chapter has mentioned just a few: encryption, anonymous remailers, and firewalls.

Cryptographic systems, perhaps the simplest to work with, are available as either hardware or software—that is, encryption chips, or software programs. Both have advantages and disadvantages. One popular software system is Pretty Good Privacy (wryly named by creator Philip Zimmerman after "Ralph's Pretty Good Grocery," a staple of humorist Garrison Keillor's "Prairie Home Companion" on National Public Radio).

PGP—as it's widely called—is an easy-to-use, highly secure program that turns computer messages into a jumble of letters and numbers unreadable to anyone except the intended recipient. It's virtually uncrackable and, though there are competing crypto systems, PGP is the de facto world standard software for e-mail security.

New encryption systems are likely to emerge in the years to come. But, for now, PGP, first published in 1991, is the closest thing to a standard system and has spread all over the world. PGP, like many computer programs, has evolved in steps, so various versions exist, such as 2.4, 2.6, and so on. You can obtain it two ways. There is a commercial version of PGP sold by Pretty Good Privacy, Inc. (formerly ViaCrypt), licensed for private or commercial use in the United States and Canada (http://www.pgp.com). On the other hand, if you're a member of the ''digiterati''— that is, a computer sophisticate—you can find it on the Internet or various BBS systems: an informative web site can be found at MIT's server, http://web.mit.edu/network/pgp.html.

3. Take consistent action to maximize your online privacy. Among the things you can do:

• Create a secure password and change it frequently.

• Assume that your online communications are not private and act accordingly. Do not send sensitive or personal information by computer.

• Be cautious of ''startup'' software of online service providers. These programs often require you to provide credit card, checking account and/or Social Security numbers, or other personal information.

• Be aware that you leave ''footprints'' for others to see when you use your online service. These show when and where your log-ons occurred, as well as where and what commands you have executed.

• Remember that the ''delete'' command doesn't make your messages disappear. They can still be retrieved by others from backup systems and from archives of posted messages.

• Keep in mind that online identities are not always what they seem. Many network users adopt one or more online disguises.

• Teach your children about appropriate online privacy behavior. Caution them against revealing information about themselves or your family.

- If you want to reply to private messages posted in an online newsletter, be sure you address it specifically to that person's e-mail address, not the newsletter's e-mail address.

- If for any reason you need to safeguard your identity, don't create an online biography. And don't create an e-mail address that replicates your name in whole or in part. Avoid ''jdoe@anyservice.com''.

- Never reveal your name, address, phone number, credit card number or computer password while online unless you're dealing with a trusted entity or are using an encryption system.

4. Get software that blocks your children from accessing certain kinds of material.

It is very easy for small hands to inadvertently access information in your computer. In one case, children fighting over a mouse opened their parents' finance program and, with one click of the Enter key, managed to write 240 identical checks to pay off twenty years of a thirty-year mortgage. You can buy programs that will allow children to execute only the programs you want them to.

Check that the blocking software you purchase, such as Net Nanny and Cyber Patrol, blocks not only access to offensive material but also blocks transmission of personal information such as name and address.

5. If you use e-mail or other online services at work on your employer's computer, limit it to business-related activity.

Most employers can and do claim that any computer communication made during business hours is the property of the company, and therefore subject to inspection. This can lead to embarrassment and maybe job loss. So use your home computer for personal messages or to visit non-job-related Internet sites.

6. Be cautious about copying free software.

Be careful when downloading free software from cyberspace

and putting it into your computer. The freebie (often called "freeware" or "shareware") may do what it promises. But it also may make a copy of your credit card number or other sensitive information in your files and send it elsewhere.

7. Clean out your computer before you get rid of it.

If you give away or throw away your computer, you should use the "wipe" feature on many popular PC utility programs to delete the information on your hard drive. Experts say that any amateur hacker can bypass the "delete" function. The same applies to information on old floppy disks.

In fact, even the "wipe" feature may not be adequate, experts say. Physically destroying the hard drive and the floppies may be the best protection, especially if they contain highly sensitive information such as trade secrets.

8. Know the downside of having your own Web site.

It's trendy to develop your own "home page," but keep in mind that you're practically begging direct marketers and others to collect your address, phone number, résumé data, and any other information that you provide via the Web site.

9. Be alert to the possible social dangers of being online.

Among them are harassment, stalking, being "flamed" (getting verbally attacked), or "spamming" (being sent frequent, unsolicited messages). Women can be particularly vulnerable if their e-mail addresses are recognizable as women's names. Females should consider using gender-neutral online IDs as well as declining to post online service biographies.

10. Contact the following groups for more information:

PUBLIC INTEREST GROUPS

Several public-interest groups advocate on behalf of online users. They also have extensive information about privacy issues available via their online archives.

- **Center for Democracy and Technology**
  1634 I St., NW, No. 1100
  Washington, D.C. 20006
  (202) 637-9800
  http://www.cdt.org
  This is a nonprofit public-interest organization whose mission is to develop and advocate public policies advancing civil liberties and democratic values in new computer and communication technologies.

- **Computer Professionals for Social Responsibility**
  P.O. Box 717
  Palo Alto, CA 94302
  (415) 322-3778
  http://www.cpsr.org
  CPSR is a public-interest alliance of computer scientists and others interested in the impact of computer technology on society.

- **Consumer Project on Technology**
  P.O. Box 19367
  Washington, D.C. 20036
  (202) 387-8030
  http://www.cptech.org
  Created by Ralph Nader in 1995, this group focuses on telecommunications regulation, copyright, and the impact of technology on privacy, among other issues.

- **Electronic Frontier Foundation**
  1550 Bryant St., No. 725
  San Francisco, CA 94103
  (415) 436-9333
  http://www.eff.org
  A nonprofit civil-liberties organization, EFF seeks to protect privacy, free expression, and access to public resources and information online, as well as promote responsibility in new media.

- **Electronic Privacy Information Center**
  666 Pennsylvania Ave., SE, No. 301
  Washington, D.C. 20003
  (202) 544-9240
  http://www.epic.org
  EPIC is a public-interest research center which seeks to focus attention on emerging civil-liberties issues and to protect privacy, the First Amendment, and constitutional values.

- **NetAction**
  601 Van Ness Ave., No. 631
  San Francisco, CA 94102
  (415) 775-8674
  http://www.netaction.org
  This nonprofit group is dedicated to promoting effective grassroots citizen-action campaigns and educating the public, policymakers, and media about technology-based social and political issues.

- **Privacy International**
  http://www.privacy.org/pi
  Based in London, with its U.S. operation administered by Electronic Privacy Information Center (see above), PI is an international watchdog on surveillance by government and corporations.

- **Utility Consumers' Action Network**
  CyberCop Project
  1717 Kettner Blvd., No. 105
  San Diego, CA 92101
  (619) 696-6966
  http://www.ucan.org
  The CyberCop Complaint Center Web site provides an interactive forum for lodging complaints about online privacy as well as other online consumer abuses.

PGP ENCRYPTION INFORMATION

- The **"Official PGP FAQ"** **(Frequently Asked Questions)** can be found at http://www.pgp.net/pgpnet/pgp-faq/.

- **"PGP Steps,"** a set of instructions for installing PGP on Dos/Windows, is provided at http://www.aha.ru/~szdmos. pgpsteps.txt.

- **MIT Distribution site for PGP** http://www.mit.edu/network/pgp.html

- **"Private Idaho,"** compiled by Joel McNamara. http://www.eskimo.com/~joelm/pi.html

INFORMATION ABOUT CHILDREN AND ONLINE USE

Request the publications:

- **"Child Safety on the Information Highway,"** published by the National Center for Missing and Exploited Children, (800) 843-5678. See also the Web site: http://www.missingkids.org.

- **"Project Open: Making the Net Work for You,"** published by the Interactive Services Association and the National Consumers League, (800) 466-OPEN. See also the Web site: http://www.isa.net/project-open.

- **"Web of Deception: Threats to Children from Online Marketing,"** from Center for Media Education, 1511 K St., N.W., Washington, D.C. 20005, (202) 628-2620. See also the Web site: http://tap.epn.org/cme.

- Investigate "parental control" software programs. These online filters limit the types of sites children can visit. Some prohibit online users from disclosing certain information, such as names and addresses. The commercial online services also provide parental control mechanisms.

  Cyber Patrol   http://www.microsys.com

Cybersitter   http://www.solidoak.com

Net Nanny   http://netnanny.com/netnanny

Net Shepherd   http://www.netshepherd.com

SurfWatch   http://www.surfwatch.com

The debate surrounding parental control software is heating up. To learn more about such concerns as censorship and proprietary blocking standards, visit these sites:

Voters Telecommunications Watch, "Internet Parental Control FAQ"   http://www.vtw.org/parents

Neosoft   http://www.neosoft.com/parental-control

CompassNet   http://www.ccom.net/ccom/censor

FOR FURTHER READING

- André Bacard, *The Computer Privacy Handbook: A Practical Guide to E-Mail, Encryption, Data Protection, and PGP Privacy Software*. Peachpit Press, 1995.

- Edward Cavazos and Gavino Morin, *Cyberspace and the Law*. MIT Press, 1994.

- Karen Coyle, ed., *Coyle's Information Highway Handbook*. American Library Association, 1997.

- Robert Gelman and the Electronic Frontier Foundation, *Civilizing the Electronic Frontier*. HarperEdge, 1997.

- Lance Rose and Jonathan Wallace, *Syslaw*. LOL Productions, 1992.

- Bruce Schneier, *E-Mail Security: How to Keep Your Electronic Messages Private*. John Wiley & Sons, 1995.

- Philip R. Zimmerman, *The Official PGP User's Guide*. MIT Press, 1995.

Online Newsletters Discussing Cyberspace Privacy:

- **Computer Privacy Digest:** CPD can be read as a Usenet newsgroup—comp.society.privacy. Alternatively, to receive CPD via e-mail, send a request to the newsletter's moderator at: comp-privacy-request@uwm.edu.

- **Privacy Forum:** For subscription information, send an e-mail message consisting of the word "help" (without quotes) in the *body* of the message to: privacy-request@vortex.com.

Powerful search tools are now available to find information contained in public postings to Internet newsgroups. To see if your own contributions are listed, you may wish to visit the following Web sites.

If you do not want your Usenet postings to be accessible by these search tools, add the line "x-no-archive: yes" (no quotation marks) to the header or to the first line of the posting.

- **Alta Vista** at http://www.altavista.digital.com

- **Deja News** at http://www.dejanews.com

- **Excite** at http://www.excite.com

- **HotBot** at http://www.hotbot.com

The following search and directory services offer "people-finding" tools. Several provide a name-removal option if you don't want your e-mail address, home address and phone number to be accessible online. (This is not an all-inclusive list.)

- **Bigfoot** at http://www.bigfoot.com

- **Four11** at http://www.four11.com

- **Infoseek** at http://www.infoseek.com

- **Infospace** at http://www.infospace.com

- **LookupUSA** at http://www.lookupusa.com

- **Lycos** at http://www.lycos.com

- **Switchboard** at http://www.switchboard.com

- **WhoWhere** at http://www.whowhere.com

- **Yahoo!** at http://www.yahoo.com

For information about **anonymous remailers**:

- **"Anonymous Remailers FAQ,"** compiled by André Bacard. http://www.well.com/user/abacard/remail.html

- To find the addresses of remailers, visit http://www.cs. berkeley/~raph/remailer-list.html.

- Find out about the Internet privacy utility "Private Idaho" at http://www.eskimo.com/~joelm/pi.html.

●

PART IV

PROTECTING YOUR PRIVACY
ON THE JOB

What's Your Future Boss Entitled to Know?

You thought you came across well in the interview, confident but not cocky, interested but not overly eager. Everyone said your résumé—well organized and professionally printed on quality paper—was impressive. You didn't spill your waterglass into your lap during lunch, and you talked in more or less complete sentences.

So why didn't you get the job?

Maybe . . . maybe, it had to do with information gathered by the employer—information that you'll rarely hear about or see, let alone have a chance to respond to.

Firms, stung by "negligent hiring" lawsuits, are checking into new hires more deeply than in the past. Databases containing millions of personal records allow them to do so easily and cheaply. From the firms' point of view, it makes a lot of sense. Who would want to hire, say, a chief financial officer who was on parole for larceny? Or an explosives-truck driver with a string of DUIs on his record? Or a convicted child molester as an elementary-school teacher?

If you're none of those things and have nothing to hide, why worry? Because you might be sabotaged by information that is irrelevant, taken out of context, or just plain wrong.

Today there are a lot of different services available that use computer databases containing personal information about millions of Americans. More employers are using them than ever before because they offer quick, relatively inexpensive background searches.

Privacy advocates are concerned that the scope and easy availability of this data make this material seem more authoritative than it really is. They also fear that the newer, perhaps less responsible, background-check services may not fully verify the accuracy of their information.

In truth, many databases are chock full of errors.

For example, Larry is a retail worker who had his wallet stolen. Apparently, the thief committed crimes while carrying Larry's ID. As a result, information about this criminal conduct, wrongfully attributed to Larry, made its way into the database of a firm which does background checks for the retail industry. Bottom line: Larry was fired and couldn't find work for a long time. Eventually, he learned of the erroneous information in the database, and he has filed suit against the background-check firm.

Further, some information in such databases may not be legal to use for hiring purposes, or may come from questionable sources. Rosa applied for a job and had a promising first interview by phone. She was buoyed when the company called back to arrange an in-person meeting. But Rosa's euphoria turned to distress when the firm then sent her a packet of forms to sign: waivers allowing a private eye to do a background check, an authorization form for a credit report, a release for her school records, and a request for permission for the company to conduct interviews with her neighbors. Although the firm may have been within its rights, Rosa was understandably confused about whether—and why—she needed to agree to all those intrusions.

While you can't stop prospective bosses from checking into your background, you can know your rights and you can minimize the chances that what's unearthed will be wrong or misleading. In this chapter, you'll learn what future employers may go looking for and how to make sure that, if they find it, the facts will be complete and accurate.

WHAT'S CHECKED IN A BACKGROUND CHECK?

Employers use background checks for many reasons, such as to verify the accuracy of information provided by job seekers, to uncover information left out of an application or interview, or to protect themselves from lawsuits that can spring from hiring an employee whose actions hurt someone, whether another employee or a customer.

Background checks can reveal a variety of personal information, from both public records and commercial databases. This can range from merely the verification of an applicant's Social Security number to a detailed account of the candidate's history and acquaintances.

Here are some of the pieces of information that might be included in a background check:

- Driving record
- Vehicle registration
- Social Security number
- Bankruptcy
- Property ownership
- Education records
- Character references
- Employment verification
- Credit records
- Court records

- Interviews with neighbors

- Military service records

- Criminal records

- Workers' compensation cases

- State licensing records

Before obtaining certain types of information, an employer must get permission from a potential employee. This includes:

• **Education records** Under the Family Education and Right to Privacy Act, transcripts, recommendations, disciplinary records and financial information are confidential. A school should not release student records without the authorization of the student or parent. However, a school may release "directory information"—such as name, address, dates of attendance, degrees earned, and activities—unless the student (if over age 18) or the parent of a minor expressly forbids that in writing. (See also Chapter 6, "From Cradle to Grave: Government Records and Your Privacy.")

• **Military service records** Under the federal Privacy Act, service records are confidential and can only be released under limited circumstances. Inquiries must be made under the Freedom of Information Act. Even without the applicant's consent, however, the military may release name, rank, salary, duty assignments, awards, and duty status.

• **Medical records** Medical records generally are confidential. However, if an employer requires a physical examination after making a job offer, the company can get the results. The Americans with Disabilities Act allows a potential employer to inquire only about an employee's ability to perform specific job functions.

WHAT CAN'T BE CONSIDERED?

Meanwhile, certain types of information either can't be gathered, or may be gathered but can't be considered by a potential employer. Federal and state laws generally exclude employers from using the following types of information in hiring decisions:

• **Arrest information** Although arrest record information is public record, in many states employers cannot seek out the arrest record of a potential employee. However, in California, for example, if the arrest resulted in a conviction, or if the applicant is out of jail pending trial, that information can be used. Other states may deny access to arrest records altogether, or at least first convictions for minor offenses.

• **Criminal history** Generally, criminal histories or "rap sheets" compiled by law enforcement agencies are not public record. Depending on your state's laws, only certain employers such as public utilities, law enforcement, security-guard firms, and child-care facilities may have access to this information.

However, with the advent of computerized court records and arrest information, private firms can and do compile virtual "rap sheets" from public records.

• **Workers' compensation** When an employee's claim goes through the state system or the workers' compensation appeals board, the case becomes public record in most states. Only if an injury might interfere with one's ability to perform required duties may an employer use this information in making a hiring decision. Under the federal Americans with Disabilities Act, employers cannot use medical information or the fact than an applicant filed a workers compensation claim to discriminate against applicants.

• **Bankruptcies** While bankruptcies are public record, employers cannot discriminate against applicants because they have filed for personal bankruptcy.

Commonly Asked Questions About Background Checks

Q: **Do you have a right to be told when a background check has been requested?**
A: **Only in certain circumstances.**

The only times you must be told about a background check are when the employer requests an "investigative consumer report" or a credit report. Both are regulated by the federal Fair Credit Reporting Act and laws in many states. The investigative consumer report may contain information about your character, general reputation, personal characteristics, and lifestyle. The information in the report is typically compiled from interviews with neighbors, friends, associates, and others who might have information about you.

Ideally, you should have the right to see the background checks done on you, whether or not those are classified as "investigative consumer reports," but because there's no requirement for disclosure on other types of background checks, that usually doesn't happen. If you ask to review your background check, you run the risk of being perceived as a troublemaker.

Q: **How do companies conduct background checks?**
A: **They may search computerized data bases, or have someone do it for them.**

There are numerous companies and private investigators that specialize in conducting preemployment background checks. These include Avert, Equifax Employment Services, EMA-SPA, Employers Information Service, and Pinkerton Security and Investigation Service. The Yellow Pages under "Investigators" lists many more.

Some background-check companies can be reached via the Internet, or through the online systems of the information vendors. For a fee, hirers can use them to access criminal records, driving citations, and credit histories of potential employees. The information vendors that compile data from the many public records and commercial sources include CDB Infotek, IRSC (both of California), and Information America.

Employers sometimes also create a "clearinghouse" of information about potential employees by establishing a shared database. Each participating firm submits information about its employees, and when a job seeker applies to a member company, that employer can check with the clearinghouse for information on the applicant.

Q: What can my former employer say about me?
A: Anything truthful about your performance.

Often, a potential employer will contact an applicant's past employers. Many employers have a policy of confirming only the dates of employment, final salary, and other limited information. Additionally, some states prohibit employers from intentionally interfering with former employees' attempts to find jobs by giving out false or misleading references.

Documents (except for medical data) in your personnel file generally are not confidential and can be revealed by an employer. If you're a federal employee, however, your personnel file is protected under the federal Privacy Act of 1974. Some states have similar safeguards, allowing disclosure only under limited circumstances.

Q: Can an employer ask about an applicant's past or current drug use?
A: No.

Under the Americans with Disabilities Act, an employer may

not ask about an applicant's past drug use. However, the ADA does not protect current users of illegal drugs and, thus, drug testing is often included as a part of a preemployment physical. If the employer has a postemployment drug-testing or employee-investigation policy, you must receive notice of such a policy before a job is offered.

Q: Can an employer talk to friends, neighbors, former teachers, or relatives of the applicant?
A: Yes.

While an employer's safest course of action is contacting and interviewing only the references provided by the applicant, it's not against the law for an employer to interview other acquaintances. However, unless the applicant has signed a waiver, contacting other references may expose the employer to claims of invasion of privacy. An employer's best bet is to contact only the references provided, along with former employers and coworkers.

Q: What can an employer really learn from my credit report?
A: Potentially, a lot.

Although less detailed than an investigative report, a credit report can still tell an employer a great deal. For example, it may contain public-records information such as finance-related court cases, judgments, bankruptcies and liens; also, outstanding credit accounts and loans, and the payment history for each account. Credit report entries remain in the report for up to ten years. A recent amendment to the federal credit reporting law requires employers to obtain the consent of the job applicant before using a credit report for employment determination. (See also Chapter 4, "How Private Is Your Credit Report?")

Although federal and some state laws allow credit bureaus to include criminal record information, it's a policy of the credit-reporting industry not to do so.

●Privacy Pointers: What You Can Do Now●

1. Check public records.

If you have an arrest record or have been involved in court cases, go to the county where this took place and inspect the files. Make sure the information is correct and up to date. Also, request a copy of your driving record from the department of motor vehicles, especially if you are applying for a job that may involve driving.

2. Ask to see a copy of your personnel file from your old job.

Even if you no longer work there, you may have a right to see your file, usually up to at least one year from the last date of employment. Some states allow you to make copies of documents in your file that have your signature on them. You may also want to ask if your former employer has a policy about the release of personnel records. Many companies limit the amount of information they disclose.

3. Read the fine print carefully.

When you sign a job application, you may also be authorizing the disclosure of other personal data, such as education, medical, and financial records. Unfortunately, job seekers are in an awkward position, because refusing to authorize a background check may jeopardize the chances of getting the job.

4. Notify neighbors and colleagues.

Let people know that they may be asked to provide information about you. This helps avoid suspicion and could alert you to possible problems.

5. If you feel comfortable doing so, ask the interviewer about the company's employee-privacy policies.

Many responsible employers have developed written policies to guide their background-checking practices. Find out if your potential employer plans to do a background check and, if it seems appropriate, ask to see a copy.

6. Contact the following for more information:

- **U.S. Equal Employment Opportunity Commission**
  (EEOC)
  1801 L St., NW
  Washington, D.C. 20507
  (202) 663-4900
  http://www.eeoc.gov

- **Your state's equivalent of the EEOC.**
  The government pages of your phone book has listings for both federal and state equal-opportunity offices. Call them and request their brochures on lawful hiring practices.

7. Learn more about the background-check process.

One source is the book *Netspy* (Wolff New Media, 1996). It contains the Internet addresses of many background-check firms and provides an eye-opening look at the amount of online information available to employers and investigators.

Another resource is *Naked in Cyberspace* by Carole Lane (Online, Inc., 1997). It provides a comprehensive guide to the many online services which compile information about individuals.

Employee Monitoring: Is Your Boss Spying on You?

At some point long ago, Cave Man No. 1 must have peered around a corner to see how diligently Cave Man No. 2 was wielding his sharpened rock. And so began employee monitoring.

Workplace surveillance is as old as organized work itself. Few would question a boss's right to prevent crimes or check how his employees are performing. But computers, video cameras, tape recorders, and a raft of Tom Clancy-like devices have added new tension to this age-old impulse.

Now, every act and every conversation can be tracked almost every minute of the workday. If they choose, employers can explore your computer screen and memory, get a count of how many keystrokes you make per hour, read your e-mail and voice-mail, keep track of your phone calls, and even chronicle how much time you spend away from your computer. Some employees may soon wear electronic badges signaling their whereabouts at all times, and *Business Week* even reported that some bosses are buying special chairs to measure wiggling (with the idea being that wigglers aren't working).

Most workplace monitoring springs from the desire to measure performance, but too often, it's more than the work that ends up being scrutinized. For instance:

- John, a gay man who's worked for a junior college for ten years, was alarmed to learn that messages on the campuswide voice-mail system are backed up and stored. He had thought that by using the "delete" feature, he was truly deleting his messages. One of his colleagues has already hinted that he's aware of some of John's messages, and John fears that old messages referring to his sexual orientation could imperil his chances for promotion.

- Two systems administrators at a Nissan subsidiary in California were fired in a dispute involving their use of e-mail to criticize their supervisor. The supervisor, referred to in a derogatory manner in the e-mail exchanges, intercepted the messages. A judge held that the company had the right to read the e-mail because it owned and operated the equipment.

- Charlene, an airline reservations clerk, complained that her telephone headset records the amount of time she takes with each call, what she says to customers—and to coworkers between calls—and how long she takes for bathroom and lunch breaks.

- Charles was stunned to accidentally discover that his company car was outfitted with a location detector. He understood that his firm might have reason to know his whereabouts when he was supposed to be making sales calls. But what about over the weekend when he kept the car? Was the firm logging where he met friends, how many trips he made to the liquor store, or whether the car remained overnight at his girlfriend's house?

Of course, there are lots of good reasons for keeping a close eye on workers. Court rulings have held firms liable for a worker's crimes or negligence. With sexual harassment such a volatile issue, there's a need to ensure proper decorum. And to remain competitive, employers must provide quality control and customer satisfaction.

But workplace monitoring is essentially unregulated, and workers' dignity can be a casualty. A Maryland hospital, for example, suspecting narcotics theft, secretly planted a camera in the nurses' locker room. The nurses were outraged when they discovered that the camera was connected to a closed-circuit TV monitored by a male security chief, who could watch them undress.

Sometimes it's not just privacy but job security that gets steamrollered. A telephone company representative in the Midwest phoned the state wage-and-hour board to ask how to file a complaint against her employer for commission money she believed was owed her. Two hours later, her supervisor grilled her about the call, playing a tape of the conversation.

Or take Evelyn, who worked for the customer-services department of a utility for 27 years. Her employer tapes some incoming calls to check quality of service. Evelyn was fired after being told that her tapes showed poor performance. But she claims a number of older employees, nearing retirement age, are being let go for the same stated reason. When she asked to listen to some of the tapes, company officials told her they'd been destroyed.

IS MONITORING EMPLOYEES LEGAL?

Neither Congress nor the state legislatures have effectively spelled out the respective rights of employers and employees in this area. But the bottom line is this: By and large, when you walk into the workplace, you check your privacy at the door.

That is not new. As mentioned, jobsite monitoring has been going on as long as there have been bosses and workers. In the early decades of the twentieth century, Henry Ford supposedly had 100 investigators who would visit the homes of his workers unannounced to see if they were living a proper, family-oriented lifestyle.

The main difference today is that technology allows employers to monitor you without your knowledge. Surveillance equipment is now cheap enough and small enough—some cameras and audio monitors are the size of thimbles—that almost any company can, if it chooses, observe what you do, say, and write—without being detected.

Macworld, a respected computer magazine, surveyed executives at more than 300 large, medium, and small businesses in a wide range of industries to find out how much they peek at employees' work on their computers. The results:

- 22% admitted having searched employees' computer files, voice mail, e-mail, or other such networking communications.

- 66% said they didn't warn employees of any searches.

- Only 18% of the companies had a written policy regarding electronic privacy for employees.

The larger the firm, the more likely the snooping, *Macworld* discovered. Extrapolating to the workplace at large, the magazine estimated that as many as 20 million Americans may be subject to electronic monitoring through their computers (not including telephones) while on the job. Another study predicted 30 million American workers will be monitored continuously by the year 2000.

Various studies have found links between employee monitoring and stress, both physical and psychological.

Among the other issues:

- Is monitoring used manipulatively to punish union activists, dissenters or whistle blowers?

- Are monitoring records used to discipline employees without proper due process?

- Is monitoring done in such a way as to rob employees of their basic dignity?

- Is monitoring discriminatory because it usually takes place at the lower end of the pay scale—such as clerks and factory workers—whose ranks are often disproportionately comprised of women and minorities?

Privacy advocates and labor unions have been pushing for fair monitoring laws since the mid-1980s. Bills introduced in Congress over the last several sessions have asserted the right of employees and customers to know if they're being monitored, perhaps by means of a signal light or a beep tone.

These bills also generally would require employers to tell all employees and new hires that they may be monitored via phone, computer, or e-mail and to explain how collected data will be used. Monitoring, according to these bills, should be part of a systematic program to collect information about people's work—not a license to snoop indiscriminately. A telephone company, for instance, may need to listen to directory assistance operators to ensure they're giving out accurate information in a courteous manner. But managers shouldn't be allowed to randomly go on electronic fishing expeditions.

So far such bills have died amid legislative gridlock, and there's little indication they will be passed anytime soon. Meanwhile, existing federal and state laws are less exacting. Generally, federal law prohibits employers from listening in on employees' personal phone calls but acknowledges that supervisors probably won't know if the calls are personal until they do listen.

Make no mistake: The legal deck is stacked in the boss' favor. But if any of those issues strike a chord with you, if you feel your boss may be crossing the line between checking on your work and intruding on your personal space, there are some steps you can take and organizations you can contact. We'll list those later in this chapter.

E-MAIL AND OTHER MESSAGES

E-mail has become the gossip medium of choice. Conversations once whispered around the watercooler now are sent from computer to computer—often with a wholly unrealistic sense of privacy. A number of workers have paid a heavy price for such naïveté when they sent careless, inappropriate, or even defamatory or offensive missives that they wouldn't want their bosses to read. For example:

• When a married McDonald's manager carried on a love affair with a coworker in New York, his amorous voice-mail messages were retrieved by a fellow manager, who played them for the manager's supervisor and for the manager's wife. The manager was fired.

• A Pillsbury manager logged onto his home computer, and in the course of exchanging messages with colleagues, said he'd like to ''kill the bastards'' in the sales department. He also referred irreverently to the company's upcoming Christmas party. Several months later, he was fired for making tasteless, unbusinesslike remarks.

Ninety percent of all firms with more than 1,000 workers use e-mail. Altogether, some 40 million workers send more than 60 billion messages annually. Unlike telephone conversations which go out over public wires, e-mail is usually sent over the employer's equipment. Thus, courts have ruled the employer owns the system and with it the right to monitor, save, and review such messages. Even after a message is deleted, it continues to reside in the computer's hard disk drive and in many cases is routinely backed up and saved by the company.

The courts have ruled that employers can't listen in on office phone calls unless they have a business reason. So bosses are supposed to stop when they realize a conversation is personal rather than work related. No such restriction exists for e-mail or voice-mail.

For the sake of both employers and employees, it's recommended that firms and organizations spell out privacy policies in general and e-mail policies in particular—and they should announce such rules frequently. For one thing, that's the fair and above-board way. For another, it's becoming a practical necessity to prevent costly litigation.

E-mail records now are routinely requested in lawsuits involving discrimination, harassment, and other workplace issues. E-mail archives often can provide the smoking gun. (Chevron paid $2.2 million in a sexual-harassment case in which an employee sent around on e-mail a list of "25 reasons beer is better than women.")

It's not just the "little" guy who can get hurt. The indiscretion of one corporate executive, who reportedly sent the message "I don't care what it takes. Fire the bitch!" contributed greatly to a reported $250,000 settlement for the discharged employee.

INTERNET ISSUES

As more and more employees are granted access to the Internet, that's another worry. Some workers may visit sexually explicit Web sites, gambling sites, or sites that transmit hate mail, leaving companies open to harassment charges from other workers who may not appreciate what appears on a colleague's screen.

Such fears have led to counter measures. New software programs, such as Net Nanny and WebSense, allow companies to monitor and regulate their employees' Internet activities. With them, the bosses can read e-mail and selectively block certain Internet sites, though the proliferation of new sites threatens to outstrip that capability. Further, such programs can generate reports that detail everything a worker has done on the Net.

So, wherever you work, the lesson is clear: You shouldn't have any expectation of privacy when you use the office computer. A dramatic case in point was Jean Lewis, a witness in the federal investigation of President Clinton and the Whitewater land deal. She was visibly shaken when Senate investigators produced an incriminating letter she had written on her computer, then deleted. A technician, hired by the congressional probers, had been able to reconstruct the contents of a subpoenaed disk.

THE FUTURE OF MONITORING

With terrorism now a part of the American landscape, there's an increased demand from employers for sophisticated employee identification, and technology is rushing to fill that need. Already, some firms use a hypersensitive bar code scanner that reads a strip of numerical information on the badge of every employee. Soon, such machines could track workers throughout the day.

Similarly, fingerprint-identification and voice-recognition software may help maintain security—but also could be used to make sure workers are busy every minute of the day. In monitoring and security, as we've seen in other areas of privacy, we are on the cusp of technological breakthroughs. Whether they'll be used to enhance privacy, or abuse it, is still unclear.

◉Commonly Asked Questions About Workplace Privacy◉

There are other workplace privacy issues, such as psychological testing, drug testing, polygraph or lie-detector testing and off-the-job surveillance of employees. But let's address the most commonly-asked questions in the three main areas of electronic monitoring: telephone, computer, and voice-mail/e-mail. Then, *Privacy Pointers* will outline avenues for self-help and outside assistance.

TELEPHONE MONITORING

Q: Can my employer legally listen to my phone calls at work?
A: In most instances, yes.

For example, employers may monitor calls with clients or customers for reasons of quality control. However, in some states (such as California, Pennsylvania, and Florida), the law requires that workers be informed that the conversation is being recorded or monitored by either putting a beep tone on the line or playing a recorded message.

However, not every business is aware of this requirement. So your calls might still be monitored without a warning even if state laws require it. Federal law, which regulates phone calls with persons outside the state, does allow unannounced monitoring for business-related calls.

Personal calls are treated differently, though. Under federal law, when an employer realizes the call is personal, he or she must immediately stop monitoring the call. However, when employees are told not to make personal calls from specified business phones, the employee assumes the risk that calls on those phones may be monitored.

It used to be that only large corporations could afford to monitor employees' phone calls. But now that monitoring systems have become a lot cheaper, even smaller companies are getting into the act.

Q: Are my phone conversations with coworkers subject to monitoring the same as conversations with customers?
A: Yes.

Your chats with coworkers are subject to monitoring by your employer in the same way that your business calls are. You should use the same care you would if you were talking to a customer or client on the phone.

Q: Can my employer obtain a record of my phone calls?
A: Yes.

Telephone numbers dialed from phone extensions can be recorded by a device called a pen register. It allows the employer to see a list of phone numbers dialed from your extension and the length of each call. This information may be used to evaluate the amount of time spent by employees with clients.

Employers often use pen registers to monitor employees with jobs in which telephones are used extensively. Frequently, employees are concerned that the information gathered from the pen register is unfairly used to evaluate their efficiency with clients without consideration of the *quality* of service.

COMPUTER MONITORING

Your computer terminal may be your employer's window into your workspace. Every time you sign onto your computer, you're creating a permanent record.

There are several types of computer monitoring:

- Employers can use computer software that enables them to see what is on the screen or stored in the employees' hard disks.

- People involved in intensive word processing and data-entry jobs may be subject to keystroke monitoring. This tells the manager how many keystrokes per hour each employee is performing. It also may inform employees if they are above or below the standard number of keystrokes expected.

• Another computer monitoring technique allows employers to keep track of the amount of time an employee spends away from the computer or idle time at the terminal.

• Some employers may use programs—such as SurfWatch, Net Nanny, WebSense, or Cybersitter—to block out pornography and news groups.

Q: Is my employer allowed to see what is on my terminal while I am working?
A: Generally, yes.

Because employers own the computer network and the terminals, they're free to use them to monitor employees. Employees are given some protection from computer and other forms of electronic monitoring under certain circumstances.

Union contracts, for example, may limit the employer's right to monitor. Also, public-sector employees may have some minimal rights under the U.S. Constitution, in particular the Fourth Amendment, which safeguards against unreasonable search and seizure.

Q: How can I tell if I am being monitored at my terminal?
A: Usually, you can't.

Most computer monitoring equipment allows employers to monitor without the employees' knowledge. Ideally, employers should notify employees that monitoring takes place. This policy could be communicated in memos, employee handbooks, union contracts, at meetings, or on a sticker attached to the computer.

In reality, employees often find out about computer monitoring during a performance review when the information collected is used to evaluate the employee's work.

ELECTRONIC MAIL AND VOICE MAIL

Q: Isn't electronic mail private?
A: In most cases, no.

Electronic mail (e-mail) systems are a convenient and wonderful tool, and it *seems* so private when you're sitting at your screen typing a note to someone else. In truth, your message is neither private nor impermanent.

Legally, the employer owns the e-mail system and is allowed to review its contents. Messages sent within the company as well as those that are sent from your terminal to another company or from another company to you may be monitored by your employer.

Lawsuits have been filed dealing with work-related e-mail messages transmitted over public networks, but so far the results have been inconclusive.

Q: What about voice-mail?
A: Ditto.

Voice-mail systems are also generally seen as the property of the employer. Voice-mail messages do not necessarily vanish when deleted; the system may store them, much as with e-mail. Although it appears they are erased, they are often permanently "backed up" on magnetic tape, along with other important data from the computer system.

Q: My office's e-mail system has an option for marking messages as "private." Are those messages protected?
A: In most cases, no.

Many electronic mail systems have this option, but it does not guarantee your messages are kept confidential. An exception is when an employer's electronic mail policy states that messages marked "private" are kept confidential.

Q: Is there any circumstance in which my messages are private?
A: Some employers have begun to use encryption to protect the privacy of their employees' electronic mail.

Encryption involves scrambling the message at the sender's terminal, then unscrambling the message at the terminal of the receiver. This ensures the message is read only by the sender and his or her intended recipient. While this system prevents industrial "spies" or third-party coworkers from reading your electronic mail, your employer still may have access to the unscrambled messages by holding the key to unlock the code.

●Privacy Pointers: What You Can Do Now●

1. Always ask yourself: Would I want my boss—or, say, a jury—to read this e-mail message?
You should get out of the habit of sending gossip or frivolous or malicious messages via computer. Try to keep your chatter professional and, for best results, limit personal messages altogether. (One study found that more than 40% of e-mail was extracurricular to the job at hand.) Steer away from anything that could be construed as derogatory or an offensive joke.

Remember, not only can e-mail be retained, it can be easily forwarded to hundreds of people, in and out of the company. Think of your e-mail as the electronic equivalent of a postcard—sent to one person but potentially read by many.

2. Protect your password.
Always log off when not using the system, or use a password-protected screen saver. Otherwise, someone can—playfully or otherwise—use your keyboard while you're gone and send out messages in your name, or snoop in your files.

Guard against giving your password to anyone, including

e-mail and systems administrators, and report any effort to obtain your password.

3. Work out problems face-to-face, not on e-mail.

E-mail, as mentioned, is a marvelous tool for certain tasks, but dispute resolution is not one of them. If you're having a problem with someone, emotions are clearly involved. Feelings—especially where one's work is concerned—are best handled in person. In fact, the CEO of a New York software firm gave up his personal e-mail account and ordered the entire e-mail system shut down for four hours each day to encourage workers to interact face-to-face.

Whether you're the superior or the subordinate, you'll be better off using the phone or, even better, talking over the dispute in person. Humor and sarcasm, for example, just don't translate well on the computer screen. Even a brief, polite message can be misconstrued as brusque if feelings are already running high.

4. Urge your company to create an official privacy policy.

When an employer issues a policy about any issue in the workplace, including privacy, that policy is legally binding. For example, if an employer explicitly states that employees will be notified when telephone monitoring takes place, the employer must honor that policy.

Policies can be communicated in various ways: through employee handbooks, via memos, or in union contracts. If you are not already aware of your employer's workplace privacy policies, it's a good idea to become informed. Information about what should be included in such a policy can be obtained from the ACLU, the Electronic Messaging Association, and some of the other groups listed at the end of this chapter.

Keep in mind, however, that even if a company promises you e-mail privacy, there's no guarantee that your e-mail won't be subpoenaed in a lawsuit.

5. Don't store anything in your computer you wouldn't want management to see.

Despite the fact that you have a personal password, the law recognizes the computer and its contents as belonging to the boss. So it's not the place to store the x-rated novel you're writing, notes from your union meeting, letters to prospective employers, or anything else you wouldn't want your supervisors to see.

6. Try to avoid using your desk phone for personal matters.

Remember, you may be monitored on the phone or at the computer, so be careful what you say in your e-mail or voice mail as well as on the telephone.

Find out if personal calls are permitted on company phones.

If they're not, don't use them for that purpose. Even if occasional personal calls are okay, you'd be better off making confidential calls on highly sensitive matters from a public pay phone. The best way to ensure privacy for your personal communication—whether by phone or computer—is not to use office equipment.

7. Read carefully any privacy waiver, a document some employers require as a condition of employment.

These waivers may give management the option to conduct surreptitious monitoring and random searches as well as to eavesdrop using electronic devices. You may not be able to avoid signing it, but you should be alert to what it entails.

8. If you are concerned about this issue, contact your federal legislators, especially the members of these House and Senate committees.

• **U.S. Senate**
  Committee on Labor and Human Resources
  Washington, D.C. 20510

- **U.S. House of Representatives**
  Committee on Economic and Education Opportunities
  Washington, D.C. 20515

9. Call or write for more information.
The following groups and publications are actively involved in workplace-monitoring issues.

GENERAL GROUPS

- **American Civil Liberties Union National Task Force on Civil Liberties in the Workplace**
  166 Wall St.
  Princeton, NJ 08540
  (609) 683-0313
  http://www.aclu.org

- **Electronic Messaging Association**
  1655 N. Ft. Myer Dr., No. 500
  Arlington, VA 22209
  (703) 524-5550
  http://www.ema.org
  EMA sells an e-mail "privacy toolkit" for developing company policy.

- **9 to 5, the National Association of Working Women**
  231 W. Wisconsin Ave., No. 900
  Milwaukee, WI 53203
  (414) 274-0925
  hotline: (800) 522-0925

- **National Employee Rights Institute**
  414 Walnut St., No. 911
  Cincinnati, OH 45202
  (800) 469-6374
  NERI provides information about workplace rights and makes referrals to attorneys.

LABOR GROUPS

Labor unions are beginning to take a stronger interest in workplace monitoring. One that is particularly active is:

Communications Workers of America
501 Third St., NW
Washington, D.C. 20001
(202) 434-1100
http://www.cwa-union.org

For further information on labor groups involved in workplace-monitoring issues, contact:

Coalition on New Office Technology
Office Technology Education Project
650 Beacon St., 5th Floor
Boston, MA 02215
(617) 247-6827
This is a state-based group that organizes office workers and advocates for legislation around issues of workplace rights, privacy, and health and safety.

PART V

●

GUARDING YOUR PERSONAL SAFETY

Coping with "Identity Theft": What to Do if an Imposter Strikes

It began routinely. John applied for an auto loan and dutifully filled out the paperwork. His credit was good, he got the car, and he drove away, thinking he'd have nothing more serious than the payments to worry about. *Wrong!*

Someone—apparently an employee of the dealership—filched John's information off the loan application, used it to open several accounts in John's name, and began buying things. The imposter even leased an apartment in John's name, forgetting, of course, to pay the rent. The bills began piling up, and John thinks his clone called and listened to his answering-machine tape several times so he could learn to mimic John's speech patterns. Yet John had difficulty getting the police to take an interest in his case.

John had become a victim of identity theft, a form of robbery that nets much more money than the kind with guns. Eventually, he had to hire a private investigator to track down the criminal, and finally, the imposter was arrested. But as John learned after much debt and much hassle, identity theft—the misuse of personal identifying information to commit various types of financial fraud—is a frightening problem. It's also one that's often hard to get anybody—except the victim—to take seriously.

Police may not want to make a report because, they ask, who was the victim: you or your creditors? The department of motor vehicles prefers not to issue new licenses because that, in itself, may be an invitation to fraud. The Social Security Administration doesn't like to give out new numbers because one is supposed to last a lifetime and, again, creating a new SSN can lead to abuse.

Indeed, it's the SSN—the most often used (indeed, vastly *over-used*) recordkeeping number in the United States—that's frequently at the heart of identity theft. While there will always be ways for an imposter to violate your privacy, this chapter will walk you through steps that will ensure you aren't an easy target. You'll learn, for example, when you can legally withhold your SSN. The chapter will prescribe many other ways to protect your vital information as well as outline what actions to take if you are victimized.

HOW THEY DO IT

Stealing wallets used to be the easiest way for a thief to take on your identity. That still happens. Now, however, the same information is often obtained through subtle means as white-collar criminals become much more sophisticated.

Identity theft is a huge problem, with credit card fraud losses alone estimated to be $3 billion a year. Automation and computerization have made life more convenient for us—and more lucrative for the identity thieves. Their approaches include:

- Stealing mail from mailboxes to obtain bank and credit card statements, preapproved credit offers, telephone calling cards, driver's license numbers, or tax information.

- ''Dumpster diving'' in trash bins where unshredded credit card and loan applications may have been tossed.

- Posing as you and reporting an address change, often reporting a "lost" card at the same time and ordering a new one. This is called "account takeover," the fastest-growing type of credit card fraud. This crime often has more of an emotional impact than even the use of stolen or fake cards, because the thieves may go to great lengths to obtain information about the customers they're impersonating. It's also difficult for merchants to detect because the thief has a valid credit card.

- Accessing your credit report fraudulently by, for example, posing as an employer, loan officer, or landlord and ordering a copy. Or they can also illicitly obtain victims' SSN and credit information while actually employed by a company with access to a credit bureau database.

- "Shoulder surfing" at ATM machines and phone booths in hopes of capturing personal identification (PIN) numbers.

Once he's assumed your identity, the crook may lessen chances of detection by spending as much money as he can in as short a time as possible before moving on to someone else's name and account information. By the time you notice the big bills cascading in and can notify authorities, he's long gone.

THE UBIQUITOUS SSN

A major advantage to an identity thief is the pervasiveness of the Social Security number. First issued in 1936, the SSN was supposed to be used just for Social Security programs. Its use has gradually widened, and in 1961 its use got a big boost when the IRS began employing the SSN as taxpayer ID numbers. As a result, SSNs are required on records of any transaction in which the IRS is interested—such as most banking, stock market, property, or other financial dealings, plus employment records.

Because your SSN must be included on all of these sensitive financial documents, it's important to limit *other* uses of the number. However, the trend is to broaden its use, and today, those nine-digit numbers often are used for all manner of other purposes, including employee IDs, medical records, credit reports, various account numbers—and, sometimes, for absolutely no good reason at all, such as registering your child for Little League or signing up for a club or an adult education course.

Without a doubt, the SSN is the key to defrauding someone. Despite that, many abuses of SSN use have been documented, including:

- A large medical facility routinely posts employees' names, job ranks, and SSNs on its office bulletin boards.

- A local soccer league required parents to list their SSN and driver's license number as well as their children's SSN on the league forms. At season's end, the league tossed the forms into a Dumpster without shredding or burning them.

- A widow received a letter from the Social Security Administration with the name and SSN of her deceased husband on the outside of the envelope.

- Several states use the SSN as a driver's license number while others record it on applications and store it in their databases.

- A college professor posted students' SSNs along with their grades. A stalker got Jennifer's SSN and has tracked her for years, finding her wherever and whenever she moves. He doesn't physically threaten her, but just lets her know he knows where she lives.

The SSN has become the most frequently used record-keeping number in the country because accurate retrieval of information works best if each file is assigned a specific, one-of-a-kind number. (In fact, a SSN is now required for dependents over one year of age!)

With the SSN accessible to so many people, it's relatively easy for someone to fraudulently use your SSN to assume your identity and gain access to your bank account, credit services, utility billing information, and other sources of personal information. Your SSN is also frequently used as your identification number in a wide variety of computer databases, giving access to information you may want kept private and allowing an easy way of linking databases.

When a criminal obtains it, the consequences can be devastating. With just your name and SSN, an unscrupulous person can apply for credit with your name and their address, then avoid paying the bills; falsely apply for a welfare check or an income tax refund; get a job under your name, then avoid paying taxes; or create an entire new identity to elude law enforcement or creditors.

A few real-life examples include:

- Peter got the phone call he'd always dreamed of. The state lottery called to say he'd won the big prize. Just give me your SSN and driver's license number, the caller said, and a limousine will be by tomorrow to drop off the $50,000 check and whisk you and your wife away to a life of luxury. Peter complied, but when the limo failed to show, he began to worry. Indeed, it wasn't long before lots of phony credit card charges began flowing in.

- Cheryl and her seven-year-old daughter went to the bank to open an account for the daughter. But the bank told Cheryl her child had a bad credit report. It turned out someone had been using the child's SSN to open credit accounts, then not paying the bills.

- Kathy learned she had a bad credit report when she was

turned down for a loan. She discovered that someone in a distant state had fraudulently used her SSN to obtain credit cards, then failed to pay off the accounts. The unpaid bills, of course, eventually made their way onto Kathy's credit report.

- Gerhard, a physician, doesn't know how they did it, but someone found out his SSN, date of birth, and driver's license number. Thus armed, the imposter was able to access Gerhard's bank account, as well as order a credit card in Gerhard's name. At last count, the amount of the fraud was up to $30,000.

- Mary, also a doctor, didn't know anything was amiss until she realized she wasn't receiving her favorite magazine. By that time, a gang had diverted her correspondence to a New York address, forged her name on documents, raided her bank accounts, and effectively destroyed her credit rating.

As several of these victims learned, most law-enforcement and government agencies are slow to help because, strictly speaking, the one who's been defrauded is not you but your creditor. That's because federal law limits your liability to $50—with few, if any, creditors even demanding that in repayment from victims.

Nonetheless, you're the one who's been put through the emotional wringer, whose credit has been blemished, who may have to spend months or even years trying to untangle the web of deception. Thus, unfortunately, the buck stops with you. *You* have the prime responsibility to protect your personal identification numbers.

PREVENTIVE MEASURES YOU CAN TAKE

There are numerous ways to prevent becoming a victim of an identify thief. Here are a some ideas on ways to protect your credit cards, PIN numbers, and SSN:

Credit Cards

• Reduce the number of credit cards you actively use. Carry only one or two of them in your wallet or purse, and cancel all unused credit card accounts. (Even if you don't use them, those account numbers are recorded in your credit report and, if that report falls into the wrong hands, those numbers could come back to bite you.)

• Make a detailed list of all your credit cards, the account numbers, expiration dates and telephone number of the customer-service departments. Update it as needed and keep it in a secure place so you can quickly contact your creditors if your cards are stolen.

• Never give out your credit card number or other personal information over the phone unless you have a trusted business relationship and *you* have initiated the call.

Passwords and PINs

• When creating passwords and PINs, don't use the last four digits of your SSN or any obvious word or number that can be discovered by thieves.

• Ask your bank to add extra security protection to your transactions. Most will allow you to use an additional code when accessing your account. Don't use your mother's maiden name. Instead, use a nonsense word or series of numbers and letters that won't be obvious to anyone but you.

• Shield your hand when using a bank ATM machine or making long-distance phone calls with your phone card.

Social Security numbers

• Release your SSN only when absolutely necessary. (This will be discussed more a little later.)

• Don't have your SSN printed on your checks, and don't let

merchants handwrite it onto your checks, either. (Explain to them how you could become a fraud victim if someone were to use your SSN and account number to gain access to your bank account.)

• Order your Social Security Earnings and Benefits Statement once a year to check for fraud. You can order the form from the Social Security Administration by calling (800) 772-1213.

WHAT TO DO IF YOU BECOME A VICTIM

What if despite your best efforts, someone does assume your identity? Then what? For starters, it's important to act *immediately* to let authorities know and, thus, limit the damage. Because identity theft comes in all shapes and sizes, you'll need to pick and choose among the other steps those which are relevant to you. (Not all identity theft involves bank accounts, for example, so skip that one if it doesn't pertain to you.)

Here's the master list of sixteen actions to take:

1. Call the fraud units of the three big credit-reporting companies: Experian (formerly TRW), Equifax and Trans Union.

Report the theft of your credit cards and/or numbers. Ask that your accounts be flagged. Also, add a victim's statement to your report ("My ID has been used to apply for credit fraudulently. Contact me at 555-123-4567 to verify all applications.") Be sure to ask for how long the fraud alert will be posted on your account and how you can extend it if necessary.

Ask the credit bureaus for a free copy of your credit report every few months. (As a fraud victim, you are entitled to one free report per year, but you're likely to need more to monitor your file effectively.) Also urge them to send all corrected information to the other major bureaus as well as to any person who has requested your credit report within the past six months, or the last two years if for employment purposes.

2. Immediately cancel all your credit cards.

Get replacement cards with new account numbers. Ask that the old accounts be processed as "account closed at consumer's request." (This is better than the label "card lost or stolen," because when that statement is reported to the credit bureaus, it can be interpreted as blaming you for the loss.)

3. Report the crime to the police at once.

Give them as much documented evidence as possible. In return, get a copy of any police report they generate.

Credit card issuers, your bank, and the insurance company may require you to show that report in order to verify the crime. Some police departments have been known to refuse to write police reports on such crimes, so you may have to be persistent.

4. Notify your bank(s) of the theft.

Cancel your checking and savings accounts and obtain new account numbers. Ask the bank to issue you a secret password that must be used in every transaction. Put stop payments on any outstanding checks that you are unsure of.

To prove your innocence, you may need to fill out fraud affidavits with banks and credit grantors where fraudulent accounts have been established in your name.

In some cases, you might be asked to have affidavits notarized, which can be costly. Attempt to persuade the requestors to waive the notary requirement. They may be willing to accept other forms of proof and save you the expense of notarizing documents.

5. Get a new ATM card, account number, and password.

Don't use your old password. When creating a password, avoid such commonly used numbers as the last four digits of your Social Security number, your birthdate, or consecutive numbers.

6. Make a report if your checks were stolen or bank accounts were set up fraudulently.

Contact TeleCheck, National Processing Co. (NPC), or Equifax Check Services, whose phone numbers are listed under *Privacy Pointers.*

7. Notify the Secret Service.

The Secret Service has jurisdiction over credit card fraud cases. While the Secret Service doesn't usually investigate individual cases—especially those under $10,000 in losses—it may be interested in evidence of crime rings. You might ask someone in the fraud department of your credit card companies and/ or banks to notify the particular Secret Service agent they work with, or call the local Secret Service office listed in the government pages of your phone book.

8. Consider changing your SSN.

If your number has become associated with bad checks and credit, this may be a good idea. However, this step should be reserved for only the most extreme situations—in particular, if the imposter uses your SSN for employment.

You will need to notify *all* credit grantors and credit reporting bureaus of your new SSN. Otherwise, your financial affairs could really get tangled. If you decide to go this route, contact the Office of the Inspector General of the Social Security Administration.

9. Contact the postal inspector if you suspect mail theft.

Theft of mail is a felony. Also, notify this office if you suspect an identity thief has filed a change of address with the post office or has used the mail to commit credit or bank fraud.

10. Notify your nearest passport office.

If you have a passport, even if it wasn't stolen, alert authorities there that someone might be fraudulently ordering a new passport in your name. Ask them to check photographs carefully.

11. Alert your public utilities.

Call your telephone, electrical, gas, and water utilities. Warn them of the possibility that someone may attempt to open new service using your identification. Give them a password that will be required when any account changes will be made.

Also contact your long-distance telephone company. You also may need to cancel your long-distance calling card if it has been stolen or if the account number has been accessed by "shoulder surfers."

12. Consider changing your driver's license number.

You may want to change your driver's license number if someone has been using yours as identification on bad checks. Be prepared to prove to the department of motor vehicles that you have been damaged by the theft of your driver's license. You may need to be persistent.

13. Seek to clear up any incorrect legal information.

If your credit report reflects a legal judgment against someone who used your name, contact the court where the judgment was entered. Document for the court that you were an identity theft victim and seek to have that judgment deleted. This may prove difficult, so be prepared to be persistent.

Similarly, if someone using your identity was prosecuted for a crime, be aware you may be listed as a criminal in a state or federal database. Call your state's department of justice as well as the FBI to find out if charges were brought against someone using your name and how to remove such a stigma.

14. Keep a detailed log of your efforts.

In dealing with the authorities and financial institutions, keep a log of all conversations in this matter, including dates and names, so you can effectively follow up. Send correspondence by certified mail. Keep copies of all letters and documents. Provide your police report number to expedite reporting the crime.

15. Consider seeking legal counsel.

Especially if you have difficulty clearing up your credit history, or if your case is complex and involves a lot of money, an attorney can help you recover from the fraud and determine whether your rights under various credit, banking, social security, and other laws have been violated.

16. Pay attention to your own mental health.

Victims of identity theft report that they are often made to feel as if they are somehow to blame. They can also feel violated, even powerless.

For example, someone has been impersonating Jessica for more than a year: renting apartments in her name, then moving out without paying the rent, as well as opening telephone accounts and running up other bills. Collection agencies have come after Jessica, and an unlawful-detainer judgment has been put in her credit report. For Jessica, the stigma has been "almost like a rape case," with people treating her as if she's the crook.

Few, if any, of the authorities have the time or inclination to step forward to help such a victim. So, discuss your situation with a trusted friend or counselor.

17. Enlist the help of your elected representatives.

Write to your state and federal legislators. Ask them to support stronger privacy protections, especially assistance for consumers victimized by fraud.

●Commonly Asked Questions About Identity Theft●

Q: **Am I financially responsible for debts run up by crooks who use my name?**
A: **Usually not. But you're probably in for plenty for other kinds of problems.**

Under federal law, credit-fraud victims are only liable for the first $50 of their losses if they notify financial institutions within two days of learning of the loss. Most financial institutions will waive even that amount. But while you may not be saddled with paying an imposter's bills, you will likely be left with a bad credit report and perhaps months or years of trying to regain your financial health.

A word of caution. Debit and ATM cards don't give you the same protection against fraud as credit cards. You must notify the bank within two business days if your card is lost or stolen, or risk being liable for up to $500 if the bank can prove you were negligent in reporting to them. If you are not aware that your card has been lost or stolen, or if the imposter is using your account *numbers* to make fraudulent purchases, you have 60 days from the date the account statement has been mailed to you to report to the bank. If you do not notify the bank, you could find your entire account wiped out with no ability to recover those funds.

Q: Am I required to give my SSN to government agencies?
A: It depends on the agency.

Some government agencies, including the IRS, welfare agencies, and the DMV, can require your SSN. Others may request the SSN in such a manner that you're led to believe you must provide it.

The Privacy Act of 1974 requires all government agencies—federal, state, and local—that use your SSN to provide a "disclosure" statement. This statement tells whether you're required to provide your SSN or if it's optional, how the SSN will be used, and what will happen if you refuse to provide it. If you're asked to give your SSN to a government agency and no disclosure statement is included on the form, complain and cite the Privacy Act.

Q: Must I provide my SSN to private businesses?
A: Most of the time, no. But they can refuse you service if you don't.

You're not legally compelled to provide your SSN to a business—including private healthcare providers and insurers—unless you're involved in a transaction in which the IRS requires notification. (Medicare and parallel state health plans are part of government and, thus, can require a SSN.)

There is no law, however, which prevents businesses from *asking* for your SSN, and there are few restrictions on what businesses can do with it once they've got it. Also, even though you are not required to disclose your SSN, the business may refuse you its goods or services if you don't furnish your number.

Credit card applications usually request Social Security numbers. Your number is used primarily to verify your identity in situations where you have the same or a similar name to others. Although credit grantors will insist on having your SSN, you may be able to find one which will give you credit without knowing your SSN, especially if you are persistent. That's very rare, though.

If a business insists on knowing your Social Security number when you cannot see a reason for it, speak to a supervisor who may be authorized to make an exception, or who may know that company policy doesn't strictly require it. If the company won't allow you to use an alternate number, you may want to take your business elsewhere.

Q: Can my employer use my SSN as an employee-ID number?
A: Yes, but it's not a good idea.

While an employer may use your SSN for identification purposes, the Social Security Administration discourages employers from displaying SSNs on documents that are viewed by other people, such as badges, parking permits, or lists distributed to employees. Employers do, however, need each employee's SSN to report earnings and payroll taxes.

Q. Should a school be using my Social Security number?
A: No, though many do.

Schools that receive federal funding must comply with a federal law requiring written consent for the release of educational records or personally identifiable information, with some exceptions. The courts have stated that SSNs fall within this provision.

Thus, an argument can be made that if such a school displays students' SSNs on identification cards or distributes class rosters or grade lists containing SSNs, it's illegally releasing personally identifiable information. However, many schools and universities have not interpreted the law this way and continue to use SSNs as student identifiers. To succeed in obtaining an alternate number to the SSN, you will probably need to be persistent and cite the law.

If the school is private and receives no federal funding, your only recourse is to work with the administration to change the policy or at least let you use an alternate identification number as your student ID.

Two other important points on this issue:

- SSNs may be legally obtained by colleges and universities for students who have university jobs and/or receive federal financial aid.

- Public schools, colleges, and universities that ask for your SSN must adhere to the Privacy Act of 1974, requiring they provide a disclosure statement telling students how the SSN is used. If you're required to provide your SSN, be sure to look for the school's disclosure statement. If one isn't offered, you may want to file a complaint with the school, citing the Privacy Act.

Q: How can I reduce the likelihood of my wallet or purse being stolen or lessen the repercussions if it is?

A: By taking some or all of these steps:

- Know exactly what's in it. Some experts recommend getting into the habit of inventorying your wallet or purse on a daily basis.

- In crowds, keep your wallet in a front pocket or keep your purse in front of you. Other options: keep your wallet in a pocket with a Velcro enclosure, or put rubber bands around it so it won't slip out your pocket so easily. Or, wear a "fanny pack" in front of you.

- Consider subscribing to a credit-security service that registers all your credit cards and important documents.

●Privacy Pointers: What You Can Do Now●

1. Minimize the amount of data a thief can steal.

Carry as little as possible. Don't bring along anything you don't use frequently or that can't be replaced. For example, don't carry your SSN, birth certificate, or passport in your wallet or purse, except when you will be using them that day. Memorize all your passwords and don't record them on anything obvious, such as a card carried in your wallet or purse.

2. Reduce the amount of available information about you.

To do so, consider removing your name from the marketing lists of the three large credit-reporting bureaus. The flyers and promotions you receive, when tossed into the garbage, are a potential target of identity thieves who use them to order credit cards in your name.

Also, sign up for the Direct Marketing Association's Mail Preference Service and its Telephone Preference Service. These will delete your name from lists used by nationwide marketers.

3. Reduce your credit card exposure.

Carry no more than one or two in your wallet or purse. Cancel all unused credit cards. Even though you may not use them, someone who steals your wallet or gets a copy of your credit report could.

4. Don't give out credit card data over the phone.

Never give out your credit card number or other personal information over the telephone unless you have a well-established business relationship and you have initiated the call.

Identity thieves have been known to call victims with a fake story that goes something like this: "Today is your lucky day! You've been chosen by the Publishers Consolidated Sweepstakes to receive a free trip to the Bahamas. All we need is your credit card number and its expiration date in order to verify you as the lucky winner." Or, "Hello, I'm Tim Jones, the security officer, calling from the bank to verify your account number and PIN."

5. Order a copy of your credit report once a year.

Get it from each of the three large credit bureaus and check for inaccuracies and fraudulent uses of your accounts.

6. Don't give out your SSN unless it's vital.

Adopt a policy of not giving out your SSN unless you are convinced it's required (tax forms, employment records, and most banking, stock and property transactions), or if it is to your benefit. Make people show you why it's needed. If a business insists, ask if there's an alternative number that can instead be used. Demand to speak to a manager, if need be.

If a form asks for your SSN, leave the space blank or write "refused" in that space. Speak to someone in authority and explain why you don't want your SSN used to identify you. If all else fails, take your business elsewhere.

Being so assertive may make you uncomfortable or unpopular with sales clerks and others, but it's important. Remember, the SSN is the key to your credit and banking accounts and is thus a prime target of criminals.

A cautionary note: While it's good to be assertive, it's not so great to be obnoxious. In some cases, consumers have been so demanding that their SSN not be used, the police have been called in, to the detriment of both the customer and probably the issue of privacy in general. So be dogged, but not rude. And if you get nowhere, consider writing a letter to a higher-up and, as mentioned, finally taking your business elsewhere.

7. Don't display your SSN in obvious places.

Never print your SSN on your checks, business cards, address labels, or other identifying information. Try to convince your employer to do the same. Do not carry your SSN card in your wallet, and don't allow merchants to write your SSN on your checks.

8. If your employer uses your SSN as an identification number, talk to him or her and try to change the policy.

Many employers fail to treat SSNs as confidential information. They may be willing to change their policy when they understand the twin dangers of invasion of privacy and fraud.

9. Demand that financial institutions safeguard your data.

Discourage your bank, credit union, or savings and loan from using the last four digits of the SSN as your PIN number, or as the identifier for banking by phone. Tell them this constitutes irresponsible information-handling and makes their customers vulnerable to fraud.

If need be, write a letter of complaint. Demand to have a different PIN and/or identification number assigned. Explain why the SSN is an extremely poor choice for a banking security or identification code.

Ask if your financial institution has a policy of shredding *all* paper before disposing of it, or if it uses locked recycling bins. Take your business elsewhere if it seems sloppy disposal methods are used. (See also Chapter 15, "Respecting Others' Privacy: How to Handle Information Responsibly.")

10. When you fill out loan or credit applications, find out how the firm disposes of them.

If you aren't convinced that it stores them in locked files or shreds them, take your business elsewhere. Similarly, when you pay by credit card, ask the company how it stores or disposes of the transaction slip. Avoid paying by credit card if you're uncertain if the business safeguards such data.

11. Buy a paper shredder for your home.

Many office-supply stores sell inexpensive models. Make it a habit to shred pre-approved credit offers and other sensitive information, such as credit-card receipts and phone bills.

12. Don't put your address or license-plate number on your key ring.

That will merely point the thief to your home and car. If your keys have been stolen or lost and there is a way for a thief to find you, remember to change the locks on your house and automobile.

13. Take precautions with your mail.

• Install a secure, locked mailbox at your home, or use a post office box to reduce mail theft.

• When you order new checks, don't have them sent to your home. Pick them up at the bank instead.

• When you pay bills, don't leave the envelopes containing your checks at your mailbox for the postal carrier to pick up. If stolen, your checks could be altered and then cashed by the imposter, or the account numbers could be copied and used.

• Also, because of the rise in mail theft, it's best to mail bills and other sensitive items at the post office rather than using neighborhood drop boxes.

14. Store your canceled checks in a safe place.

In the wrong hands, they could reveal a lot of information about you, including the account number, your phone number, and driver's license number.

15. Contact the following groups for more information:

CREDIT REPORTING BUREAUS

- **Equifax**
  To report fraud: (800) 525-6285 or (800) 685-1111
  To order copy of report ($8 in most states):
  P.O. Box 740241
  Atlanta, GA 30374
  (800) 685-1111
  To opt out of preapproved offers of credit:
  (800) 556-4711

- **Experian (formerly TRW)**
  To report fraud: (800) 301-7195 or by fax
  (800) 301-7196
  To order copy of report: ($8 in most states)
  P.O. Box 2104
  Allen, TX 75013
  (800) 682-7654
  To opt out of preapproved offers of credit:
  (800) 353-0809

- **Trans Union**
  To report fraud: (800) 680-7289
  To order copy of report ($8 in most states):
  P.O. Box 390
  Springfield, PA 19064
  (800) 888-4213
  To opt out of preapproved offers of credit:
  (800) 680-7293

To Report Fraudulent Use of Checks

- **CheckRite**: (800) 766-2748

- **ChexSystems**: (800) 428-9623 (regarding closed bank accounts only)

- **Equifax Check Services**: (800) 437-5120

- **National Processing Co.**: (800) 526-5380

- **TeleCheck**: (800) 710-9898

Other Groups and Agencies

- **Social Security Administration**
  To order Earnings and Benefits Statement:
  (800) 772-1213

  To report fraudulent use of your SSN or impropriety by Social Security Administration officials, call the Office of the Inspector General of the SSA: (800) 269-0271

  The Social Security Administration's web site is http://www.ssa.gov.

- **Computer Professionals for Social Responsibility** is a nonprofit organization that is actively involved in efforts to control the misuse of Social Security numbers. For more information, write:
  CPSR
  Box 717
  Palo Alto, CA 94302
  (415) 322-3778
  For a useful FAQ (Frequently Asked Questions) about SSNs, visit the CPSR's Web site: http://www.cpsr. org/cpsr/privacy/ssn/ssn.faq.html.

- **Public Interest Research Groups**
  U.S. PIRG
  218 D St., S.E.
  Washington, D.C. 20003
  (202) 546-9707
  http://www.pirg.org

  CalPIRG
  11965 Venice Blvd., No. 408
  Los Angeles, CA 90066
  (310) 397-3404
  From either group, you can order its 1996 report,
  Theft of Identity: The Consumer X-Files *($20).*

- **For Victims of Identity Theft**

  If you are a victim of identity fraud, you can benefit
  from the experiences of other victims. The "Identity
  Theft Survival Kit" (1997) includes a booklet with
  tear-out letters addressed to government agencies,
  credit grantors, credit reporting agencies and law enforcement, plus a computer disk containing the letters,
  and an audio tape with interviews of victims and identity theft experts. For order information, contact:

  Identity Theft Kit
  28202 Cabot Rd., No. 215
  Laguna Niguel, CA 92677
  (714) 364-1511

  Contact a support group for victims:

  Victims of Identity Theft
  c/o CALPIRG
  (See address above.)

14

Are You Being Stalked?
Tips on Protecting Yourself

Being harassed, stalked, and perhaps killed or injured by a cunning, relentless pursuer is perhaps everyone's worst nightmare. Emerging technology makes the ease of such predatory acts all the more disturbing.

Such personal fixations have cropped up in movies (such as *Fatal Attraction*) and, much more troubling, in real life, where the easy availability of personal information has fostered high-tech stalking. A recent high-profile victim was Rebecca Schaeffer, costar of a popular television program, who answered her doorbell in West Hollywood one summer day in 1989 and was shot to death by an obsessed fan. He had hired someone to track her down via computer.

Similarly, comedian David Letterman has been harassed for nearly 10 years by a woman who's been found wandering in his Connecticut home, driving his Porsche, camping out on his tennis courts, and even washing her clothes in his swimming pool. Madonna, Theresa Saldana, Sharon Gless, Kathie Lee Gifford, Princess Anne, Jodie Foster, Whitney Houston, and other celebrities have also been pursued.

News of famous people being stalked has raised public awareness of this crime. However, the majority of stalking vic-

249

tims are ordinary people, mostly women, who are followed and threatened by someone with whom they have had a prior relationship.

The disturbing truth is that a stalker doesn't even need high-tech equipment. Public records available at courthouses or departments of motor vehicles frequently allow anyone with a little bit of information to access your records. In fact, about a million people a year in the United States are said to be stalked, 80% of them women hounded by ex-boyfriends and former husbands. Other cases often involve ex-employees obsessed with having lost a job or a promotion.

Either type of stalking case can, and too often does, end violently. Knowing where the dangers lie and lowering your profile can lessen your chances of being a victim. This chapter will try to help you reduce the likelihood that your personal information will get into the hands of a stalker or a harasser. If those preventive measures fail and you are actually stalked, this chapter also will detail more extreme responses.

However, it's important to remember that this is a problem you probably can't solve by yourself. You must involve the authorities: police, telephone company, postal investigators, and prosecutors. The process of bringing a stalker to justice is often long and cumbersome. You'll need to be patient and to persist at a time when you're under great emotional stress. It's a high-risk situation that requires you to be careful, thorough, and mentally strong.

DEALING WITH A HARASSER

When a coworker, classmate, acquaintance, former spouse, or ex-lover seems obsessed with you—whether fondly or angrily so—that can be annoying. We'll call that kind of attention "harassment." Unwanted phone calls and letters, repetitive e-mail, propositions, and undesired gifts pose problems for thousands of people in such situations. More important, this harass-ment can evolve into "stalking." That's when you feel in danger or have been physically threatened.

Although you probably won't get much help from law-enforcement authorities in the harassment stage, you needn't wait for actual stalking to occur before taking action. You can send signals to the obsessed person that you have not the slight-est interest in responding to any kind of overture from him or her.

For example, you can:

1. Say "no" clearly and firmly.

Well-meaning people often make excuses or delay the ulti-mate showdown out of respect for the other person's feelings. But such mixed messages may further tantalize the obsessive person.

It's potentially too dangerous a situation to beat around the bush. Forget about *their* feelings, focus on your own. Say some-thing like, "No, I don't really want to see you. I don't even want to think about you, and I don't want you to think about me. Do not talk to me, do not call me, do not write to me, do not contact me in any way. Am I being clear?"

2. Never agree to a "guilt" date.

Don't ever accept a date or social invitation if your pursuer threatens suicide, claims his/her life "will be over" if you turn them down, or uses other guilt-inducing tactics. This is manipu-lative, and the mere fact that you spend time together may fuel further advances.

3. Remain cool and composed.

Some obsessed people thrive on seeing you fearful or flus-tered. Try not to show that they're having an impact on you.

4. If the situation persists and is within a structured situa-tion, invoke the chain of command.

For example, if the unwanted approaches occur at work,

school, or in a group social situation and your personal rejection doesn't work, then appeal to the boss, teacher, or host or hostess to intercede. Often, it's more effective to have an authority figure tell the obsessed person to back off.

5. If it still continues, consider hiring an attorney.

Even if violence hasn't yet been threatened, you may want a lawyer to write a stiff warning, perhaps mentioning trespassing, harassment, or other forms of criminal prosecution, or the threat of a civil suit.

WHEN HARASSMENT BECOMES STALKING

Stalking is an extreme form of obsession. It's harassment taken a step further. A stalker will purposely, maliciously and repeatedly harass or follow you to the point that you fear for your safety.

Such preoccupations, psychologists tell us, almost always occur in someone with poor social skills and low self-esteem. Often lonely, the stalker desperately seeks a sense of worth outside the usual channels of home, job, or friends. Stalking may give him the sense of power and control he otherwise lacks.

Stalkers are not necessarily street criminals. In New York, for example, former high-ranking judge Sol Wachtler was convicted of stalking a woman who'd been his lover. "Many abusers, and particularly stalkers, have above-average intelligence," a spokesman for the National Victim Center told a congressional subcommittee. "But in the vast majority of cases, the hunter needs no specialized training or knowledge to find their prey. They need only find a post office or a DMV office."

HOW TO COMBAT STALKING

Being stalked changes your life. Stalking victims are in a state of fear twenty-four hours a day. The ongoing nature of stalking can be quite traumatic for the victim.

"I was scared of not knowing what his next move may be or if he was going to hurt me," remembers Marlena, a woman stalked by an ex-boyfriend who was so relentless that he was eventually sentenced to prison for 16 years. "I was confused. I kept thinking he has more rights than I do, why won't anybody listen to me or help me, and what can I do to make this person leave me alone?" She said she also felt depressed, trapped, angry, and threatened, as well as sad and guilty.

If you are stalked, or feel that you may become a victim, then you need to take some or all of the following steps:

1. Notify the police immediately.

In recent years, police have become more sensitive to this issue, and new laws have been enacted that make it easier to protect yourself from a stalker. Often, though, there is no intervention by authorities until an actual threat or near violent act has occurred.

2. Be consistent in reporting to authorities.

Law-enforcement officers get a lot of false alarms, where one party calls the police as a means of one-upping their domestic partner rather than in response to a genuine, physical crisis. If you're serious about wanting and needing police help, make that clear and call them each time there's a problem. That way, they'll take you more seriously.

3. Seek a temporary restraining order.

This is a court order legally compelling a harasser to stay away from you or risk going to jail. Be aware, though, that this is for serious cases only. It will require hiring a lawyer or being represented by a public defender and going to court.

Keep in mind, too, that papers filed for a TRO or police report may become public record. Put minimal amounts of information on the order and only provide a post office box address.

Restraining orders do not always prevent a tragedy, but if violence is threatened, getting a TRO is a good idea, and it is another way of showing police that you're serious.

4. Consider arming yourself with pepper spray.

In many states, pepper spray now can be bought without taking a training class. However, you should take the class anyway. Learning how to properly use pepper spray can greatly improve your chances of successfully warding off an attacker.

5. Take a self-defense class.

Personal-defense classes can also make you feel more secure. Being more prepared in the event of an assault can dramatically affect the outcome. Almost all police departments provide such classes, or can refer you to a private organization that does.

6. Seek help from a support group.

A victims' support group can help you deal with the anxiety and depression associated with being stalked. Many counties and states operate services for crime victims.

Also see *Privacy Pointers* for names of other support services.

●Commonly Asked Questions About Stalking●

Q: Aren't there laws against stalking?
A: Yes.

California was the first to pass an antistalking law in 1990 in response to the murder of actress Rebecca Schaeffer. Now all states have enacted some form of anti-stalking law.

Q: Don't federal laws cover stalking?
A: Only one deals with it directly, but other federal statutes seek to restrict stalking in other ways.

A recent federal Violence Against Women Act includes an anti-stalking provision. One of its sections is aimed at domestic-violence cases where stalking by a "prior intimate" may be involved.

Other federal laws authorize grants to law-enforcement agencies which develop antistalking programs and for states to improve the processing of stalking-related data. There's a training program for judges to ensure that when they issue orders in stalking cases, they'll have all the available criminal history.

Although it does not specifically address stalking, a new federal law—effective in fall 1997—assists victims by allowing them to prohibit the release and use of certain personal information from the records of state departments of motor vehicles.

Q: Are there other legal remedies?
A: A civil lawsuit is a possibility.

In most states, stalking victims may bring a civil suit against the stalker and try to recover money damages. In some cases, victims may also request that the department of motor vehicles prevent their automobile registration and driver's license records from being released to anybody but court and law-enforcement officials, or other specified agencies. To have these records suppressed, the victim must submit verification from the police or courts showing the plaintiff has reasonable cause to believe he or she is a victim of a stalker.

Q: Should a stalking victim carry a gun?
A: Generally, police discourage that, especially for victims without experience or training with firearms.

Carrying concealed weapons is against the law in most communities unless you have a permit. Permits are issued by local law-enforcement authorities, and one criterion may be if an applicant's life is in danger. So that option exists, though the potential dangers—such as accidental discharge or a mistake in judgment that results in a wrongful death or injury—may far outweigh the benefits.

If a firearm is available for home protection, it's imperative that all adult members of the household be trained in its use. And, of course, it should be stored out of reach of children.

●Privacy Pointers: What You Can Do Now●

Throughout this book, numerous ways have been mentioned to lessen your visibility. These will serve you well in confounding a stalker, too. A key is shielding your new address and phone number when you've moved to evade the stalker. That's the most critical time to safeguard your personal data.

This section will repeat some of those earlier tips as well as suggest some additional steps you might take to make yourself a more elusive target. Some may be fairly inconvenient. How far you're willing to go will depend on how serious a threat you believe you face.

In addition to the many suggestions which follow, Appendix B reprints "Security Recommendations for Stalking Victims." This is a list covering residential, office, personal, and vehicle security which has been compiled by the Los Angeles Police Department's Threat Management Unit.

1. Keep your address and phone number confidential.
This is one of the most important things you can do.

- Don't print your street address on checks or on your driver's license. Instead, use a postal box number, preferably a private postal box (not one at a U.S. Post Office). Private postal outlets generally have stricter rules for releasing your box number.

  Find a private postal outlet where you can use a street address and an "apartment" number instead of a box number. This makes your return address seem as if it's a residence. Use this address for all your correspondence. Print it on your checks instead of your residential address. Avoid using your home address for anything that is mailed or shipped to you. For instance, don't use your home address when you subscribe to magazines.

- Make sure your telephone number is unlisted. Don't pre-print it on your checks. If you're asked to give a phone number when making a purchase, use your work number. If you're receiving harassing phone calls, change your number immediately. If your area has Caller ID, be sure to order Per Line Blocking so that your phone number is not disclosed when you make phone calls from your home.

  Don't call "800," "888," or "900" numbers with which you're not familiar. Remember, your phone number, whether blocked or not, is transmitted if you call any number with those prefixes. Some stalkers have been known to obtain a personal "800" number and then create a ruse to lure the victim into calling them. If you do need to call an "800" number, use a pay phone.

- Have your name and/or address removed from reverse directories or any kind of professional directories you may be in. Don't forget college alumni associations, church groups, and other sources. Potential stalkers can also use this information to discover your address or phone number.

- Be particularly careful not to allow your residential address to be obtained by banks, credit card firms, and other sources that may find their way onto your credit report. "Credit header" data is a powerful, popular tool of private investigators and professional snoops. This header consists of name, address, place of employment, SSN, and year of birth, and is often the most up to date of any records about you.

  The three major credit-reporting companies sell credit header information to data compilers and information vendors as well as to online services that maintain electronic directories. Currently, there is no way for stalking victims to suppress this data. (Consider lobbying your legislative representatives and the Federal Trade Commission, which oversees the credit-reporting companies, to allow individuals to "opt out" of having their credit header data sold.)

2. Don't fill out the change of address card at the post office.

The U.S. Postal Service shares this information with the National Change of Address system. The NCOA updates mailing lists and files of marketing companies, credit bureaus, and government agencies. The change of address card is also kept on file at the post office of your last known address. Instead, create your own letter with your new address and mail it to family, friends, and specific businesses.

One relatively new post office service does aid stalking victims, however. If the victim shows postal officials that she has a court-ordered restraining order, the post office will not give out her new address. It will mark "Moved Left No Address" on mail returned to sender.

3. Let people know that information about you should be held in confidence.

Tell your employer, coworkers, friends, family, and neighbors to be suspicious of people inquiring about your whereabouts or schedule. Let your associates know that information about you should be held in confidence.

4. Avoid using your middle initial.

Middle initials are often used to differentiate people with common names. For example, someone searching the voter registration records or credit report files might find several people with the name Jane Doe. If you have a common name and want to blend in with the crowd, don't add a middle initial.

5. When conducting business with a government agency, only fill in the required pieces of information.

Many government records, as we have seen, are public. Files containing voter registration, property assessments and transfers, and business licenses are especially useful for finding people. Ask each such agency in your area if it allows address information to be confidential in certain situations. If possible, use a postal box address and do not provide your middle initial, phone number, or your Social Security number.

6. Don't put your name on the list of tenants on the front of your condo complex or apartment building.

If necessary, use a variation of your name that only your friends and family would recognize.

7. Be very protective of your Social Security number.

As mentioned previously, your SSN is the key to much of your personal information. Don't preprint it on your checks or elsewhere. Only give it out after satisfying yourself that you're required to do so.

8. If you're having a problem with harassing phone calls, put a beep tone on your line so callers think you are taping your calls.

Use an answering machine to screen your calls, and put a "bluff message" on your machine to warn callers of possible taping or monitoring. However, be aware that there are legal restriction on taping of conversations. (See Chapter 8, "How You Can Stop Harassing Phone Calls.")

9. Get a car phone and/or a beeper.

A cellular phone, though somewhat expensive, could be a lifesaver if you're seriously threatened. It allows you to remain inside your locked car and call for help.

Having a pager number forces callers to go through an intermediary, steers them away from your residence phone, and gives you the option of returning calls, or not.

10. Carry a camera, or a video camera, so you can take pictures of suspicious activity.

This could be very helpful in documenting your case, and its presence may also help deter the stalker.

11. Keep a log.

Record every stalking incident, including names, dates, and

times of your contact with law enforcement officers and others. Save phone message tapes and items sent to you in the mail.

12. Be careful when in your automobile.

Park only in well-lighted areas. Avoid parking lots where doors must be unlocked and keys surrendered. Keep the doors locked while driving, be alert for vehicles that may be following you, don't stop to assist stranded motorists (instead, phone in), and use a different route and a different time of travel each day.

13. Use caution in cyberspace.

If you use e-mail and other online computer services, change your e-mail address if necessary. Do not use a variation of your name as a sign-on. Do not enter any personal information into online directories. (For other protective measures, see Chapter 10, "Privacy in Cyberspace: How to Protect Your Personal Computer.")

There are several "people-finding" services on the Internet, each containing millions of names, addresses, and phone numbers. Remember, staying out of these online directories involves the same process as staying out of phone books, reverse directories, and the files of data compilers. The online directories are based on those same sources. Follow the suggestions in Chapter 1 ("How to Turn Off the Junk-Mail Juggernaut") and Chapter 2 ("Telemarketing: What Happened to a Quiet Evening at Home?") in order to keep your profile low.

14. Consider alternative forms of property ownership.

If you own real estate or a car, you may want to consider alternative forms of ownership, such as a trust. This could further shield your personal address from the public record. Consult an attorney for details.

15. Contact these groups for more information:

- **National Organization for Victim Assistance** (NOVA) is a nonprofit information and referral group. Contact it at:

NOVA
1757 Park Rd., NW
Washington, D.C. 20010
(202) 232-6682. Hotline: (800) 879-6682
http://access.digex.net/~nova

- **National Victim Center** offers a guide for victims of stalking. You can obtain it by writing or calling:

National Victim Center
2111 Wilson Blvd., No. 300
Arlington, VA 22201
(800) FYI-CALL or (703) 276-2880
http://www.nvc.org

- **Survivors of Stalking, Inc.** is a membership organization that provides support for stalking victims.

Survivors of Stalking
P.O. Box 20762
Tampa, FL 33622
(813) 889-0767
http://www.soshelp.org

- **National Domestic Violence Hotline** provides crisis intervention, referrals to shelters, and information about sources of assistance.

National Domestic Violence Hotline
3616 Far West Blvd., No. 101–297
Austin, TX 78731
(800) 799-SAFE 24-hour hotline
(800) 787-3224 TDD
(512) 453-8117 Administration
http://www.inetport.com/~ndvh

PART VI

●

WHAT MORE CAN YOU DO NOW?

15

Respecting Others' Privacy: How to Handle Information Responsibly

- Joe received an invitation from his phone company to attend a small-business conference on telecommunications. He was shocked to see his unlisted phone number—which he'd kept private for 35 years—printed on the mailing label. He called the phone company, which apologized and said it'd never happen again.

- Yolanda requested a copy of her student-loan file from the state. But when it arrived, she was surprised to find that in addition to her file were the names, addresses, SSNs, and phone numbers of 29 other borrowers.

- Terry is a police officer who was called by another cop who'd discovered a suspect carrying the driver's license of Terry's wife. It turned out Terry had been recently married, and his wife had gone to the DMV to get a new license with her married name on it. But the DMV discarded old licenses by tossing them away, intact and in clear plastic bags—a treasure trove for local crooks.

As these real-life examples show, many abuses of privacy

spring from ignorance or thoughtlessness, not malice—but the victim feels just as abused.

A few years ago, for example, residents of an entire Vermont town—about 1,200 in all—were erroneously designated as tax deadbeats due to a coding error at a major credit-reporting agency. Other surveys of credit reports have shown errors as high as 48%, including some mistakes—such as a delinquent debt—which could cause denial of credit.

Changing such innocent but harmful acts requires the efforts of everyone concerned about privacy. This chapter will provide a detailed checklist of ways you can further sensitize yourself and your colleagues to issues involving personal information.

It's up to you to urge your company and other organizations you're involved with—such as churches, synagogues, and non-profit groups—to protect the privacy of customers, employees, and members. Being assertive about privacy probably isn't going to make you popular, but you have an obligation to speak up when you see blatant errors or bad practices.

Samantha did. Her doctor's billing office sent her a copy of her Blue Cross bill, as she requested. Attached to it was the record of another patient, complete with name, SSN, and treatments administered. Samantha called to complain. The mailing, she was told, had been meant for her doctor, not her.

Or take Charles. He ordered a copy of his credit report and discovered an additional report of someone else in the same envelope. To make matters worse, the stranger's report was flagged "security alert." Charles complained, but the credit bureau told him it thought the woman was his wife, even though she had a different last name.

Samantha and Charles made the effort and took the time to complain, to call attention to egregious practices. If we all were so conscientious, we'd soon get better handling of confidential material. In the future, how much personal privacy we possess will probably depend on how many of us are sufficiently outraged to protest dangerous practices.

LOW-TECH VIGILANCE

Much of this book has dealt with the dark side of technology, how going high-tech brings with it enormous potential for abuse of personal privacy. This chapter will also show how our computers and other office machines are only as effective as the minds operating them.

There's definitely a low-tech side to protecting privacy. Poor information-handling usually springs from human behavior, not technology. While it's important, for instance, to have the best possible protection against computer hackers, it's also critical not to discuss confidential information in elevators, or leave sensitive documents in the copying machine, or fax them to the wrong phone number. In the final analysis, it's how we think and act—or, sometimes fail to think and act—that causes many security breaches.

The truth is, we don't have what Jeff Smith of Georgetown University's School of Business calls a "culture of confidentiality" in this country. We are chronically careless with information. You would rarely find treasurers, or anyone else responsible for handling money, scattering currency or checks about their desks like so many autumn leaves on a lawn. But you can walk into just about any office and see personal information treated cavalierly.

This chapter will encourage you to take a proactive stance, to combat carelessness and assert control over policies and equipment. First, we will suggest yardsticks by which you can measure the privacy quotient of your organization. Then, we will explain what provisions you should push for in your firm's internal policies—and we will urge you to be more careful in your everyday handling of information of all kinds.

PRIVACY FOR CUSTOMERS

Here are some questions to help you analyze your firm's attitude toward the privacy of its customers or clients:

- For starters, does your company have any privacy or information policies? (*It should.*)

- If so, how are they communicated? In writing? Or informally by supervisors? (*Clearly, they should be written. And, for that matter, clearly written!*)

- Are the policies reiterated regularly—in initial orientations, in regular organization-wide training programs, in employee handbooks, on posters and posted signs, and in brochures available to clients? (*The policies need to be widely, repeatedly disseminated.*)

- Are all employees who handle personal information included in the training programs, including temporary employees, back-up personnel, and contract staff? (*No one should be exempted or overlooked, including top management.*)

- When copying information for others, are employees told to make sure that nonessential data is deleted? (*That which has no relevance to the transaction should be removed or obscured.*)

- Are all employees who handle personal information trained to be able to detect when they are being "pumped" for personal information by unauthorized or unscrupulous persons? (*"Pretext" interviews are often used by persons bent on learning confidential personal information to which they're not entitled.*)

- For employees who work at home, including temporary and contract staff, are there policies and training programs which emphasize responsible information-handling practices? (*The trend toward allowing employees to operate from home widens the possible range of unauthorized access, such as friends or family members, and perhaps "hackers," too.*)

Your organization or firm may or may not score well on these questions. But, if it's to protect privacy, it will need an effective set of policies as a foundation. The stakes are just too high to allow unknowing, or unscrupulous, employees to have indiscriminate access to people's records. In one case, for example, an employee of the Social Security Administration was accused of searching that agency's huge database for people with similar names and years of birth close to hers. Then she would allegedly use their SSNs to open up credit accounts.

What should an organization's policies cover? The Organization for Economic Cooperation and Development developed some guidelines almost 20 years ago. Since then, these policies have formed the basis of numerous privacy laws and business practices and have come to be known as "fair information practices":

1. Openness. There should be open discussion about *what* personal information is to be collected. The existence and nature of personal data held by the organization should be readily verifiable.

2. Purpose specification. *Why* is it being collected? This should be specified at the time the data is collected. Subsequent uses should be limited to those purposes. Secondary uses shouldn't be made without consent by the person whose information is involved.

3. Collection limitation. *How* is the data being collected? It should be obtained lawfully and fairly and with the knowledge and consent of the subject. Only that information necessary for the stated purpose should be collected, nothing more. Information shouldn't be collected simply because it might be useful sometime in the future.

4. Use limitation. *Who* gets to share this personal information? It shouldn't be revealed to others without the consent of the subject or without legal authorization.

5. **Individual participation.** *Everyone* should get to inspect and correct his or her personal information.

6. **Quality.** Personal information should be *accurate*, complete, timely, and relevant to the purposes for which it's to be used. Whenever possible, personal information should be collected directly from the individual.

7. **Security.** There need to be reasonable security *safeguards* against risks such as loss, unauthorized access, destruction, or alteration. Only those with a need to know should have access.

8. **Accountability.** Who is accountable for applying these principles? The higher up that person is in the organization, the better. Many businesses now assign the job to the chief information officer (CIO). Privacy audits to ensure *compliance* must be conducted regularly, as should employee-training programs.

In addition to those broad principles, there are additional, specific guidelines which your firm or organization should follow, which we will now discuss.

RETAINING AND DISPOSING OF RECORDS

As far as personal records go, out of sight should not mean out of mind. To the contrary, it's essential your organization think about how it disposes of records. Many fraud and identity-theft cases start with old records being carelessly handled.

In Sacramento, for example, a large drugstore chain tossed old job applications in the trash. An imposter, or possibly a crime ring, found them and used them to make fake IDs. With the bogus IDs, they then wrote checks and opened credit accounts, causing many of the erstwhile job applicants untold grief.

So, inquire:

1. Does your organization have a proven method and timetable for disposing of personal information, regardless of what form (e.g., paper, microfilm, computer disks) it's stored in?

2. When disposing of computers, diskettes, magnetic tapes, hard drives, and any other electronic media which contain personal data, are they erased with an ''initialize'' process or a ''wipe'' or ''overwrite'' function of utility software? Are the diskettes physically destroyed?

3. When disposing of waste and recycling paper, are all personal documents placed in secure, padlocked containers, or shredded? Does your recycling company certify its disposal/destruction methods?

USING FAXES SAFELY

In most offices, facsimile machines are not at all private. They have become such a ubiquitous tool of home and office that we tend to use them reflexively, without much thought as to who might see the material at the other end, or even on *our* end. Worse yet, especially in a busy office with lots of fax traffic, it's easy for a harried user to dial a wrong number.

For instance, a medical doctor who was filing for bankruptcy meant to fax a financial document to his attorney. But he dialed incorrectly, sending the document instead to the local newspaper. In a similar case, a secretary at a large corporation was sending a fax about a pending merger when she reportedly pressed the wrong speed-dial button. Instead of the fax going to the merger partner, it went to the editorial office of *The Wall Street Journal*, which promptly ran a story that effectively killed the merger.

Those were both accidents. However, sometimes a fax sent on purpose—but thoughtlessly—can cause problems. Franklin, for example, was having financial woes, and a debt-collection agency was after him. It faxed a nasty letter to him at work, which, of course, his colleagues saw, much to his embarrassment.

Because the confidentiality of faxes is difficult to insure, the best policy is to avoid faxing personal records, if possible. If that's not feasible, you can help guard against faxing problems by finding out:

1. Is your fax machine in a supervised area, off-limits to unauthorized persons?

2. Is the fax machine used primarily for sending *non*confidential materials? Are special procedures used for confidential documents? (See Numbers 5 and 6 below.)

3. When sending documents, do all users fill out a cover sheet which shows the sender's and receiver's names, addresses, phone and fax numbers? Does the cover sheet also include a statement prohibiting redisclosure? Does it include a statement regarding distribution? Does it include instructions for the recipient to verify receipt of the fax?

4. Do users always check the receiver's telephone number before faxing? Do they check for errors by comparing the number displayed with the number being called? Do they check the transmission report after the fax has been sent?

5. If confidential material is sent, is notice of its confidential nature indicated on the cover sheet?

6. When faxing confidential materials, is the recipient notified in advance that the document is being sent? Does the sender check with the receiver to make sure the document has been received?

7. Are separate fax machines provided for departments or units with differing needs for confidentiality?

8. Are shredders or secure disposal containers placed near fax machines so that extra copies of confidential faxes resulting from transmission or reception failures can be destroyed?

9. Does office policy designate one person and a backup as the monitors of the fax machine?

10. Are faxes sent during regular working hours when authorized personnel are most likely to be there to receive them? If the need arises for sensitive information to be faxed outside of normal working hours, can an isolated fax machine in a secure environment be used?

BEING CAREFUL ABOUT ANSWERING MACHINES

Answering machines are simple gadgets, but they're only as infallible as the person dialing the phone. For example, one woman we know got a message along these lines: "Hello, Mrs. Weaver. This is Judy from the County Parole Office. You called earlier about your daughter Crystal? She has already been taken to the juvenile detention center."

The woman's name was not Mrs. Weaver and she didn't have an incarcerated daughter named Crystal. But she sure *knew* now about Mrs. Weaver's problems! All because the parole officer misdialed and then left a message that should have been confidential.

So, at your firm or organization, you'll want to know:

1. Are precautions taken when confidential or highly sensitive messages are expected to be left on answering machines?

2. Is the number of the call recipient verified for accuracy?

3. Is permission asked of the intended recipient to leave confidential messages on the machine?

4. Are nonspecific messages left when prior permission hasn't been obtained from the call recipient?

COPING WITH COPIERS

Is there one of us who hasn't left an original of something we were copying on the copier glass? Or thrown away without much thought a copy that didn't come out quite right?

If the information is personally sensitive, there could be privacy ramifications. Questions to ask about copying practices at your office include:

1. Is there an awareness-training program that points up the peril of leaving confidential originals on the copier glass or in the copier feeder where they may be found by someone who shouldn't see them?

2. Is there a shredder or a secure disposal container placed nearby for sensitive rejects?

3. Is there a confidentiality provision in your copier-repair contract so repair persons will turn over any material encountered while clearing jams?

PROPERLY PREPARING PRINTERS

Much like the fax or the copier, a computer printer often spews out information in a vacuum. Maybe the person who asked for the printed item forgets about it, is called away, or is chatting with others in the vicinity of the printer. In any event, the machine does what it's told and pumps out the information regardless of whether anyone is paying attention, or even if the *wrong* people are paying attention.

Some questions to ask about your office's printer procedures include:

1. Are separate printers provided for departments or units based on the need to print confidential information?

2. Are shredders or secure disposal containers placed near printers for unneeded or imperfect copies?

3. Are printers located so that visitors or other unauthorized people can't see confidential information being printed?

4. Are staff members fully aware of printer locations so they don't direct confidential print jobs to the wrong location?

COMMUNICATING ON CELLULAR AND CORDLESS PHONES AND PAGERS

As people stood in line to enter the theater, the cellular phone conversation of one theatergoer was overheard by those near her. It soon became clear that the woman was a medical doctor, and her conversation was about the care of a patient. In this case, no equipment was needed to eavesdrop. A little more discretion would have avoided an awkward situation.

As we saw in Chapter 7 ("Cordless and Cellular Phones: Is Everybody Listening?"), conversations on cellular and cordless phones are vulnerable to eavesdropping because the signals are transmitted over radio waves. Thus, special precautions need to be taken. To test your organization's cellular, cordless and pager practices, ask:

1. Are cellular and cordless phones strictly forbidden for conversations involving confidential information in which personal names are revealed, such as a patient's medical care or a lawsuit? If they are used, do they employ the newer, digital technology that makes eavesdropping more difficult?

2. Is there a policy against sending confidential messages to voice pagers?

LIMITING PERSONAL IDENTIFIERS

As noted many times in this book, the SSN can be a dangerous number. It's the key that can open many doors to fraud or
privacy intrusion. Yet, sometimes the carelessness of its use is
shocking. For example:

- Bernie gets mail from his bank that shows his SSN right
  above the mailing address. It's visible through the plasti-
  cene window for all to see.

- A large Midwestern newspaper offered a $100,000 sweep-
  stakes contest. Readers could enter by sending in their
  name, address, and SSNs. In fact, the more often they entered, the greater the chance would be that they'd be picked
  in the drawing.

As should be clear by now, use of SSNs for recordkeeping
purposes and personal identifiers should be strongly discouraged, and preferably prohibited. So you might want to find out
the following about your employer:

1. If it uses the SSN as a recordkeeping number, does it offer
clients or customers the option of using an alternative number?

2. Does it have a strict policy prohibiting the display of SSNs
on any documents that are widely seen by others, such as on
mailing labels?

3. If it requires an access code or PIN for certain transactions,
does it prohibit the use of SSNs, or any part of the SSN?

HANDLING TRANSACTION-GENERATED DATA

With increasing computerization, a great many of our transactions can be tracked, stored, and used for purposes other than

simple recordkeeping. As we've seen, when you call someone who subscribes to Caller ID or you call an "800" or "900" number, for example, your phone number can be captured. Some companies use that information for subsequent marketing solicitations. Other types of transaction-generated data include: ATM-use records, credit card usage, supermarket purchases, and utility meter readings.

For instance, when Fred moved, he didn't give his new, unlisted phone number to his credit card company. Thus, he was a little surprised when his new phone number appeared on his next monthly bill. He realized the company probably captured his new number when he called its customer service "800" number.

His surprise turned to anger when, reading the fine print of his credit account contract, he noticed the card company claimed "the right to share information" with others. He was understandably upset: who else had they given his unlisted number to?

At your organization, try to learn:

1. Are customers and clients notified of the uses made of the transaction-generated data when usage goes beyond recordkeeping?

2. Is consent obtained in such cases?

KEEPING COMPUTERS SECURE

As we saw in Chapter 10 ("Privacy in Cyberspace: How to Protect Your Personal Computer"), computer security can be a big problem, especially for organizations. It's also a field where the technology is complex and constantly changing. The following pointers are only the tip of the iceberg and are offered for assessment purposes. For a thorough diagnosis of your organization's computer security, you'll definitely want to consult with experts.

Meanwhile, though, here are some basic questions to ask about your organization's data and network security:

1. Does it have staff specifically assigned to data security? Do staffers participate in regular training programs to keep abreast of technical and legal issues?

2. Are sensitive files segregated in secure areas or systems and, thus, are available only to authorized persons?

3. Are there procedures to prevent ex-employees from gaining access to computer and paper files?

4. Are audit procedures and strict penalties in place to prevent information being accessed by unauthorized persons?

5. Do all employees follow strict password and virus-protection procedures? Are employees required to change passwords often and to use "foolproof" password-creation methods? (See Chapter 10 for tips on password creation.)

6. Is encryption used to protect extremely sensitive information, especially when transmitting personal information over public networks such as the Internet?

7. Does the organization regularly conduct "systems-penetration tests" to determine if its systems are "hacker" proof?

8. If your organization is susceptible to "industrial espionage," does it take extra precautions to guard against leakage of information?

9. Are employees trained never to leave computer terminals unattended when personal information is on the screen? Are password-activated screen-saver programs used? Are PCs located so that screens can't be seen by unauthorized people?

10. Are there policies and procedures for safeguarding personal information when transported outside of the office by portable computers? Is the network connection between home and work secure?

GUARDING YOUR ORGANIZATION'S LISTS

Lists are the lifeblood of almost any organization. Not just businesses and governments, but Little League, churches and synagogues, Neighborhood Watch groups, book clubs, Masonic groups, 4-H, Rotary—you name it! They all keep lists of members, and maybe former members and prospective members, too.

In both the workplace and in the nonprofit arena, these lists too often are handled inappropriately and carelessly. Take Roger, for example. He went to a chiropractor once for a treatment. The office receptionist read his medical file and later contacted him on her own. It turns out she was an independent salesperson for a home-remedy product. She'd noticed that he and she had the same ailment. Having been helped by the home-remedy product, she tried to interest him in purchasing the product from her. Roger complained to the chiropractor about this dreadful lapse in privacy.

Whether you're responsible for something as simple as your soccer team's roster, or as complex as your company's customer database, the same principles of "fair information practices" that were introduced earlier in this chapter should apply. Particularly critical for list-handling are:

Openness
Be sure that those on the list are aware that the list is being compiled and what is being done with it. As we've seen, all too often marketing lists are put together without the knowledge of those listed.

Purpose Specification
If your business or group strays from the initial reason for

collecting the data, then you should get consent from the listed individuals before beginning a secondary use. A common, but unfortunate, practice is turning a membership or customer list into a money-maker by selling it to others. Doing so without consent is probably the most flagrant abuse of fair information practices in the marketplace today. Responsible list managers—whether at a large corporation or a small volunteer group—make disclosure and get consent before selling anyone's name.

Security
Ensure a safe environment for lists. Keep them out of the hands of those who are not entitled to access.

Many of the stories of privacy abuses contained in this book occurred because of carelessness, or ignorance of the sensitivity of personal information. Make it your goal to stamp out slipshod handling of such data in your company or organization.

PRIVACY FOR EMPLOYEES

In all likelihood, how your organization regards the privacy of its customers mirrors how it treats the privacy of its employees. Just as it should have written—and frequently voiced—policies about customer data, so, too, should it have policy statements about e-mail, phone monitoring, and other privacy issues facing employees.

As we learned in Chapter 12 ("Employee Monitoring: Is Your Boss Spying on You?"), technology has greatly boosted the ability of firms to observe the behavior of employees. An increasing number of employers are checking up on their workers in a variety of ways, from monitoring telephones and computers to planting cameras and listening to voice mail.

Such "advances" bring with them a great many concerns

about whether such monitoring is violating workers' rights. For example:

- Paul, a computer technician, discovered that his boss, a former policeman, had placed hidden microphones and cameras around the building to monitor employees.

- Jan's employer made a "private" line available for employees to make personal calls. But Jan felt duped when she learned the boss was monitoring that line, too.

- Pamela would often spend her lunch hour writing personal letters on her office computer. After she printed them out, she would delete the letters from the computer system. She had no idea her deleted files could be read by supervisors until she got into trouble for supposedly disclosing "confidential company information" in letters to friends or relatives.

To scrutinize your organization's policies and practices, here are some of the issues you will want to explore:

E-MAIL AND VOICE-MAIL SYSTEMS

As mentioned in Chapter 12, many workers mistakenly believe e-mail and voice-mail at work are private. But the law and reality say otherwise, as numerous employees have learned to their chagrin.

Chuck, for example, was absent from work for a month on disability leave. Upon his return, he was shocked to discover that his supervisor had changed his password and listened to his voice-mail messages.

In order to find out where you and your organization stand, you need to find out:

Does it have a policy that states what degree of privacy can be expected by employees, as well as third parties (such as clients or customers) who use the e-mail and/or voice-mail systems? How is that policy communicated? Is it made clear to all employees and third-party users?

Points to include in any e-mail/voice-mail policy:

- The purpose for which the system is to be used (e.g., Business only? Personal matters allowed? No trade secrets discussed?)

- Penalties for misuse.

- Who's authorized to access e-mail/voice-mail messages?

- Under what circumstances will files be kept for possible use as legal evidence?

- What are employees' expectations for privacy? (Total? None? Only files marked "private"?)

- Password creation/change procedures.

- Use of encryption. (Prohibited? Allowed? Required for sensitive communications?)

- Safeguards for copying and forwarding messages, especially messages containing personally identifiable data.

ELECTRONIC MONITORING

In Chapter 12 ("Employee Monitoring: Is Your Boss Spying on You?"), we saw several cases of employees being surprised by unknown monitoring practices. Sometimes, the employees lost their jobs, and often lawsuits resulted. All that could have been avoided had the employers prepared policies and clearly communicated them to the workers.

Some questions you should ask about your organization's monitoring:

1. Is there a policy about the kind of monitoring allowed and the uses made of the results? Are there procedures to safeguard sensitive, personal information encountered while monitoring?

2. If telephones are monitored, are nonmonitored phones provided for personal calls? Are employees notified of the "private" phones?

3. Are employees given a clear explanation of who has access to files kept in their office computer and under what circumstances?

PERSONAL INFORMATION

Just as organizations must be careful with personally identifiable data concerning clients and customers, they must help limit their employees' exposure to fraud or embarrassment. Too often, though, there is a blasé attitude or, at worst, an intentional violation.

For instance:

- The supervisor of a unit within a large state agency sent an e-mail message to every employee, listing all their names and SSNs, disregarding—or maybe not even being aware of—the privacy and fraud potential.

- Stan, a salesperson for a long-distance phone company, objected to the fact that his firm uses employees' SSNs so indiscriminately—it's his company ID number; it's required on his business card; and when he makes a sale, it's even on the paperwork the customer receives.

- Skip, a retired railroader, agreed to appear as an expert witness in a lawsuit involving someone struck and killed by a train. When he took the stand, the attorney didn't ask him about railroad switches, his area of expertise, but instead focused on his mental health. Years earlier, Skip had had psychiatric treatment. His employer released that sensitive information to the attorney, who used it to intimidate and discredit Skip.

Obviously, the use of SSNs for recordkeeping purposes and personal identifiers should be strongly discouraged, and mixing medical records and personnel files is legally prohibited in many states. In addition, wisdom and common sense have to be applied to what kinds of information are released.

At your organization, you might want to find out:

1. If it uses the SSN as a recordkeeping number for employees, does it offer them the option of using an alternative number?

2. Does it have a strict policy prohibiting the display of SSNs on any documents that are widely seen by others, for example, time cards, parking permits, employee rosters, and ID badges?

3. If it requires an access code for certain transactions (e.g., security system, building-access cards, passwords), does it prohibit the use of SSNs, or any part of the SSN?

4. Does it keep paper and microfilmed files of personnel records under lock and key? Are computerized personnel files strongly secured?

5. Does it strictly forbid the commingling of medical data with employees' personnel files?

Many books, journals, trade magazines, and conferences are devoted to the subject of the security of personally-identifiable information. You may wish to consult the following for more information in safeguarding your business:

●Organizations●

▓Computer Privacy

• **Association for Computing Machinery**
  1515 Broadway
  New York, NY 10036
  (800) 342-6626
  http://www.acm.org

• **Electronic Messaging Association**
  1655 N. Ft. Myer Dr., No. 500
  Arlington, VA 22209
  (703) 524-5550
  http://www.ema.org
  Request "Access to and Use and Disclosure of Electronic
  Mail on Company Computer Systems: A Tool Kit for For-
  mulating Your Company's Policy," *available for $45.*

• **National Computer Security Association**
  1200 Walnut Bottom Rd.
  Carlisle, PA 17013
  (717) 258-1816 or (800) 488-4595
  http://www.ncsa.com
  Request its catalogue of publications.

▓Other Groups:

• **American Health Information Management Association**
  919 N. Michigan Ave., No. 1400
  Chicago, IL 60611
  (312) 787-2672
  http://www.ahima.org
  AHIMA publishes the newsletter In Confidence.

- **American Society for Industrial Security**
  1655 N. Ft. Myer Drive, No. 1200
  Arlington, VA 22209
  (703) 522-5800
  http://www.asisonline.org
  This is the major U.S. professsional organization for security managers and directors, public and private.

- **Association for Records Managers and Administrators**
  4200 Somerset St., No. 215
  Prairie Village, KS 66208
  (913) 341-3808
  ARMA is a nonprofit organization of records and information management professionals.

- **Business Espionage Controls and Countermeasures Association**
  P.O. Box 260
  Ft. Washington, MD 20749
  (301) 292-6430
  This group promotes awareness of the threat of espionage in the business community.

- **Direct Marketing Association**
  1120 Avenue of the Americas
  New York, NY 10036
  (212) 768-7277

  1111 19th St., NW, No. 1100
  Washington, D.C. 20036
  (202) 955-5030
  http://www.the-dma.org
  Request its Fair Information Practices Manual *(1994) for those responsible for handling your organization's lists.*

- **Privacy & American Business: A Comprehensive Report and Information Service**
Two University Plaza, No. 414
Hackensack, NJ 07601
(201) 996-1154
http://shell.idt.net/~pab
This is an independent, bimonthly newsletter ($395 annually). P&AB sponsors an annual conference and leadership forums for businesses interested in adopting sound privacy policies.

●Literature●

- Decker, Kurt H., *A Manager's Guide to Employee Privacy Laws, Policies, and Procedures* (Wiley, 1989).

- *Privacy in the Workplace: Rights, Procedures, and Policies* (LRP Publications, 1994).

- Smith, H. Jeff. *Managing Privacy: Information Technology and Corporate America* (University of North Carolina Press, 1994).

- Wood, Charles Cresson. *Information Security Policies Made Easy: A Policy Construction Kit.* (Baseline Software, 1996). $495. Contains over 730 already-written policies in a printed manual and computer diskette. Call (800) 829-9955 or order from National Computer Security Association (see above).

16

How to Become an Advocate for Privacy Rights

Lisa had already won her fight with the community college about using her SSN as a student ID number. The school registrar had backed down, agreeing to give her an alternate number. But now the campus bookstore refused to honor the new number and said it wouldn't accept Lisa's checks unless she added her SSN.

Lisa refused. Instead, she went to the college president and showed him information, such as is contained in this book, explaining how easy it is to use a fraudulently obtained SSN to gain access to someone else's bank or credit records. The president was impressed with her research and with her passion. He changed the policy, and now the bookstore doesn't require the SSN on checks. Lisa is one of the best examples we know of someone who perceived an issue, took a stand, did her research, persisted, and as a result, got a bad policy changed.

One of the reasons not much gets done about protecting privacy is that it's an arena with largely invisible combatants. Almost everyone in America *says* they're pro-privacy. You name them—Lisa's college, insurers, credit agencies, government, even the big information brokers—they're all staunch supporters of the right of privacy . . . until, and unless, there's some detail in a bill, a legal opinion, or a procedure that might make their job slightly more difficult or slightly less profitable.

Not surprisingly, proponents of privacy tend to keep a low profile. Privacy doesn't have much going for it in the way of organized activism, except for a handful of tireless individuals and small organizations that try to sweep back the tide of intrusion. The right of privacy lacks powerful lobbying groups like those that seek to protect farm subsidies, win corporate tax breaks, and establish the rights of smokers or nonsmokers. A legislator's campaign war chest is not likely to be enriched by his or her sponsorship of stricter privacy laws. In fact, a lawmaker who tries is usually rewarded with more headaches than kudos.

As a result, *you* are your best privacy protector. That's true in asserting control over your own personal information as well as in banding together with others to change laws and industry practices.

Little will get done in terms of protection until and unless many are educated and speak out. Only when citizens, businesspeople, and government officials understand the growing dangers will they be able to work together to guard against erosion of our privacy. This chapter will suggest some goals to shoot for and also introduce you to people—like Lisa—who caused changes, small and large.

THREE AREAS FOR ACTIVISM

As an individual, there are three areas in which you can take a stand for stronger privacy: the **workplace**, the **marketplace**, and the **policy arena**. The preceding 15 chapters have made you more aware of what's at stake when you give out your personal information, or even worse, when it's collected without your consent. You're now in a position to beat the drums for some changes.

I—Workplace

Chapter 12 told of the wide range of employee-monitoring that's legally and technologically possible. In Chapter 15, you learned privacy criteria by which progressive organizations can be judged. The rest is up to you.

Look around your office. Is information—whether belonging to customers and clients, or to your fellow employees—being responsibly handled? If not, take your newfound knowledge and put it to work. Educate others, including your supervisors.

Bob, for example, works for a company which asked all employees for their medical histories dating back to birth, including information on their spouses. The company pays 80% of the employees' health-insurance premiums and apparently thought it needed all that information to manage its healthcare costs.

But Bob and other employees thought that request was extreme. They researched the law in that state and learned that employers could access medical information *only* to the extent needed to determine insurance payments. Faced with this information and a united front among the workers, the firm backed down.

In addition to scrutinizing how your employer uses your data, you need to make sure you handle others' personal information with confidentiality, accuracy, and security. A concerted "information sensitivity" campaign should be conducted in all workplaces—businesses, government agencies, and nonprofits—where personal information is gathered, stored, and disseminated.

Not only should all employees and volunteers be trained, but professional and trade associations should inform their members. Similarly, proper information-handling should be taught to college students in business schools.

Most important, be prepared to take a stand if it's *you* who's in a position to handle information more responsibly. Margaret, for instance, works as human-resources manager for a software company. She was approached by a head-hunting firm which promised to pay her for giving it copies of résumés of unsuccessful job applicants. Further, if any of the individuals whose résumés Margaret provided were hired by the headhunter's clients, Margaret would share in the commission.

Margaret was shocked at the idea of peddling applicants' résumés without their knowledge. She turned down the proposal, lucrative though it might have been. Would you have done the same?

HOW TO ENCOURAGE PRIVACY PROTECTION

How should much-needed reform of information-handling in the workplace occur? Through laws, or voluntarily?

This is a time of great flux in the workplace. One trend that's clear, at both the federal and state level, is a desire for less, not more, regulation. Thus, positive reinforcement may work best, at least for businesses that sincerely desire to be socially responsible. We, as employees and as customers, must reward firms that are progressive about privacy. It's up to us to add privacy-friendly policies and practices to the list of criteria—such as day-care centers, pension plans, worker retraining programs—that we use to judge the best places to work and to support as customers and clients.

To those who do not respect privacy, we should say, "I don't support companies that snoop on their employees or their customers." Then take our business elsewhere. And if we're in a position as an employee to do so, take our skills to a company which better respects worker privacy.

Look for companies that have well-crafted privacy policies addressing both customer and employee privacy. If you're active in a union, campaign for your organization to include in its contract negotiations such privacy issues as disclosure of workplace-monitoring practices.

This isn't to say that legislation be ignored as a way to ensure fair workplace-privacy practices. But in the short run more progress is likely to be made with the carrot rather than the stick.

II—Marketplace

Probably more so than with your employer, you have a trump card in dealing with the information practices of businesses. They may need you more than you need them. Because competitors usually are easy to find, you can always walk.

We've urged repeatedly in this book that you guard against giving out too much information to merchants. We've cautioned you to avoid common ploys—such as sweepstakes, grocery store "clubs," and product "registrations"—used to get your personal information with, or without, your knowledge.

But you also can be more proactive about careless or deceptive marketing. You can demand to speak to the manager or supervisor if you think the merchant is, for example, gathering too much data, selling it to others, or perhaps disposing of it haphazardly.

As a general rule, you should, at the very least, be told when personal information is being collected. Further, you should be given the ability to determine how, if at all, that information will be used by others.

Senator Edward Markey of Massachusetts is said to have coined the phrase "knowledge, notice and no" to sum up the way the marketplace should work. First, consumers should be informed that their personal information is being collected. Second, they should be alerted when that information is going to be shared with other parties. Lastly, consumers should be able to restrict those third-party uses; their "no" should be respected.

Some activists are more aggressive. For example, Barney's pet peeve is that many banks and brokerage houses don't bother to shred their files before tossing them in the Dumpster. So he periodically goes on "fishing" expeditions, sorting through the trash bins behind those institutions and gathering documents. Barney then writes two letters: one to the customer whose data was thrown away so carelessly and one to the firm. He tells the customers how their personal financial information was found, adding, "With a little additional effort, these documents provide everything a crook needs to work up phony credit cards, checks, driver's license, etc.," and he suggests the customer complain to the firm.

And he also tells the firm where he found the material and how it could damage the company's customers. "Don't you 'financial advisers' realize that crosscut shredders have existed for years and that you have a legal responsibility to protect and secure client identification?" he asks. (Does Barney risk prosecution for picking through the Dumpsters? Apparently not. The U.S. Supreme Court has ruled that one can't expect trash to remain private once it's been put out for pickup.)

We don't all have Barney's tenacity, but we can take a lesson from his passion and sensitivity by being alert to careless use and disposal of personal information.

III—POLICY

The toughest but most far-reaching advocacy arena is the creation of privacy policy itself. As mentioned before, the law is slow, the pace of technology is swift, and there's usually little incentive—and lots of resistance—when it comes to substantive change.

Still, it's possible. One of the best ways is to join a group that lobbies on behalf of privacy. Many are listed in Appendix C and elsewhere in this book.

You also can advocate on your own behalf. For example, Martha is married to an undercover policeman. They both take precautions to safeguard their home address because of his sensitive job. When Martha went to the hospital to have a baby, she insisted that her home address not be released to *anyone*.

But three days after she returned home with the newborn, she began receiving mail solicitations for baby-care products. The hospital hadn't honored her wishes. Martha complained to her state legislator. An aide to the legislator found a loophole in the state's medical confidentiality law that allowed the hospital to release the information despite the patient's lack of consent.

Martha worked with a privacy group and the legislator to draft legislation to close that loophole. At last report, the legislation hadn't passed. But the point is, Martha didn't suffer in silence. She perceived a threat and committed herself to working to lessen it, and may yet succeed.

Another activist has filed and won several suits against telemarketers who violate the Telephone Consumer Protection Act by calling him after he has told them not to. He has also won suits against companies which fail to send him their written "Do Not Call" lists when he so requests. Taking his crusade to the media, he's inspired others, too.

Other privacy advocates have discovered the Internet as a powerful tool to become informed about privacy issues and to take part in privacy-promoting initiatives. Although cyberspace is the scene of a great deal of privacy abuse, it also holds out hope for remedies because the online world can be a powerful force for organizing like-minded people. The World Wide Web provides excellent resources on privacy as well as constructive discussion groups. Many such sites are listed in Appendix C. If you are not already online, take that step. Participate in forums on privacy and take advantage of the vast amount of material that is available.

Make your voice count. For every person who has taken on privacy as a personal cause, there are thousands who mutter to themselves "There oughta be a law . . . " or "That just isn't fair . . . " and then leave the hard work to others. It behooves us all to do what we can and not just bemoan inequities.

SOME WORTHY GOALS

This book has mentioned many steps individuals can take to protect their personal information. But, in addition, there are a number of ways we as a society could heighten our sensitivity to privacy. Here are five broad privacy goals that we might work toward. Gathered from various sources, they combine high points from corporate and trade-association policies as well as the views of privacy advocates.

1. Predict and Prepare.

Both the public and private sector need to analyze and address the effect that new products and services will have on privacy. Just as the ecologically concerned prepare environmental-impact reports, we should assess damage and tradeoffs before they occur by preparing "privacy-impact statements" or "privacy audits."

Similarly, anyone who introduces a new product or service that's dependent on technology and that could threaten personal privacy should have extra obligations. They should be required to conduct an educational campaign to explain the privacy implications of using that product or service.

That's just what the state of California did when Caller ID was introduced in 1996. The state's Public Utilities Commission required the local phone companies to conduct an extensive consumer-education campaign. Full-page newspaper ads, TV spots, and radio announcements described the privacy impacts of Caller ID and told consumers about their free call-blocking options. As a result of California's unprecedented campaign, a majority of households selected the blocking option that gave them maximum privacy.

2. "Opt-in," Not Out.

This book has suggested taking advantage of "opt-out" provisions under which consumers can choose to remove themselves from mailing lists or telemarketing databases. But why not take that a step further and create an "opt-in" system? You would be put on the lists only if you asked to be. That's better yet.

In fact, if every data collector would simply ask for consent at the very *first* instance that information is gathered—say, on a magazine subscription form, or when money is contributed to a worthy cause, or when you log on to a Web site—then, "opt in" would be the de facto standard of information gathering.

3. An Effective Central Registry.

There ought to be a central registry where you can sign up to delete yourself from lists used for junk mail, unsolicited e-mail, or even telemarketing calls. Clearly, the present mechanisms for taking yourself off such lists don't work well.

The Direct Marketing Association's Mail Preference and Telephone Preference Services (see Chapters 1 and 2) are not well known by consumers, and are used only by the largest of the national marketers. You can't access these preference services by phone, so only those who bother to write are placed on them.

A central registry would be used by all marketers who solicit uninvited goods and services. Marketers would face a penalty if they failed to use the registry to purge their distribution lists of those who don't want to be contacted.

4. Own Your Own Information.

You ought to own the rights to your personal information. Just as a soap company can't use a movie star's likeness to peddle its product without the star's consent, you shouldn't have your name, address, product preferences, and other personal information sold without your okay and without some form of compensation.

Thus, all consumer databases used for direct marketing would be consensual. The consumer would agree to be on the list and would be compensated for surrendering his or her information. That compensation might be in the form of a royalty, much as musicians are paid each time a radio station plays their songs. Or perhaps the payment could be some kind of bonus or reward. In return, let's say, for filling out a questionnaire about products and services you might like to receive, you would be promised early access to new products, or receive special discounts.

In short, this policy would adhere to the basic premise that it's up to the individual to choose what information about himself or herself is revealed to others and under what conditions.

5. Level the Information Playing Field.

Government and business have far more access to information about us as consumers than we have. It should be at least as easy for you to get information about yourself as it is for others to obtain it. Here are just a few suggestions for what needs to be done:

Credit reporting. Because your credit report is increasingly being used to make important decisions about you, it's critical for you to be able to readily access that information. Thus, credit-reporting bureaus should be required to provide one free credit report per year upon request.

Right now, four states (Georgia, Maryland, Massachusetts, and Vermont) require that their residents be allowed to get at least one free credit report annually. Let's make that all fifty states. Rather than wait for Congress to pass a bill, or the remaining forty-six states to each pass laws giving us free access, we should ask the credit bureaus—Experian, Equifax and Trans Union—to voluntarily adopt a free credit report policy. It can only be to their benefit if more consumers check their reports and correct any errors.

In addition, credit bureaus should be required to divulge our credit scores to us. Credit-related decisionmaking, such as whether a department store will give you instant credit or if a landlord will rent to you, is becoming increasingly automated. A single number—the credit "score"—often determines your fate. It's time we see what the creditors see.

Information vendors. Consumers should be allowed access to the ever-growing dossiers that are gathered on them by the information vendors. These companies, such as CDB Infotek, Information America, Lexis/Nexis, and IRSC, specialize in compiling information about us from many different sources— including government agencies, credit-reporting companies, consumer-survey data, and magazine-subscription files. And these firms are virtually unregulated.

Almost 30 years ago, Congress passed the Fair Credit Reporting Act to rein in the burgeoning credit-reporting industry. As a result, consumers have access to their credit reports as well as a right to have errors corrected and to see who else has looked at their credit files.

Today, we need a similar set of "fair information practices" applied to the information-brokering industry. The power of computers and telecommunications networks to compile, analyze and distribute information about each of us is virtually without limit. What's needed is a strong set of rules guiding the information-vendor industry's use of personal information.

Government records. Let's stick to the basics. Government records are public so we, the people, can monitor how our government is working. Not so we can be marketed to or surveilled. The challenge we face is to maintain the spirit of public records—scrutinizing government operations—while at the same time giving individuals some control over the uses made of those records for commercial purposes.

Clearly, the sale of government records for commercial purposes is increasing. Let's work to develop systems that allow us to "opt out" of secondary uses of this information if we so choose. After all, we usually have no choice but to divulge our personal information to government agencies (just try to get a driver's license without divulging your name, address and SSN). So shouldn't we at least be able to choose whether or not we want that information made available for nongovernmental purposes?

6. A Privacy Watchdog

An independent federal agency should be created to deal with national privacy protection. The current political climate isn't hospitable to adding further layers of government. But, in truth, there are privacy "police" in many other countries because citizens there believe business and government can be checked only by some independent representative. Most European nations, along with Australia, Canada, Hong Kong, Japan, and New Zealand, have data-protection commissioners who make sure that organizations maintaining databanks of personal information meet standards of confidentiality and accuracy.

By contrast, the United States has tended to rely on voluntary codes of practice and a patchwork of laws. No government agency reviews privacy issues comprehensively or tries to map out an overall policy on the wide range of consumer, business, or workplace privacy issues.

In fact, America is the biggest exception to the privacy-protection movement worldwide. That's probably because free speech and free access to information are viewed here as entwined. Americans, while fearing a loss of privacy, also fear the heavy hand of government. According to a 1995 Louis Harris poll, more Americans (51%) fear Big Government than fear Big Business (43%). Yet that same poll found more than 80% of Americans say they're very worried about maintaining their privacy.

It will be hard to reconcile our aversion to government regulation and our aversion to further loss of privacy. But we need to try. At the very least, we need an entity that will:

- Shine the spotlight on good privacy practices as well as bad, whether in the public, private, or nonprofit sectors.

- Foster extensive consumer education to make citizens more privacy vigilant. This could be done both by the agency itself engaging in educational activities itself and by encouraging and perhaps funding nonprofits, libraries, and schools to reach the masses.

- Encourage enhancement of privacy standards in all information-handling organizations and serve as a stamp of approval for those agencies and businesses which adhere to an effective set of privacy standards.

- Conduct research and publish reports on policy alternatives, uses of technology, and other issues. Similarly, convene forums to discuss controversial issues.

- Promote mediation as a way to resolve disputes over privacy.

- Serve as a clearinghouse for the federal government's information policy. This would both promote effective federal policymaking and help citizens seeking information under the Freedom of Information Act or Privacy Act.

FRIEND OR FOE?

We don't yet know whether the Information Age will ultimately be consumer friend or consumer foe. If we were keeping a running score, "foe" would likely be ahead right now.

In the final analysis, the test will be whether technology and privacy can be made to coexist. That's not as far-fetched as it sounds. Technology has already eliminated some intrusions (while, of course, creating many more). For example, X-ray machines have made hand searches of airport luggage rare. With magnetic strips in books and clothing, searches at libraries and retail stores are becoming obsolete.

Technology itself doesn't have to be the enemy of privacy. Traditionally, it's been used to increase the amount of information gathered, but it could be used to enhance privacy as well as threaten it.

If we had the collective will to protect privacy, we could doubtless find the way. What's required now is to educate business and government about the need for more enlightened approaches and raise consumers' awareness level so they can protect themselves. It will be a monumental challenge to develop technologies that protect privacy faster than we develop those that threaten it . . . to educate people about their rights before those rights have vanished . . . to make government and business sensitive to personal privacy, given the vested interests that profit from invading that privacy.

That's where you as a privacy advocate can make a difference.

APPENDICES

●

Appendix A: Sample Letters
1. Freedom of Information Act Request Letter
2. Freedom of Information Act Appeal Letter
3. Privacy Act Request for Access Letter
4. Privacy Act Denial of Access Appeal
5. Privacy Act Request to Amend Records

Appendix B: Security Recommendations for Stalking Victims

Appendix C: Other Sources of Information
1. Lobbying and Consumer-Advocacy Groups
2. Newsletters
3. Privacy-related Websites
4. Books Recommended for Further Reading

Appendix A: Sample Letters

1. Freedom of Information Act Request Letter

Agency Head (or Freedom of Information Act Officer)
Name of Agency
Address of Agency
City, State ZIP

Re: Freedom of Information Act Request

Dear————:

This is a request under the Freedom of Information Act.

I request that a copy of the following documents [or documents containing the following information] be provided to me: [Identify the documents or information as specifically as possible.]

In order to help determine my status regarding access fees, you should know that I am [insert a suitable description of the requester and the purpose of the request].

[sample requester descriptions:

an individual seeking information for personal, not commercial, use.

a representative of the news media affiliated with (name of organization) and this request is part of news-gathering efforts in the public interest and not for a commercial use.

affiliated with an educational or noncommercial scientific institution (name of organization) and this request is made for a scholarly or scientific purpose and not for a commercial user.

affiliated with a private corporation and seeking information for use in the company's business.]

[Optional] I am willing to pay fees for this request up to a maximum of $_____. If you estimate that the fees would exceed that limit, please inform me first.

[Optional] I request a waiver of all fees for this request. Disclosure of the requested information to me is in the public interest because it is likely to contribute significantly to public understanding of the operations or activities of government and is not primarily in my commercial interest. [Include a specific explanation.]

Thank you for your consideration of this request.

Sincerely,

Name
Address,
City, State ZIP

2. Freedom of Information Act Appeal Letter

Agency Head (or Appeal Officer)
Name of Agency
Address of Agency
City, State ZIP

Re: Freedom of Information Act Appeal

Dear———:

This is an appeal under the Freedom of Information Act.

On (date), I requested documents under the Freedom of Information Act. My request was assigned the following identification number:——————. On (date), I received a response to my request in a letter signed by (name of official). I appeal the denial of my request.

[Optional] The documents that were withheld must be disclosed under the FOIA because . . .

[Optional] I appeal the decision to deny my request for a waiver of fees. I believe that I am entitled to a waiver of fees. Disclosure of the documents I requested is in the public interest because the information is likely to contribute significantly to the operations or activities of the government and is not primarily in my commercial interest. (Provide details.)

[Optional] I appeal the decision to require me to pay review costs for this request. I am not seeking the documents for a commercial use. (Provide details.)

[Optional] I appeal the decision to require me to pay

search charges for this request. I am (provide details) and am seeking this information not for commercial use.

Thank you for consideration of this appeal.

Sincerely,

Name
Address
City, State ZIP

3. Privacy Act Request for Access Letter

Privacy Act Officer (or Records Manager)
Name of Agency
Address of Agency
City, State ZIP

Re: Privacy Act Request for Access

Dear———:

I request a copy of any records [or specifically named records] about me maintained at your agency.

[Optional] To help you locate my records, I have had the following contacts with your agency: [Mention job applications, period of employment, loans or agency programs applied for, etc.]

[Optional] Please consider that this request is also made under the Freedom of Information Act. Please provide any additional information that may be available under the FOIA.

[Optional] I am willing to pay fees for this request up to a maximum of $_____. If you estimate that the fees will exceed this limit, please inform me first.

[Optional] Enclosed is [a notarized signature or other identifying document] that will verify my identity.

Thank you for your consideration of this request.

Sincerely,

Name
Address
City, State ZIP

4. Privacy Act Denial of Access Appeal

Agency Head (or Appeal Officer)
Name of Agency
Address of Agency
City, State ZIP

Re: Appeal of Denial of Privacy Act Access Request

Dear———:

This is an appeal under the Privacy Act of the denial of my request for access to records.

On (date), I requested access to records under the Privacy Act of 1974. My request was assigned the following identification number:_____. On (date), I received a response to my request in a letter signed by (name of official). I appeal the denial of my request.

[Optional] The records that were withheld should be disclosed to me because . . .

[Optional] Please consider that this appeal is also made under the Freedom of Information Act. Please provide any additional information that may be available under the FOIA.

Thank you for your consideration of this appeal.

Sincerely,

Name
Address
City, State ZIP

5. Privacy Act Request to Amend Records

Privacy Act Officer (or Records Manager)
Name of Agency
Address of Agency
City, State ZIP

Re: Privacy Act Request to Amend Records

Dear————:

This is a request under the Privacy Act to amend records about myself maintained by your agency.

I believe that the following information is not correct: [Describe the incorrect information as specifically as possible.]

The information is not (accurate) (relevant) (timely) because . . .

[Optional] Enclosed are copies of documents that show that the information is not correct.

I request that the information be (deleted) (changed to read) as follows: . . .

Thank you for your consideration of this request.

Sincerely,

Name
Address,
City, State ZIP

Appendix B:
Security Recommendations for
Stalking Victims

The following is reprinted with the permission of the Los Angeles Police Department, Threat Management Unit, Detective Headquarters, 150 N. Los Angeles St., Los Angeles, CA 90012.

RESIDENCE SECURITY

1. Be alert for any suspicious persons.

2. Positively identify callers before opening doors. Install a wide angle viewer in all primary doors.

3. Install a porch light at a height which would discourage removal.

4. Install dead bolts on all outside doors. If you cannot account for all keys, change door locks. Secure spare keys. Place a dowel in sliding glass doors and all sliding windows.

5. Keep garage doors locked at all times. Use an electric garage door opener.

6. Install adequate outside lighting.

7. Trim shrubbery. Install locks on fence gates.

8. Keep fuse box locked. Have battery lanterns in residence.

9. Install a loud exterior alarm bell that can be manually activated in more than one location.

10. Maintain an unlisted phone number. Alert household members to unusual and wrong number calls. If such activity continues, notify local law enforcement agency.

11. Any written or telephone threat should be treated as legitimate and must be checked out. Notify the appropriate law enforcement agency.

12. All adult members of the household should be trained in the use of any firearm kept for protection. It should be stored out of reach of children.

13. Household staff should have a security check prior to employment and should be thoroughly briefed on security precautions. Strictly enforce a policy of the staff not discussing family matters or movement with anyone.

14. Be alert for any unusual packages, boxes, or devices on the premises. Do not disturb such objects.

15. Maintain all-purpose fire extinguishers in the residence and in the garage. Install a smoke detector system.

16. Tape emergency numbers on all phones.

17. When away from the residence for an evening, place lights and radio on a timer. For extended absences, arrange to have deliveries suspended.

18. Intruders will attempt to enter unlocked doors or windows without causing a disturbance. Keep doors and windows locked.

19. Prepare an evacuation plan. Brief household members on plan procedures. Provide ladders or rope for two-story residences.

20. A family dog is one of the least expensive but most effective alarm systems.

21. Know the whereabouts of all family members at all times.

22. Children should be accompanied to school or bus stops.

23. Routes taken and time spent walking should be varied.

24. Require identification of all repair and sales people prior to permitting entry into residence.

25. Always park in a secured garage if available.

26. Inform trusted neighbor regarding situation. Provide neighbor with photo or description of suspect and any possible vehicles.

27. Inform trusted neighbors of any anticipated extended vacations, business trips, and other absences.

28. During vacations and other extended absences have neighbors pick up mail and newspapers.

29. If residing in an apartment with on-site manager, provide the manager with a picture of the suspect. If in a secured condominium, provide information to the doorman or valet.

OFFICE SECURITY

1. Central reception should handle visitors and packages.

2. Office staff should be alert for suspicious people, parcels, and packages that do not belong in the area.

3. Establish key and lock control. If keys possessed by terminated employees are not retrieved, change the locks.

4. Park in secured area if at all possible.

5. Have your name removed from any reserved parking area.

6. If there is an on-site security director, make him/her aware of the situation. Provide him/her with suspect information.

7. Have secretary or coworker screen calls if necessary.

8. Have a secretary or security personnel screen all incoming mail (personal) or fan letters.

9. Be alert to anyone possibly following you from work.

10. Do not accept any package unless you personally ordered an item.

PERSONAL SECURITY

1. Remove home address on personal checks and business cards.

2. Place real property in a trust, and list utilities under the name of the trust.

3. Utilize a private mail box service to receive all personal mail.

4. File for confidential voter status or register to vote utilizing mail box address.

5. Destroy discarded mail.

6. Phone lines can be installed in a location other than the person's residence and call-forwarded to the residence.

7. Place residence rental agreements in another person's name.

8. The person's name should not appear on service or delivery orders to the residence.

9. Do not obtain a mailbox with the United States Post Office.

10. Mail box address now becomes the person's official address on all records and in all rolodexes. It may be necessary or more convenient to list the mail box as "Suite 123" or "Apartment #123" rather than "Box 123."

11. File a change of address card with the Post Office giving the mail box address as the person's new address. Send letters [rather than U.S. Post Office Change of Address cards] to friends, businesses, etc., giving the mail box address and requesting that they remove the old address from their files and rolodexes.

12. All current creditors should be given a change of address card to the mail box address. (Some credit reporting agencies will remove past addresses from credit histories if a request is made. We recommend this be done.)

13. File a change of address with the DMV to reflect the person's new mail box address. Get a new driver's license with the new address on it.

VEHICLE SECURITY

1. Park vehicles in well-lit areas. Do not patronize parking lots where car doors must be left unlocked and keys surrendered; otherwise surrender only the ignition key. Allow items to be placed in or removed from the trunk only in your presence.

2. When parked in the residence garage, turn the garage light on and lock the vehicle and garage door.

3. Equip the gas tank with a locking gas cap. The hood locking device must be controlled from inside the vehicle.

4. Visually check the front and rear passenger compartments before entering the vehicle.

5. Select a reliable service station for vehicle service.

6. Keep doors locked while vehicle is in use.

7. Be alert for vehicles that appear to be following you.

8. When traveling by vehicle, plan ahead. Know the locations of police stations, fire departments, and busy shopping centers.

9. Use a different schedule and route of travel each day. If followed, drive to a police station, fire department, or busy shopping center. Sound the horn to attract attention.

10. Do not stop to assist stranded motorist. (Phone in.)

Appendix C:
Other Sources of Information

1. Lobbying and Consumer-Advocacy Groups

- **American Civil Liberties Union**
  132 W. 43rd St.
  New York, NY 10036
  (212) 944-9800
  http://www.aclu.org
  or
  122 Maryland Ave., NE
  Washington, D.C. 20002
  (202) 675-2322
  E-mail: privaclu@aol.com

- **Center for Democracy and Technology**
  1634 I St. NW, No. 1100
  Washington, D.C. 20006
  (202) 637-9800
  E-mail: info@cdt.org
  http://www.cdt.org

- **Computer Professionals for Social Responsibility**
  P.O. Box 717
  Palo Alto, CA 94302
  (415) 322-3778

E-mail: cpsr@cpsr.org
http://www.cpsr.org

- **Consumer Project on Technology**
  P.O. Box 19367
  Washington, D.C. 20036
  (202) 387-8030
  E-mail: love@cptech.org
  http://www.cptech.org

- **Electronic Frontier Foundation**
  1550 Bryant St., No. 725
  San Francisco, CA 94103
  (415) 436-9333
  E-mail: ask@eff.org
  http://www.eff.org

- **Electronic Privacy Information Center**
  666 Pennsylvania Ave., SE, No. 301
  Washington, D.C. 20003
  (202) 544-9240
  E-mail: info@epic.org
  http://www.epic.org

- **FACTNET, Inc.**
  P.O. Box 3135
  Boulder, CO 80307
  E-mail: factnet@rmi.net
  http://www.factnet.org

- **Illinois Privacy Council**
  Center for Information Technology and Privacy Law
  John Marshall Law School
  315 S. Plymouth Ct.
  Chicago, IL 60604
  (312) 987-1419

- **NetAction**
  601 Van Ness Ave., No. 631
  San Francisco, CA 94102
  (415) 775-8674
  E-mail: akrause@igc.org
  http://www.netaction.org

- **Privacy International**
  666 Pennsylvania Ave., SE, No. 301
  Washington, D.C. 20003
  (202) 544-9240
  E-mail: pi@privacy.org
  http://www.privacy.org/pi

- **Privacy Rights Clearinghouse**
  5384 Linda Vista Road, No. 306
  San Diego, CA 92110
  Voice: (619) 298-3396
  E-mail: prc@privacyrights.org
  http://www.privacyrights.org

- **Private Citizen, Inc.**
  P.O. Box 233
  Naperville, IL 60566
  (800) CUT-JUNK
  E-mail: prvtctzn@private-citizen.com
  http://www.private-citizen.com

- **Stop Junk Mail Association**
  3020 Bridgeway, No. 150
  Sausalito, CA 94965
  (800) 827-5549

- **U.S. Office of Consumer Affairs**
  808 17th St., NW, 8th Floor
  Washington, D.C. 20006

(202) 565-0040
National Helpline: (800) 664-4435, 10 A.M. to 2 P.M., M-F

- **U.S. PIRG**
  218 D St., SE
  Washington, D.C. 20003
  (202) 546-9707
  E-mail: uspirg@pirg.org
  http://www.pirg.org

- **U.S. Privacy Council**
  P.O. Box 15060
  Washington, D.C. 20003
  (202) 829-3660

- **Voters Telecommunications Watch**
  E-mail: vtw@vtw.org
  http://www.vtw.org

- **Wisconsin Data Privacy Project-ACLU**
  122 State St., Rm. 407
  Madison, WI 53703
  (608) 250-1769
  E-mail: acluwicmd@aol.com

2. Newsletters

- **Privacy Journal**
  Box 28577
  Providence, RI 02908
  monthly; $118 or $145 overseas
  (401) 274-7861

- **Privacy Newsletter**
  Box 8206
  Philadelphia, PA 19101

monthly; $99/yr U.S. or $149 abroad
(215) 533-7373

- **Privacy Times**
  Box 21501
  Washington, D.C. 20009
  bi-monthly; $250
  (202) 829-3660

3. Privacy-related Websites

- American Civil Liberties Union: http://www.aclu.org

- Center for Democracy and Technology: http://www.cdt.org

- Computer Professionals for Social Responsibility:
  http://www.cpsr.org

- Consumer Project on Technology:
  http:/www.essential.org/cpt

- Electronic Frontier Foundation: http://www.eff.org

- Electronic Privacy Information Center:
  http://www.epic.org

- FACTNet: http://www.factnet.org

- InfoWar: http://www.infowar.com

- NetAction: http://www.netaction.org

- Network Observer and Red Rock Eater (Phil Agre):
  http://weber.ucsd.edu/~pagre

- Privacy Forum: http://www.vortex.com/privacy.htm

- Privacy International: http://www.privacy.org/pi

- Privacy Rights Clearinghouse: http://www.privacyrights.org

- Voters Telecommunications Watch: http://www.vtw.org

Appendices

23

4. Books Recommended for Further General Reading:

- Ellen Alderman and Caroline Kennedy, *The Right to Privacy*. Knopf, 1995. (Describes how the right to privacy has been perceived throughout our country's legal history and catalogues recent precedents.)

- André Bacard, *The Computer Privacy Handbook: A Practical Guide to E-Mail, Encryption, Data Protection, and PGP Privacy Software*. Peachpit Press, 1995. (Includes sections of general privacy questions.)

- Anne W. Branscomb, *Who Owns Information? From Privacy to Public Access*. Basic Books, 1994. (A dissection of the issues by a distinguished attorney and communications scholar.)

- Ann Cavoukian and Don Tapscott, *Who Knows: Safeguarding Your Privacy in a Networked World*. McGraw-Hill, 1996. (An analysis of the ways government and corporations invade our privacy. The authors bring their Canadian perspective to the discussion of policy solutions.)

- Evan Hendricks, et al., *Your Right to Privacy: A Basic Guide to Legal Rights in an Information Society*. Southern Illinois University, 1990. (An overview in Q&A form by the publisher of *Privacy Times* and published in conjunction with the American Civil Liberties Union.)

- Carolole Lane, *Naked in Cyberspace: How to Find Personal Information Online*. Online Inc., 1997. (A comprehensive guide to online services, primarily fee-based, that compile information about individuals.)

- Eric Larson, *The Naked Consumer: How Our Private Lives Become Public Commodities*. Holt, 1992. (A journalistic view of marketing research's relation to privacy.)

- David Linowes, *Privacy in America: Is Your Private Life*

in the Public Eye? University of Illinois, 1989. (A scholar's look at the many facets of privacy.)

- David Lyon, *The Electronic Eye: The Rise of the Surveillance Society*. University of Minnesota Press, 1994. (An examination of the issues arising from increased electronic surveillance.)

- *Netspy: How You Can Access the Facts and Cover Your Tracks Using the Internet and Online Services*. Wolff New Media, 1996. (A revealing look at online snooping and how to avoid it while finding privacy-enhancing technologies.)

- *Privacy Powerpak*. The Privacy Group, 1996. (A guide for consumers seeking information about privacy issues and laws. Contains full text of selected U.S. privacy laws as well as sample letters that are ready to mail.)

- Jeffrey Rothfeder, *Privacy for Sale: How Computerization Has Made Everyone's Life an Open Secret*. Simon & Schuster, 1992. (A popular account of the privacy problems brought on by computerization.)

- Robert Ellis Smith, *Our Vanishing Privacy: And What You Can Do to Protect Yours*. Loompanics Unlimited, 1993. (A broad look at privacy issues written by a well-known privacy-newsletter publisher.)

Index